NOTRE DAME REMEMBERED

Notre Dame Remembered

An Autobiography

EDWARD FISCHER

UNIVERSITY OF NOTRE DAME PRESS
NOTRE DAME, INDIANA

Photographic section credits:

Second page: *The Dome*, 1936 and 1937.

Third page: John M. Cooney photo courtesy of Catherine Anne Carroll; John T. Frederick photos courtesy of University of Notre Dame Archives.

Fourth page: upper photo courtesy of University of Notre Dame Archives; lower photo courtesy of *Notre Dame Magazine*.

Sixth page: James Withey photo courtesy of University of Notre Dame Archives; all others courtesy of Notre Dame Department of Public Relations and Information.

Seventh page: Sister Madeleva photo courtesy of Saint Mary's College Archives; Marion McCandless photo courtesy of Saint Mary's College Alumnae Office.

Eighth page: *Pieta* photo courtesy of *Notre Dame Magazine*; Ivan Mestrovic photo courtesy of Syracuse University News Bureau and *Notre Dame Magazine*.

Ninth page: Richard Sullivan photo courtesy of *Notre Dame Magazine*; Joe Boland photo courtesy of University of Notre Dame Archives.

Twelfth page: Courtesy of M. Bruce Harlan.

Library of Congress Cataloging in Publication Data

Fischer, Edward.
   Notre Dame remembered.

   1. Fischer, Edward. 2. University of Notre
Dame—History. 3. College teachers—Indiana—Notre
Dame—Biography. 4. Journalists—United States—
Biography. I. Title.
LD4112.9.F57   1986   378.772'89   86-25109
ISBN 0-268-01465-5
ISBN 0-268-01466-3 (pbk.)

FOR FATHER THEODORE M. HESBURGH, C.S.C.

*who brought with him
the grace of reconciliation*

Contents

– 1 –

Reaching Back

Alumni came back that day mainly to search for their lost youth among the paths. The early June migration helped to recall salad days, all fresh and crisp and green. In sunlight they rolled across highways from New York, Massachusetts, and Illinois and up roads from Kentucky, Tennessee, and Louisiana. License plates from all over the United States converged as cars flowed through a tunnel of greenery called Notre Dame Avenue. A golden dome glinted just ahead.

The Ford Foundation was right when its survey suggested that Notre Dame is the most national university: The distribution of its alumni population and the distribution of the nation's population match more closely than that of any other university.

At the registration desk, under Stepan's geodesic dome, a young woman clamped a golden plastic band around the wrist with an admonition, "Never take this off. Not even for sleeping or taking a shower. Not until Sunday noon." From Thursday until Sunday noon the golden band would be the "Open Sesame" to all events. She handed each of us a cap color-coded by class, a name tag, and a blue and gold folder filled with promises of things to come.

Under the heading "Thursday," the folder said, "No formal programs are scheduled today to allow you to settle in and stroll the campus at leisure." So alumni strolled at leisure across the main quad, observing that it has changed little through the years. Old footprints are more easily rediscovered here than at most places. Not much has been torn down or bulldozed over. The core is intact; the new was added to the perimeter. At night the silhouettes of Sorin towers, church steeple, and golden dome match the most ancient memory. There is something restorative in finding scenes from youth still undisturbed.

Why does this place bring an intensified sense of life and a heightened awareness? Maybe Saint Augustine came near the answer when he wrote about "the tranquility of order." Notre Dame's green acreage has order. In

1

moving from one part of the campus to another, we move from one quad to another and are always aware of the plan.

The young woman under the geodesic dome assigned the alumni to new halls, Flanner and Grace, but what they really wanted to visit were the old ones—Sorin, Walsh, Saint Edward, Lyons, and even Badin, which has never been a "stately pleasure dome." We need to return to places lived in long ago, for such space is important to us. We keep searching for something down in the deep and quiet, down where the twinges hide.

Reunions are a time to reconstruct the past. People and events are haloed with significance when seen from far off. Time's kindness puts a shine on things.

On Friday morning, those who prefer early hours before the day has hardened, took to the paths at dawn. Two alumni, wearing red caps, walked up the road between the lakes and turned left into the cemetery. Last night they had talked about Doc, Big Mac, Boozy, and other lay professors; now they were searching for the priests, Peter Rabbit, Pepper, and Daddy. In the wet grass, among the gray stone crosses disposed in serried rows, they moved about, not saying much, just pointing.

Back on the road they turned left toward Saint Mary's College. The tower of LeMans looms as it did when they walked this way to tea dances a half century ago. How dressed up everyone was on those afternoons! Photographs in old yearbooks prove it. The Sisters of the Holy Cross, back then, would have barred the door to even a casual look, and anyone wearing blue jeans might have learned where the grapes of wrath are stored.

When the two early morning alumni, in red caps, first walked this road there was a popular song called "She Went to Old Saint Mary's and I Went to Notre Dame," a lament of lost love played often on radio station WGN, Chicago.

> But I left her there
> Thought I didn't care
> Now I wonder where
> Where can she be
>
> Since the day we parted
> Life is not the same
> She went to old Saint Mary's
> I went to Notre Dame

Later Friday morning a session called "Your Questions with No Holds Barred," was held in the library auditorium. Three members of the administration were in charge of the answers. The one-hour period was filled with information: Cadavers are being dissected at Notre Dame . . . there has been a noticed return to religious observances in the past three years . . . the problem of alcoholism on the campus is waning . . . a survey shows that Notre Dame students are conservative compared with those at other universities, when it comes to opinions on such matters as abortion and the legalization of marijuana.

At five o'clock, groups met in chapels around the campus to remember their dead classmates. In the library auditorium members of our class and their wives, eighty-two souls in all, attended a memorial Mass for our 140 known dead. We have lost track of fifty-eight classmates; many of them must also be beyond the caprice of time. The 370 of us still playing out our options realize by now that life is a short season. Photographs in the 1937 *Dome* prove that we once wore the freshness of youth. Each memorial Mass reminds us that every yearbook becomes, in God's good time, one of the Books of the Dead.

After Mass we went to the penthouse on the fourteenth floor of the library for a cocktail party. Someone pointed to a classmate across the room and said, "Look at him, a gentleman and a fine fellow. He was that way as a student. And those who were sonsabitches then still are. The concrete hardens fast."

During the class dinner in the Morris Inn someone recalled the "lake parties." He counted the ways you could cause the cry, "in the lake!" to go ringing down hall corridors. One of them was to gripe too much as a freshman; the upperclassmen considered complaining about the university as their special prerogative. Another way to get doused was to walk up or down the front steps of the Main Building while still an undergraduate; you were to walk those steps for the first time in cap and gown on graduation day. The easiest way to become the guest of honor at a lake party was to stay in bed the Monday morning after the Army game; everyone was expected to walk the three miles to greet the team at the train station, especially if the team lost.

From the Morris Inn we walked across campus through a spring night evocative of commencement weekend. Inside a red and white striped circus tent, pitched on the quad in front of the North Dining Hall, a four-piece combo played with a heavy beat, and red, green and yellow lights gave a touch of the surreal to all inside. Old grads sat there looking at life through a rearview mirror, talking with the freedom that comes after a few drinks.

Talk got around to life in Corby and Sorin halls under the reign of Father Tuffy Ryan and Father Pop Farley. Those hall rectors ruled with an iron fist unencumbered by the velvet glove. They came down the corridor at dawn ringing a cowbell, and if anyone failed to get up they returned to lift the foot of the bed about fifteen inches above the floor and let it drop.

At this point several alumni decided to go to bed. Maybe deep in their memories they heard Pop Farley's stacatto: "Lights out, boy! Lights out at eleven o'clock!"

On Saturday we gathered in the library auditorium to learn the university's policy on admissions. We heard that of 8,000 applications for the freshman class, 1,275 men and 500 women were accepted.

While affection for Notre Dame is not inscribed in the genes and passed on in the gene pool, still one out of every four freshman is the offspring of an alumnus. Alumni whose offspring are not accepted often show strong reactions, said the director of admissions. One father thought that his daughter should have been admitted because of when and where she had been conceived: the weekend of the Michigan State game in the Morris Inn.

Seminars that day ranged from estate planning to stress management, from career planning to the emerging woman. Most popular were the tours of the Snite Museum of Art, where guides showed some of the 17,000 pieces from the collection valued at $30 million.

For our class photo we gathered, as the printed program directed, "on the bleachers near the beer tent." Class photos used to be taken on the long stone steps in front of the old library when we were still lithe and lean. Faces are broader now and weight in the shoulders has slipped downward "on the bleachers near the beer tent." The photos of our forty-fifth reunion suggest that none of us will ever again, on the Feast of San Firmin, run with the bulls at Pamplona. As the Second Law of Thermodynamics warns, everything is running down.

How the bells did peal that Saturday night! When Father Sorin planned Sacred Heart Church, in 1871, the naysayers must have considered him mad to build such a great edifice in the remoteness of northern Indiana. But now it could be larger, especially on reunion weekend, when alumni overflow from every door.

Father Sorin was much a part of the Solemn Mass; his chair, chalice, and paten were used in the liturgy. A brass quintet played, the alumni choir sang, and the 2,929 pipes of the great organ did their best.

After Mass a kilty band—six bagpipers and five drums—led the alumni down the main quad past Father Sorin's statue, past O'Shaughnessy Hall, and on beyond the stadium to the Athletic and Convocation Center where the round tables, with eight seats to a table, stretched on and on across the gigantic hall. There 2,478 grads sat down to a banquet. They had come from forty-seven states and Scotland, Guatemala, Uganda, Canada, Mexico, and the Virgin Islands. The banquet came to a close with thirty-five former members of the Glee Club singing "Notre Dame, Our Mother" and "The Victory March."

At ten o'clock we stepped out into a chilly night. It felt more like a football weekend than an alumni reunion. The moon was full and clear, and yellow spotlights made the dome more golden still.

Voices in the night air were mostly young. Few at the reunion went back far enough to remember when the campus bakery specialized in what was called the Notre Dame bun, a celebrated geological specimen. The crusty beige object had the shell of a turtle and the interior of caulking compound. A student once pasted a stamp on one, added his girl's address, and sent it through the mail.

Under the circus tent that Saturday night there was enough drinking to soften the present, but still a miasma of sadness hung in the air. Things that pierce the memory deeply—old photo albums, old yearbooks, old hardships—bring an uneasy mirth. We laugh when we are reminded that God has the knack of planned obsolescence.

Clustered in small groups on folding chairs, friends for many years took out memories and passed them around. The memories, blurred enough by now to be attractive, created a freemasonry that made us feel we still hold more in common than we really do. This was the time to enjoy the modified reminiscences of youth, not authenticate them. A stickler for facts is as out of place at an alumni reunion as Roman numerals on a scoreboard. Legends are not born in the midst of cross-references. And besides, to have delightful memories is to be written in the book of the blessed.

Who would want to check too closely the story about how an unsuspecting prof carried the exam answers from a student in the front row to one in the back row: "There's this Holy Cross priest, see, who paces the aisle reading his breviary during exams. He always does that, paces the aisle, and everybody knows it. So this smart student up front uses a safety pin to hook the answers onto the priest's cincture. Get the picture? The dumb student lifts them off when the priest makes his turn at the back of the room."

Alumni reunions are more restrained than they used to be. At one time they were the greatest breakdown in order since the collapse of Pax

Romana. A recurring theme used to be "how we raised hell and slid a block under it."

Why are things more restrained? Could it be *accidie*? Or the presence of wives? Or is there really such a thing as the perfectibility of man?

Sunday dawned a blue and gold day. In the morning sunshine three of us walked past Father Sorin's statue talking about how evocative a visit to the community cemetery can be. Names that we saw first in the college catalog are now on stone crosses.

We recalled the Holy Cross Fathers who meant something in our lives. In fusty classrooms under the Dome they passed along a trend of mind that is more important than data. By hinting that creation is the husk of something infinite, they opened windows onto a long view, framing problems of the day in light of eternity.

One priest used to harp on the difference between inclinations and principles. Another passed along a practical wisdom that went beyond books, for it came from spiritual experience. Most had the old-fashioned notion — it dates back to Quintilian — that the teacher must accept responsibility not only for what a student learns but for what he becomes.

They made us see it is possible to live in a way we had never considered. While trying to impose order and lucidity on our minds, they showed us how to detect the center of gravity in certain situations. What an uphill job they had, trying to help us separate sense from nonsense! Our best teachers knew that true education means teaching things that are worth being in love with.

At a reunion, vivid comraderie fades fast. The flow of reminiscence runs dry. The most garrulous is talked out. After a certain number of years, it takes courage to attend an alumni weekend. You face reflections of your mortality, seeing in others what is happening to yourself. It becomes more of a spiritual retreat than a lively celebration once you admit that not far downstream looms the Ultimate Tax Shelter. And yet those of us at the forty-fifth reunion said, "See you at the fiftieth." Such promises grow more chancy through the years.

We parted feeling more finite, knowing our horizons will move in like the wood of Dunsinane. In some well-worn classroom under the Dome we heard about "this mortal coil," but what did that mean at twenty. Now we don't need the bard, or anyone else, to tell us about mortality. Not if we were paying attention while the lessons were being taught.

"See you at the fiftieth!"

With the permission of God, of course.

– 2 –

At the Start

Notre Dame seemed as remote as the rivers of Utopia when I was growing up on a farm in Kentucky. The university first entered my awareness at the age of ten, when, in late October of 1924, I crouched beside a country road to look at a photograph in a crumpled mud-splattered newspaper. The sports page of the *Louisville Courier-Journal* featured a picture of four football players sitting astride four horses. A couple of years later a friend showed me his scrapbook containing photographs of a beaming coach, Knute Rockne, and a highly animate halfback, Christy "Fleet-Footed" Flanigan, the only pictures in the scrapbook to stick in my consciousness.

Coming events really do cast their shadows before them. That photo of the Four Horsemen was taken on old Cartier Field, where my office is now located and where this sentence is being written. The man who took the much-published photograph, Harry Elmore, drove me on my first assignment as a newspaper reporter the morning after my graduation from Notre Dame. Later I taught Fleet-Footed Flanagan's daughter at Saint Mary's College and his son at Notre Dame. And I bought Knute Rockne's house.

How little a boy foresees while reading a newspaper beside a country road!

The crumpled newspaper was lying where the Old Shepherdsville Road took a sharp turn to avoid running into a white fence. Several miles of such fencing portioned off the green pastures and the dark woods of Bashford Manor, an L-shaped racehorse farm. Our small farm fit into the pocket of the L.

It was fitting that the Four Horsemen should enter my awareness at that spot, because behind those fences had grazed four celebrated horses, three of them Kentucky Derby winners—Azra (1888), Manuel (1889), and Sir Huon (1906), the latter named after one of the knights in Charlemagne's court. The best ever to canter those pastures—at least that is what the grooms used to say—was Falsetto, who ran second in the Derby and sired three Derby winners before dying beneath a tree very near to where I was kneeling, looking at the photograph of the Four Horsemen.

7

The best-known horse in that part of the country, Proctor Knott, had been foaled a few hundred yards away. When George Scoggins bought Bashford Manor, in 1877, he kept ownership for only one day and then sold it at a profit to Colonel George Long. With the money Scoggins developed a horse farm directly across the Bardstown Road. His best horse, Proctor Knott, won the first New York Futurity in 1888 and lost the Kentucky Derby by a nose in 1889. Most spectators thought he had won, but the judges decided otherwise. Proctor Knott's fame rested on a song that became a favorite on the tent show circuit. When I was sick my mother used to sing to me about the man who had bet on Proctor Knott:

> Proctor lost, my money was gone
> Never bet from that day on.

Buechel was such a safe place while I was growing up that it was difficult to imagine that the first settlers had felt threatened there. It was, as one writer said, "a howling wilderness" when George Rogers Clark arrived in Kentucky in 1778. As a protection against Indians the early settlers built a stockade in 1779 at the south fork of Bear Grass Creek, the creek that ran through the pastures at Bashford Manor. The pioneers were scarcely inside the fort when, just to the east, an Indian ambush took the lives of nearly a hundred settlers. One of them was Abraham Lincoln's grandfather.

Abraham Lincoln later spent some time in Buechel at a place called Farmington. In passing that old Federal-style mansion on the way to school I used to picture a pair of glistening black horses, stepping high along the Bardstown road, pulling an open carriage in the back seat of which sat a tall, gaunt man wearing a tall black hat. The picture came to mind because we had been told in school that in 1841 Lincoln had come to Buechel to recover from an illness and had stayed two months with his lifelong friend Joshua Speed. The future president was suffering "a melancholic depression" caused by a broken engagement with his future wife, Mary Todd, of Lexington.

We were told in school that John James Audubon, the ornithologist and artist, had also been a guest at Farmington. The legend is that he was much taken with the old mansion, as well he might be. His artist's heart was surely warmed by the simple dignity with which the architect, Thomas Jefferson, had graced the mansion.

A hundred yards from where I crouched reading the crumpled newspaper stood Seibert's grocery store and saloon, in a triangle formed by the Bashford Manor fence, the Old Shepherdsville Road, and Bardstown

Road. Seibert's saloon when I was growing up had a magnetic attraction for Marvin Hart, later listed in *The Guinness Book of World Records* as the World's Heavyweight Boxing Champion who held the title for the shortest time, 235 days.

Years later another World Heavyweight Champion lived in Buechel, just off Fredericks Lane. After Muhammad Ali left home to become a citizen of the world, his parents continued to live on Verona Way.

In spite of its fighting champions, Derby winners, and visits from Lincoln and Audubon I never came upon anyone who had ever heard of Buechel. As a boy I felt embarrassed about being from such a countrified place and wished I could have lived in a city. While attending boarding school in Indiana I wanted to be able to say with my classmates that home was in Indianapolis or Fort Wayne or Hammond.

I used to tell people I was from Louisville, a claim with some truth in it because I had been born there in a white frame cottage on Logan Street. My mother did the laundry, as usual, on August 17, 1914, because it was a Monday. She always thought that it was the activity at the washboard and the stretching to hang clothes that encouraged my arrival at five that afternoon.

Just down the street, my father owned an ice company, a business he had started as a young man with twenty-five cents. After borrowing a horse and wagon he bought a quarter's worth of ice and sold it for thirty-five cents, then bought thirty-five cents worth and sold it for fifty. Eventually he could afford his own horse and wagon. By the time I was born, the Edward Fischer Ice Company had several routes established in the part of Louisville known as Germantown, where all of my grandparents had eventually settled after fleeing the revolutionary upheavals in Germany in 1848.

My earliest memory of Germantown is of lurching about in an ice wagon behind a runaway horse after the driver, Mr. See, had left me unattended while he visited a saloon. I could still paint from memory Mr. See's portrait. He was lean with sharp gray features; tufts of white hair sprouted from beneath his cap, and his blue eyes looked scared. He was spry, though, and proved it by his rapid pursuit of the runaway horse across the uneven bricks of Oak Street.

That was the last ride with Mr. See; from then on I went only with my father. At so many places people would say to my father, "I thought of you last night, at the motion picture show. You sure do favor William S. Hart." When in film work I used to recall this each time I came upon a photograph of William S. Hart. He and my father both had a horse-faced look, one that I inherited.

On Friday, December 13, 1918, we moved to the farm in Buechel, about three miles south of Louisville. I know December 13 was on a Friday that year because Mother often mentioned it in a tone of voice that suggested a dark omen. She would later tell of other things that occurred on Friday the thirteenth—the mules burned up and a sow died farrowing a litter that lived only a few days, and, if I remember correctly, my sister came down with scarlet fever on a Friday the thirteenth. Oh, Mother had quite a list!

She never really approved of the farm. My father said that he left the city for his health's sake. Indoors the bookkeeping ruined his eyes and outdoors the glare of the sun on ice also damaged them. I think the real reason for the move was that he had long dreamed of owning a farm, and at forty-three he knew he had to do it.

He practically gave away the ice company, or so my mother said, and I am sure she was right. Having inherited his business sense, I know just how he must have reasoned: Since the business was started with only a quarter, anything earned above that is gravy.

Once when times were lean for us he sold Mutt and Jeff, a pair of black horses. *Sold* is hardly the verb; again he practically gave them away. I can still see my mother crying. As she lifted a lid from the kitchen stove to put in a shuttle of coal, a tear dropped on the hot surface and made a hissing sound.

It was always an uneasy experience helping get ready for market. We washed the tomatoes, lettuce, potatoes, carrots, and radishes and loaded them, glistening, on the market wagon. My father drove to Louisville in early evening and slept on the wagon all night. He had not in him one ounce of market-day shrewdness and so he returned the next afternoon disconsolate.

My mother, Louise, should have been used to that, because her father, Philip Steinmetz, had much the same problem. Although he was a Lutheran and a Mason he was most generous when the Little Sisters of the Poor came begging. My mother said, "Of course they made over him. He would come home and say to my mother, 'Louisa, if I was Irish, those sisters would make me a bishop!'"

Mother complained often about my father's lack of a business sense, yet she always ended with the same sentence: "But he has been a good provider." She seemed embarrassed to catch herself complaining, because it ran contrary to her frequent use of the word *content*. She often advised, "Be content with your lot." When I was sick, which was often, she used to sing to me a Protestant hymn that she had learned as a girl:

> Count your blessings over one by one
> And it may surprise you what the Lord hath done

Mother counted it a blessing the day my father admitted he could not make a go of it as a farmer. So he took a job with the Louisville and Nashville railroad and commuted daily until he retired at age seventy, at the end of the Second World War. Through the years our land was farmed by a man with good equipment who worked several small farms on a share-crop arrangement.

Even when my father quit working the land he never lost an interest in it. He was forever walking across it, aware of every leaf and blade. From him I inherited a love of walking, a sense of quiet, and a capacity for aloneness.

Twice a week my father walked to the barbershop in Buechel for a shave. I sat with him in a row of men with bristling chins, surrounded by the heady aroma of bay rum. On a shelf stood shaving mugs covered with baroque curliques, each featuring the name of a patron. The talk was mostly about crops and politics, but no sports. On the way home I would run the mile along Bardstown Road, and if my father jogged a little way with me, I was amazed that a man of such advanced age, forty-five, could run at all.

Each Christmas I ordered his gift from Sears & Roebuck. In ordering bedroom slippers I copied what the catalog said, size 6–12. An amused clerk in Chicago returned the order form saying I had to name one definite number, and so I chose 9. Anyway they fit!

I never heard my father tell a joke, yet he had a sense of humor; he could see the amusement in the situation that prevailed. Mother, on the other hand, was full of jokes and told many of them too often. Time and again we heard the one about the man who returned from the railroad station covered with grease and grime. He said he had just put his wife on the train for a visit to her mother.

"How did you get so dirty?"

"I was hugging the engine!"

Mother marked me with some of her offbeat beliefs. She considered iodine superior to Mercurochrome, reasoning that the burning sensation it causes must surely make it more antiseptic. I thought of her years later in Burma when the Kachins belittled a new antimalarial drug because it was not bitter. Mother also believed that prayers said outdoors, flying upward unhindered, are more efficacious than those said beneath a roof. Surely she had never heard of Nietzsche's opinion that "no idea is true unless it is thought in the open air." And although she never heard of D. H. Lawrence, she would have agreed with his praise of "the high morality of the clean handkerchief," for I never left home without her asking, "Do you have a clean handkerchief?" To this day I put more trust in medicine that goes down with a shudder, and feel more at ease with prayers said out in the open, and upon leaving the house always check to see whether or not I have a clean handkerchief.

My mother's sister, Linda, came to live with us a year after I was born; her husband, Benjamin Dodt, had died in a powder plant explosion in Jeffersontown. Since I was still an infant when she joined the family, she took it upon herself to rear me, a sobering experience for a child, for Aunt Linda was a woman of ruthless piety.

At dawn each day she was always in the kitchen leading prayers. Her devotions were directed to the Infant of Prague as an everyday favorite, Saint Anthony when something was lost, and Saint Jude for impossible cases. During thunderstorms she would light a candle and make the sign of the cross after each thunderclap. One night when lightning was cracking at each tall tree in the yard she went about sprinkling holy water on us in our beds, only to learn in the morning that instead of the holy water bottle she had picked up a bottle of bluing.

Aunt Linda also contributed to my collection of fears. She warned that if I swallowed grape seeds I would get appendicitis, and that I might get cancer if I ate the dark spots of bananas. While I have come to know better, in my head, something deep down inside makes me prefer seedless grapes and avoid the dark spots on bananas.

Aunt Linda had a detailed memory for the past. She spoke often of the one-room schoolhouse, of oxen plowing the fields, and of streetcars pulled by mules. This concern for the past, however, did not dull her interest in the present. In the yellow glow of a kerosene lamp she sat at the table after dinner reading aloud the *Louisville Times*. From her I heard of the discovery of King Tut's tomb, of the electrocution of Ruth Snyder, and of Coué's self-help program, the one that encouraged frequent repetition of "Every day in every way I'm getting better and better."

When she heard that Queen Marie of Roumania would be traveling the Bardstown Road she had me go with her to stand beside the white fence at Bashford Manor. We watched a woman of icy beauty pass in a black limousine on the way to Bardstown to visit My Old Kentucky Home. We didn't know then, in 1926, that royalty had passed through Buechel as far back as 1797, when Louis Philippe traveled from Bardstown to Louisville as part of his tour of the American frontier arranged by George Washington.

Since my sister, Bertha, was seven years my senior, she was not able to be very companionable as far as playing games, but she did something much more important: she read to me. The Sisters of Charity at Presentation Academy and at Nazareth College, in Louisville, were great ones for handing out reading lists. Bertha was willing to read aloud all books required by the course, and since there was little else to do, I listened.

Perhaps the most valuable part of my education was hearing *The Adventures of Tom Sawyer*, *The Adventures of Huckleberry Finn*, and *Life on the Mississippi* read aloud at age seven. Listening to those books was better than reading them myself, considering that in time I would make a living using words: Rhythms of sentences, flavor of words, and timing in the release of ideas reach the sensibilities better through the ear than through the eye.

My, what awe I felt when hearing in the closing pages of *The Adventures of Tom Sawyer*, of how Injun Joe died of starvation, trapped in a cave. With a knife he chipped a stalagmite in such a way that it would catch the drop of water that fell once every three minutes, a spoonful in twenty-four hours.

"That drop was falling when the Pyramids were new; when Troy fell; when the foundations of Rome were laid; when Christ was crucified; when the Conqueror created the British empire; when Columbus sailed; when the massacre at Lexington was 'news'. It is falling now; it will still be falling when all these things shall have sunk down the afternoon of history and the twilight of tradition and been swallowed up in the thick night of oblivion. Has everything a purpose and a mission? Did this drop fall patiently during five thousand years to be ready for this flitting human insect's need? And has it another important object to accomplish ten thousand years to come?"

It was not the horrible death that haunted me but the vision of nature working through vast expanses of time. The question, "Has everything a purpose and a mission?" might well have been the start of *Everybody Steals from God*, a book I would not begin writing for another fifty years.

During vacations my sister's friends came from Louisville to spend some time on the farm. The girls read a great deal and spoke with enthusiasm about writers. Although I did not understand all that they said, through a kind of osmosis I absorbed the idea that reading can be interesting and that writers are important people.

Since books from the library were free, and since we lacked money, Bertha and I read and read. We enjoyed no weekly allowance, but the family did have an unusual system for the distribution of wealth, one that I took for granted was used in every household. In the upper right-hand drawer of the dining room buffet was a cigar box, "the money box," in which was all the cash the family owned. We were free to take from it what we needed for lunches, carfare, and anything we believed essential. As far as I know, neither Bertha nor I ever abused the trust.

As the years passed, the five of us—my parents, Aunt Linda, Bertha, and I—developed a sense of place. We even referred to the farm as The Place. "Some day we'll sell The Place." You could hear the capital letters in the way the words were said.

The two-story frame house had some dignity, for there was a tranquility about its long halls and its square rooms with their high ceilings and fireplaces. Stairways built south of the Ohio River in the nineteenth century were more than utilitarian: even in an unpretentious house such as ours they were made to please the eye.

A good stand of trees gave the place a calm elegance that it would not have had without them. In front a gravel driveway made an S-curve past beech, pine, and locust and carried on to the back where there were a few pear and persimmon. At one side of the house was a small orchard of apple, peach, and plum, and on the other were walnut and maple. In the barnyard, willows, oaks, and chestnuts surrounded the pond.

Among my clearest memories of those quiet days in Buechel are two sentences. At dusk my mother would say, "Time to light the lamps." Not long afterward—at least it didn't seem much later—my father would announce, "Time to hit the hay."

– 3 –

Old Friends and Neighbors

I was sitting atop the white fence that separated our property from the racehorse farm, when a nosey colt lifted his quivering muzzle toward me. In leaning down I thrust my face toward his until were were nearly nose to nose.

Uncle Dick, whose complexion was the rich brown of a well-kept saddle, rested on his hoe and watched. "Don't ever see yourself in a horse's eye," he warned. "If you do, he'll go blind."

That admonition still clings. So I have avoided seeing myself reflected in horses' eyes at the Cavalry School at Fort Riley, and on a Western movie set in Hollywood, and in the hunt country of Ireland. Just knowing better doesn't erase my superstition.

Surely, Uncle Dick was testing my gullibility when he explained, in all seriousness, how to train my pony, Snowball, to lift his feet high. To develop the elevated knee action of fancy horses, he suggested tree branches be placed a foot apart on the ground and thick glasses be strapped over the pony's eyes. "The branches look like logs. He lift his feet high to step over 'em. In time he git the habit."

Uncle Dick didn't make speeches about anything. If he spoke more than two sentences on one subject, he would grin and say, "I done said more than I know." Yet he must have spoken at some length in his sermons, for on Sunday he was a Baptist preacher in Newburgh, a community about a mile from our farm.

When he worked on our farm he was about seventy-five years old, which means he was around twenty when the Civil War ended. He may have been born into slavery; many of the old people in Newburgh had been, but he said nothing about it one way or the other. The chances are he had grown up right there in Buechel, because at Farmington Judge Speed owned seventy slaves, and at Bashford Manor there were still some cabins. The only thing he said about the Civil War is that he recollected seeing soldiers march along the Bardstown Road. It must have been the last winter of the war, for they were so ragged that they had wrapped themselves in women's and children's clothing to keep warm. Confederate prisoners of war no doubt.

Uncle Dick was a stocky man, of medium height, with kinky hair that was mainly white, and a complexion, as I said, of a rich brown. He wore a mossy green hat with a meandering brim and random sweat stains. His blue work shirt and corduroy pants were faded from many washings and many suns. On the outside of his pants, bone buttons held broad, dark green suspenders, and from his hip pocket protruded a blue handkerchief alive with white polka dots.

The old man's shoes were split here and there in deference to bunions and corns that made him shuffle with aching feet. In those days I thought he shuffled because of red peppers, for he had told me that the best way to keep feet warm is to put red peppers in your toes.

Uncle Dick often paused at the end of a long row because just inside the white fence there were trees to rest under, trees that had been planted so that horses would have shade in the summer. Along the fence ran a well-beaten dirt path, a shortcut from the interurban car station on Bardstown Road to the community of Newburgh.

My favorite person using that path was Carrie, a voluminous woman who addressed Uncle Dick as "Reverend." I felt close to her because she said that no matter how cold the night she had to sleep with her feet stuck out from under the blanket, and I was having a similar problem.

Carrie never walked the path to Newburgh without being weighted down with brown bags of groceries. Once when Uncle Dick asked her how she fared, she said, "I feel overcast today." She began to complain how "high" groceries are and how fast they disappear. "Here it is, it ain't nuthin' but Wednesday and I done carryin' groceries again. Satiday I carry 'em, and here it is an I carry 'em again."

Uncle Dick asked why she didn't have her boy, Nubbins, meet her at the station to help her "tote" those bags. She said, "You can't depend on the younguns no more." She explained how things used to be, "My Momma she had a big stick an' she'd direct it at us." Children were more "righteous" then. Just talking about it got her so riled that she said she was going home and "chastize that chile."

I often wondered if she ever did chastize him, but never asked. Not once did I break into the conversation. Too shy. Or as Carrie would say, "too backward."

The conversation was mostly one-sided, mostly Carrie's. Uncle Dick kept occupied relighting his pipe. He made his own pipes from a corncob and cane, rough-bowled things with stems that seemed blackened by frostbite at the end. He smoked mainly ashes, because the pipe was always going out and he was forever stirring up the ashes and relighting them with a thick match. The tobacco, in a black cloth sack with a drawstring at top, was a rough-cut burley that gave authority to the neighboring air as soon as he put a match to it.

Sometimes as we rested we saw Colonel Long, the owner of Bashford Manor, ride into the pasture in his car, ease himself out of it, and with a cane walk about inspecting horses. A groom would bring them to him, those that could be caught, and there was talk about teeth, hooves, and pasterns.

I looked upon the Colonel with awe because my mother had told me that each Christmas Eve he hung thousand-dollar bills all over the Christmas tree—one bill for each relative who came to Christmas dinner. I tried to picture the scene and decided it was a sight worth riding a mule over ten miles of back road just to see.

After a long rainy spell we had a beautiful sunny morning. Carrie said, "It dewed pretty heavy last night; we can *live* behind this." Uncle Dick made no reply, but not long afterward I saw him get angry over a comment someone else made about the quality of the weather.

While a penetrating rain lashed at all outdoors, Uncle Dick and I were inside the stable shelling corn. Through the wide door came Ed, a brash young fellow who worked all week to live high at the roadhouse in Newburgh on Saturday night. He came toward us, through the gloom, beating his hat against his overalls.

"Good mornin'," said Uncle Dick.

"What's good about it?" snapped Ed. "Good day for ducks!"

Even in the dusk I could see a glint in Uncle Dick's eyes. "Everything's good about it. God made it! It's good for ducks and for you, and for me and for Edward here. Good for everybody." He stopped short and said softly, almost sadly, "It's rainin' but it's a good day. God made it."

Years later I learned that Uncle Dick was quoting Psalm 118:

> This is the day which the Lord has made;
> let us rejoice and be glad.

Uncle Dick sometimes tampered with the truth to watch my eyes bug out, but never to glorify himself. Ed did it with no other reason. With the razor scar on his cheek twitching, he might say to me, "See that airplane flying round yesterday? I was flyin that airplane! Way up high!"

Ed and his friend Smokey used to sing:

> If whiskey was water
> And I was a duck
> I'd go to the bottom
> And never come up

Ed had a bad word for everybody. "That Reba, she got a bad luck look on her face. Been hit by the ugly stick." He called Ole Mose "Watermelon Head" and said, "His mouf like a satchel."

Old Mose, born into slavery, was considered ancient when I was a child. His pants and coat were ancient too, having both reached maturity but in different decades. On a frosty, damp day, with the wind from the north, he would say, "Mighty searchin' this mornin'." Or he might flutter his lips in observing, "It's trrruly cold!" When he wasn't feeling well he said, "My body just totally does wrong." His body did not do totally wrong too often, because he lived to be well past a hundred. As late as 1953 my father introduced my two sons to him.

While Uncle Dick hummed hymns, Ed and Smokey sang in brash, uninhibited voices:

> Ashes to ashes
> And dust to dust
> If the Camels don't get me
> The Fatimas must

Aunt Lindy was startled when I came into the house singing a song that Ed and Smokey had taught me:

> Minnie! Minnie!
> Minnie won't you shimmy for me now!

I don't think Uncle Dick approved of Ed or Smokey; they represented the opposite of what he and Carrie stood for. Once when they went driving off in the wagon, he muttered something that sounded like, "You need common sense . . . ole mother wit. . . ."

I never heard Uncle Dick give a sermon, but I did attend a couple of his "baptizin's" in Bear Grass Creek. The ceremony was always held where the water was nearly waist high, an unusual depth for those parts, where creeks tended to be shallow.

Uncle Dick's church in Newburgh was about a mile away. It was white frame with long rusty streaks down the side caused by the tin roof. Out back was a cemetery where the graves were dressed with ornate old medicine bottles filled with Queen Anne's lace, black-eyed Susans, rambling roses— flowers that thrived along the pikes and lanes in that part of Jefferson County.

The faithful started a procession at the church and could be heard singing long before they came out of the woods into the wide, grassy field that led to the creek. Uncle Dick, in a frock coat and carrying a tall staff, led his flock with dignity. Beside him pranced a deacon, a wiry little man, also wearing a black coat.

Those to be baptized came in white flowing gowns, with sweat glistening on their faces. They rolled across the field full of sunshine, singing about their souls and the new Jerusalem and the goodness of the Lord. They came on and on, elated over the waters of the Jordan and the sparrows that God counts. At the bank they grew solemn as the deacon assisted Uncle Dick into the water. With his staff the old man sounded the depths and raised his voice in prayer. He made us feel that God hovered just above that lazy turn in Bear Grass Creek.

Some of the faithful began to punctuate the summer afternoon with shouts. When time came for the immersion, Uncle Dick and the deacon helped the faithful wade into the water one at a time. At the deepest part, the two black-coated figures stood with a white robe between them and Uncle Dick placed his hand over the mouth of the one to be baptized. After three immersions the new Christian, especially a woman, might get the spirit and nearly drown. Even when hoisted onto the bank, she might slip back into the water, thrashing, and shouting about glory and cleansing waters.

On the way back to the church all of the newly baptized clapped their hands and shouted. The clapping more than anything else brought every stray dog in Newburgh loping and barking across the big green field of sunshine.

The next day Uncle Dick and I would be back at the end of the long row, resting beside the white fence where the ground was packed by horses' feet. Could it be the memory of those days that brings a twinge of sadness whenever I see the imprint of hooves in soft meadow turf?

Too bad that I did not appreciate those people in Buechel when they were still alive. Down the road a piece lived Henry Hikes, George Seibert, Grandad Seibert, and J. P. Cooney. All were so offbeat that a southern novelist could easily make a living off them.

Ancestors of Henry Hikes had come to Buechel in 1791. For two hundred years the various Hikes men made money galore with the first sawmill, the first gristmill, and the first carding machine, and orchards and farms. After inheriting some of that pioneering money, and a lovely house and farm, the Henry Hikes that I knew did not burn calories working, but went about carrying a rifle, shotgun, or fishing pole in pursuit of squirrels, rabbits, doves, or catfish.

The only thing he did that might be filed under the heading of work was to raise gamecocks. Although cockfighting was by then illegal, the birds were still getting together in somebody's barn. On the front porch of Seibert's store I heard a man tell how the rooster he had bet on was lying on its back in the pit, seemingly done for, when suddenly it shot out a leg and sent a steel spur through the other bird's head.

When Mr. Hikes tucked a fighting cock under his arm there was between them a remarkable resemblance: lean, bony structure; quick, dark eyes; and a sharp, definite beak. One day he brought a gamecock to our farm and turned it loose. The bird ran toward a new Maxwell, owned by a visitor, looked at his reflection in the side of it, and thinking he had found a rival, jumped high to send his spurs clashing against the reflection. By the time he could be collected, he had scarred one door.

I don't know that Mr. Hikes did much about religion in a formal way, but it must have haunted him because he often spoke of it. I recall something he said when he and my mother were sitting under a beech tree where we kept a swing and a cluster of chairs. It was one of those days that etches into the memory of a child with a deep bite, the way the memories of adult life never do. Even now I can smell the hickory smoke drifting from the smokehouse where hams and slabs of bacon were being cured.

Mother had been to Louisville and was commenting on the wonders of a new gadget she had seen and heard, called a radio. Mr. Hikes said, "You Catholics ought to use the radio. Tell about your religion. Let people know you are human beings like everybody else. When I was growing up we thought Catholics had horns. Just plain ignorance! Radio could help get rid of a lot of that."

His advice made an impression on me because at that time my parents were taking me to attend a mission at the county fairgrounds in Fern Creek. It was an improbable place for a series of sermons, but the mission was held there because the nearest Catholic church, in those days, was in Louisville.

We sat in the grandstand and the priest from Jeffersontown stood to deliver his sermon just above the finish line of the racetrack. The setting was a distraction because I used to picture trotters thundering down the stretch in that last burst of glorious speed. I recalled the mule race with the great black mule adorned with a rider equally as black, who whipped with a shingle, urging the animal to consume ground with loping strides.

And then there were the acts between races. I remembered the strong man stretched out on his back, suspended between two chairs; his wife put a great stone on his chest and pulverized it with a sledgehammer.

In one of his sermons the elderly pastor from Jeffersontown told us that right after his ordination he had been sent to a part of Kentucky that had never seen a Catholic priest. He was driving there in a buggy when he met a man on the road who told him what the people up ahead expected a priest to be. With this information to guide him, the young man removed his hat and shoes and propped his feet on the dashboard. Bareheaded and barefooted he rode through the settlement, making it clear to those people that contrary to what they had grown up believing a Catholic priest does not have horns or cloven hooves.

George Seibert, like Henry Hikes, often carried a squirrel rifle, but I never saw the two of them together. Uncle Dick said that Mr. Seibert was "pestering in the mind," for he was a morose man who seemed to be looking at life framed with a black border.

Mr. Seibert owned the saloon and grocery store mentioned earlier. Was the saloon kept mainly for nostalgia—Prohibition already parched the land—or was he selling "white mule," a bootleg likker with a fierce kick to it, I don't know. To me the mahogany bar, brass rail, and expansive mirror seemed glamorous, no matter what their use.

The grocery store catered mainly to field workers. I sometimes sat on the brick floor of the porch and watched them eat a lunch of baloney, brick cheese, and crackers, all washed down with soda pop. Between trips to the back room, where the bottles must have been kept, George Seibert stood in the doorway talking to the field workers. He often used such expressions as "be dog," "as the sayin' goes," and "as the feller says," tying them onto cliches: "Be dog, if he didn't come back again askin' for a handout. As the sayin' goes, he's as crazy as a loon. Sooner or later, as the feller says, he'll learn you don't get nuthin' for nuthin'."

Grandad Seibert was George Seibert's father. With his white hair and beard and thick black eyebrows he reminded me of one of the three kings in our Christmas set. He had a way of lurching to punctuate each sentence. In his watery blue eyes was the hunted look seen in the eyes of a wild rabbit, and on his lips, which twitched incessantly, was the powdery gray coating of age. The tip of his nose and the end of his chin were starting to keep close company.

He spoke often of age, as well he might: "When you get as old as I am, life is worth living only every other day." Several times I heard him tell about the old German who whenever he got drunk would say to his dog, "Yah, when you die you are dead. When I die I gotta go to hell yet." He used an expression, "Gott Dory," that I never heard before or since. "Gott Dory, but your bones ache when you get old!"

Grandad Seibert lived off the land, hunting mushrooms and watercress, and picking blackberries and gathering walnuts. That is how he earned toddy money. Each afternoon he went into the back door of Seibert's house and pulled down the kitchen shade in deference to the long, dark shadow of Prohibition. Into a water glass he poured two fingers of "white moon," another name for "white mule," added a cube of sugar and a splash of hot water, and after stirring thoughtfully, downed it all in a gulp or two.

He always paid for the toddy, for he was, as George Seibert observed, "an independent cuss." His independence was best dramatized by his insistence on living alone: he slept in a piano box in a shed behind the saloon.

Another old man, with the silhouette of a buggy whip, often came down the Old Shepherdsville Road atop a green wagon with "J. P. Cooney" stenciled in ornate gold lettering on its side. With a well-turned sorrell kicking up the gravel, he swung into our driveway at a good clip. A dramatic "Whoa, Heart! Whoa!" brought all of that momentum to such a halt so sudden that it annoyed my father, who disliked seeing a horse pulled up too fast, saying it damages the pasterns.

Whatever I was doing was put aside at once because J. P. Cooney was too good a raconteur to miss. He graced with zest his ancedotes, which unfolded in detail. Take, for example, the day he sat with my father and mother on the side porch speaking of medicine shows. He told of Doctor somebody-or-other who had toured that part of Kentucky shortly after the Civil War. It seems that medicine show proprietors usually carried the self-appointed title of Doctor or Professor. This particular Doctor drove an enclosed jersey wagon from town to town and after unhitching the team on the main drag, let down the tailgate, set a platform atop it, and was ready to sell.

"He walked out onto that stage wearing a broad-brimmed gray hat and a black frock coat," said Mr. Cooney, noticing I was already absorbed. "The buttons on the coat were ten-dollar goldpieces and the buttons on the vest were five-dollar goldpieces. On his right hand was a ring with a stone in it big enough to choke a moose. That's the hand he used most when he talked."

The Doctor sold a concoction called Indian Maiden Elixir, or something like that. A big brown bottle sold for a dollar. Under the label of every tenth bottle was a dollar bill. A couple of such premium bottles were always among the first sold "just to get the crowd itchy."

Before starting his pitch the Doctor turned loose a four-piece brass band that "made enough noise to be heard all over the county at once." As the crowd gathered, the Doctor's wife, billed as an Indian princess, appeared on the platform; she had stained her hands and face with walnut hulls to give herself the color of iodine. She sang Indian songs that had a mournful quality to them, "like the sound a streetcar makes going around a corner."

The climax of the show came when the Doctor shoved a chair onto the middle of the platform, calling for audience participation. He took from his pocket a pair of silver pliers and offered to pull free of charge any teeth that needed pulling. The patient was instructed to grab the rungs of the chair and hang on. The band played loud enough to drown any sounds of anguish, and the crowd twitched with the pangs of empathy.

"Did he always get some takers?" my father asked.

"Yes, because in any crowd there are some people who can't resist something for nothing. Even if it's having their teeth pulled. In the excitement he sometimes pulled the wrong tooth. He just called that a bonus and tried again."

Those neighbors deserve more attention than I gave them. Now memory sees them only fitfully and in part. How much I missed!

– 4 –

Early Solitude

During the droning summer afternoons I sat by the pond in the barnyard watching the darting and flitting of long black insects, metallic in sheen. Some people called them darning needles, but to Uncle Dick they were snake doctors. "If a snake get sick, he have a snake doctor bite him and get well."

Near the pond, cruising above the tall grass, were June bugs galore. After catching one I would tie a string to a leg and let him fly in circles.

Even clover, plentiful there in the barnyard, helped to pass the time. By tying together stems to form garlands and stretching the clover strings from tree to tree, I could create an enclosure. Sitting inside it brought a warm sense of well-being.

Not far from the pond stood a gigantic beech that I walked around and around, completing the circle often enough to wear away the bark from the exposed roots. This made Aunt Lindy nervous. She said to stop it or else I would get very dull. It must have puzzled her, for I told her nothing of the daydreams of walking a high wire in the circus, and of standing on the wing of a biplane in flight, and of playing with an imaginary younger brother.

I was a dreamer, brooding by the hours. As Sir Walter Scott confessed: "Since I was five years old I cannot remember the time I had not some ideal part to play for my solitary amusement."

All of this suggests a lonely childhood. Yet the solitude was only on the surface; inside there were adventures. Oh, there were playmates on occasion when Bill and Louise Seibert came by, or I went to Louisville to visit Joe Steltenpohl, or he came to the farm, but mainly I entertained myself.

Someone gave me an old baseball uniform, a worn-out catcher's mitt, and a cracked bat. What a strange sight, a skinny kid walking around a farm in a too-large uniform with a catcher's mitt on his left hand and a bat over his right shoulder.

My regard for adults was such that the thought never occurred to ask my father, or Uncle Dick, or anyone else to toss a baseball in my direction so that I might take a wack at it. So I threw the ball onto the tin roof of the barn and as it came flying off slammed it with the bat. Whether I flied out, or hit a home run, or did any of the other things a batter does, depended on what section of the barn the ball struck.

I also devised a way to play football in competition with myself. After I kicked the ball onto the barn roof and it came bobbling off, I would grab it and run for touchdowns. The rules that decided whether I won or lost have slipped from memory.

Just before Christmas there was usually a trip to Louisville to get a catalog at Sutcliff's. After studying photographs of games spread out in their panoramic glory, I took scissors, paste, and knife and fashioned all the parts from cardboard and bits of wood. The next problem was to dream up rules that would use all of those pieces in such a way that one person could play against himself.

Professional entertainment that came to Buechel, an occasional tent show, was one rung above a dog-and-pony show in sophistication. The owner of such is quoted in a study of American culture as saying, "We're in the entertainment business. If you're looking for art go somewhere else. We simply want to give folks a good time for an evening." Nothing gave me a better time for an evening than a small show that pitched a tent in an open field near the railroad station. The sound of creaking ropes and the smell of hot canvas and sawdust still linger.

The entertainment opened with two blackface comedians telling jokes: "Who was that lady I saw you with on the street?" "That was no street that was an alley." Next came a juggler in pink tights who kept several pie plates in the air at once, bouncing one off another. Then a rifleman, dressed as Buffalo Bill, shot cigarettes from a woman's mouth.

As far as I was concerned the most memorable act was performed by a boy not much older than myself. Wearing a checked suit and a gray derby and carrying a bamboo cane, he sang and tapped, accompanied by a tinny piano.

> The prettiest girl I ever saw
> was sippin' cider through a straw
> So cheek to cheek and jaw to jaw
> We both sipped cider through a straw
> That's how I got my mother-in-law
> A-sippin' cider through a straw.

In his repertoire was a forgettable ditty that somehow persists in memory:

> There was an old German named Fredt
> Before he went to bedt
> He ate too much
> Of a cheese that was Dutch
> And when he woke up he was deadt.

Some of the most entertaining hours of childhood were spent listening to Uncle Addie. Each summer I went to Louisville several times to visit him and Aunt Lena. The attraction was supposed to be Shelby Park, stretching from the backyard onward and outward. But I didn't find the tennis courts and swimming pool nearly as attractive as my uncle's stories and the Shelby Public Library.

How impressive it was when Addie put on his fireman's outfit, a dark blue uniform designed in imitation of those worn by Union officers in the Civil War. When he stood on the step behind the great brass stack, with smoking pouring out, and the heavy, galloping horses leaning into their rich harness, it was a sight for a country boy to see. He told me his job was to keep up the water pressure. When it was up, the engine pumped 350 gallons a minute to send a jet of water 170 feet into the air.

Uncle Addie was the slowest storyteller I have ever heard. Now if someone takes longer than necessary to tell an anecdote I get annoyed, but then the slowness added to the fascination. In sentences fragmented into a few words at a time, he told of the prowess of "The Louisvilles," a baseball club that was the smartest that ever lived.

It might take a half hour for him to tell how the pitcher and the catcher worked out a trick to get a much-needed third strike. The catcher walked out to the mound, but instead of handing the ball to the pitcher, he pocketed it deep within his glove. The pitcher faked a pitch, and the catcher slapped his mitt in a certain way and held the ball in triumph. Batter and umpire thought they had blinked at just the wrong moment. To save face the umpire called a strike.

The slow narrative pace was determined by Uncle Addie's way of chewing tobacco. Just as he reached a high peak, and I was hanging on, he would pause to spit. That is the kind of timing that writers, actors, and film directors work for—they have to know when to pause to spit.

Uncle Addie had the flattest behind ever devised by the mind of God. My mother saw it as a symbol of laziness, something acquired through years of sitting. She said that whenever she passed the fire station firemen were always sitting outside on captain's chairs, leaning back against the brick wall, with hands locked behind their heads. She felt that an occasional fire did not put enough pressure on a human being.

Across the street from Aunt Lena and Uncle Addie lived the Matures. An image of Mrs. Mature comes to mind each time pea soup is served in the faculty dining room. I see her sitting so very erect on a straight chair, a handsome woman, speaking of the glory of the pea soup she has just made. She shudders as she says, "Oh, it's so good, even though it is kind of ekelig." (*Ekelig* is a German word for something of such a texture that it is slightly repulsive.)

Mr. Mature, arriving from Germany with little money, found a way to fill a need, and, as they say down there, "he did right well." He learned that in barbershops were scissors that could use some sharpening, in butcher shops knives and cleavers needed touching up, and in most homes saws, hatchets, scissors, knives, and lawn mowers were waiting to have an edge put on them. So he arranged some sharpening equipment inside a closed wagon and drove about Louisville bringing his service to the door.

My sister knew the Matures' only child better than I did because she was nearer his age. When he went to Hollywood, years later, to try his luck, Bertha and her friends said, "When he becomes a star, we'll say we knew him when."

Victor Mature's name sounds as though it might have been made up to promote his movie career, but that is the name he has had since baptism. By coincidence he starred in roles calling for mature-looking heroes, roles he portrayed with all of the handsomeness inherited from the woman who made the *ekelig* pea soup.

I would have seen more of Victor had I spent more time in Shelby Park. But as I said earlier, Bertha and her friends made reading seem so important that the quiet of the Shelby Public Library wooed me away from the clamor of the playground.

The first books that I read on my own were about the Bobbsey Twins, followed by those telling of the Five Little Peppers, the remarkable inhabitants of Oz, and the adventures of Doctor Doolittle. The two last books read in that musty reading room, toward the end of the grade-school years, were *Ivanhoe* and *Lorna Doone*.

A book that would never rate space on a library shelf, *A Slow Train through Arkansas*, was one I read until memorized. The only part that I can still recall is that in which a woman complains about the slowness of the train and the conductor says, "Lady, if this isn't fast enough for you, why don't you get off and walk?" and she answers, "I would but my folks don't expect me until the train gets there."

In the dusky barn loft, surrounded by the sweet smell of hay, I used to sit staring into the cages of Belgian hares. In an almost hypnotic state I would catch myself wondering why I am not a rabbit and why that rabbit is not me.

When reading Malcolm Muggeridge's autobiography, not long ago, a sentence brought a pang of recognition: "Just walking along the road we lived on when I was a child I would find myself wondering, with a poignancy I find it difficult now to convey, who I was and how I came to be in that place."

This dawning of the consciousness of self as something apart from other selves comes as an experience of childhood. Jung said that from the age of eight or nine the child realizes, "I am."

The only person I mentioned it to was Uncle Dick. We were jouncing across a field in the market wagon, quiet except for the creaking of harness and wheels, and the startled cries of killdeers running ahead. Suddenly I wondered aloud why I am not a rabbit and a rabbit is not me. All he said was, "That's the way it is." His answer was about as helpful as the time I asked, "Are there ghosts?" and he said, "Only if you believe in them."

In childhood there are other haunting moments that do not fit into the ordinary pattern of experience, moments when something seems clearer, more graspable, larger than life. Such brief spells of luminous intuition were observed by Coventry Patmore years ago. He told of a seven-year-old boy saying, "What makes this ball drop when I leave hold of it? — Oh, I know, the ground pulls it." The child had never heard of the Newtonian theory of gravitation. Patmore told of another child, who while stretched out on a gravel path staring intently at pebbles, said, "They are alive. They are always wanting to burst, but something draws them in."

Intuitive moments can be so moving that they seem to cause a jolt deep down inside. "The sacred shiver," Cyril Connolly called it. When and where it will happen nobody knows, for it comes unheralded and unanticipated and refuses to be willfully induced.

In childhood the "sacred shiver" might be induced by an apparently trivial work. Gavin Maxwell said he was so deeply moved by the garish painting of a polar landscape that tears came to his eyes. At about age seven I found that a Christmas card showing a rabbit running in the snow gave a physical jolt, as though I were experiencing something on a different dimension.

In his Romanes Lectures in 1954, called "Moments of Vision," Lord Kenneth Clark said: "We can all remember those flashes when the object at which we are gazing seems to detach itself from the habitual flux of impressions and becomes intensely clear and important for us. We may not experience these illuminations very often in our busy adult lives, but they were common in our childhood, and given half a chance we could achieve them still. Such moments are the nearest many of us will ever come to the divine agitation of the artist."

Christmas in childhood was especially transcendent. A walk through the woods that morning brought a hushed awe and a restrained joy that walking those same paths the next day did not bring. At Bashford Manor even the yearlings, wooly in their winter coats, had a special look about them.

Although our family had gone to Mass well before dawn, I stayed up alone until twelve o'clock, relishing every minute of the holy day, not wanting to let go of a feeling that would not return for another year. At the fireplace I neither read nor prayed, just sat keeping watch over minutes that felt magnificent and benign. As Wordsworth said, "It is the hour of feeling."

Why do certain times, such as Christmas, and places, too, have more poignancy than other times and places? Why can a prospect please enough to bring a pang of pain? Why can a simple memory be bittersweet, such as that of my father carrying a fir tree across his shoulder, stomping through a field of snow and corn stubble? These experiences are mainly the gifts of childhood, when a turn in the road, a bend in the creek, or a lone tree in a field can make the heart leap. In travels I am intrigued by the spirit of a place, wondering what makes some places more important than others. Such things haunt me, because momentarily we nearly touch something beyond the mundane.

Sounds were also more fascinating in childhood than they are now. How haunting was that of a shallow stream running over flat rocks. Years later my memories returned to Bear Grass Creek when I came across the Greek word *nympholet*, meaning one who is under the spell of running waters.

A Carmelite nun, Mother Amata, said, "I am speaking strictly for myself, but I feel that contemplative prayer is natural to everyone because it is looking at things with wonder and joy. A child is a natural contemplative but too many of us lose that faculty as we grow older."

My first awareness of death came in the barnyard. Each Saturday chickens hopped around headless, their eyes still staring from the chopping block. Then there was the sack of kittens on the way to the creek. When pigs were ready for slaughter, J. P. Cooney put the muzzle between their eyes and pulled the trigger. An ancient horse was put down when somebody draped a burlap sack over his head and hit him between the eyes with a sledgehammer.

The first person I saw in a a casket was the first person I had fallen in love with. Mary Cooney, J. P. Cooney's daughter, must have been about twenty when I was six. She was exquisite, something of a China doll, and looked even more fragile in death. "So waxy," is the way my mother put it.

At the cemetery I watched two men straddle the grave, and with ropes beneath the casket, lower it down the lean clay walls. A few hours later Mother said, "This is Mary Cooney's first night under the sod."

When she said it, I thought of a dead squirrel found in the woods a few days earlier. After turning it over with a stick, I was startled by the seething, seething of thousands of white maggots. The image always came to mind when Mother repeated after each funeral that this is "the first night under the sod."

My feelings about death were born out of those experiences at six. Because of them I am unable to understand some people's concern with how or where they are buried.

Solitude in childhood had advantages and disadvantages. The greatest advantage was that the aloneness seemed to suit me. The disadvantage was the other children seemed better fitted for life than I was. They did better in school, were more coordinated in sports, and had some sense of teamwork. Above all they developed a sense of competition, something I lack.

– 5 –

School Years

One morning in early September of 1920, Mother and I boarded the red interurban electric that ran beside the Bardstown Road from Fern Creek to Louisville. I wore a white shirt and white trousers and a black straw hat and carried a new-smelling book with the word *Primer* printed across its yellow cover. Carefully, I held one of Bertha's old slates with a sponge and a bottle of water used to clean it. A brave show for the first day of school.

Just inside the Louisville city limits we got off at the Loop, so called because streetcars turned there to start back to the center of town. After walking three blocks we came to Saint Francis of Assisi School, a three-room frame structure with a long hitching rack in front and a long shed of toilets in back. It was almost simple enough to please its patron saint.

We had electric light, all right, bare bulbs hanging from the ceiling. Heat was supplied by a potbelly stove in the center of each room; students near it sweltered and those by the wall shivered. Atop the stove, a tin boiler of water kept moisture in the room. I soon learned from the older kids to use the boiler to heat chocolate milk brought in a pop bottle from home. That and a sandwich carried in a tin box was lunch.

Right off I found school easy to dislike. The classrooms were crowded and the playgrounds hectic. All day I looked forward to the quiet of the farm, where in late afternoon I walked around and around the beech tree, dreaming of a way to avoid school.

The answer seemed evident when my desk-partner, Jack Buscaren, fell from his bicycle and broke a leg. Since that kept him from school a few weeks, a broken leg was the way out. Perhaps the pony could help.

Snowball had the bad habit of bucking. When he threw my cousin Ida against a maple tree I cried, not for Ida's sake, but out of fear that the pony had injured himself in the effort. My father then stretched a strap from the bit to the saddle, made it taut enough so that the pony, unable to lower his head between his legs, was discouraged from bucking. Surreptitiously, I loosened the strap, hoping to get thrown and so break a leg.

31

I stopped that when Jack Buscaren died suddenly at Christmas. What caused his death I never knew, but I feared it had something to do with a broken leg. As his desk-partner I was asked to be a pallbearer. Again I watched two men straddle a grave and lower a casket. Even now I can see clearly Mrs. Buscaren in her anguish: a tall, darkly beautiful young woman. That evening I waited for Mother to say, "This is Jack Buscaren's first night under the sod," but she didn't. Perhaps she found it too painful. But I said it to myself over and over in the darkness of the big square bedroom.

In the early grades there were painful classroom experiences. For instance, it was agonizing when the teacher made me stand at the blackboard all afternoon trying to solve a problem in arithmetic. We both knew I had not the slightest idea of where to begin. How dark life seemed that day. Riding home on the interurban I couldn't look the other children in the face, and I hoped my parents would never hear about this. As we passed a field where gypsy wagons sometimes stood, I looked at the camp with longing.

When I tried to give the impression of doing homework, my parents would find that a stack of books shielded a shaky sketch, a poor imitation of a Pulaski cartoon. Each evening I pored over Pulaski's drawings in the *Louisville Times*. His political messages escaped me; I was interested only in the drawing.

Radio was another distraction from homework. When we bought a crystal set with earphones, early in the 1920s, it required a long aerial that stretched from the house to the barn. Tuning in a station required a steady hand and patience; it meant delicately scratching a fine wire, known as a cat's whisker, across a rough hunk of crystal about the size of a dime. When the wire touched the right spot, somebody usually walked across the room, jarring the cat's whisker, and that meant starting all over.

I had a radio logbook but was not allowed to stay up late enough to accumulate many listings. In the early days of radio, fans lost sleep trying to get distance on their sets. They would write to the station saying what they had heard at what hour and the station would send a card of confirmation. It was not unusual for WHAS, in Louisville, to go off the air early to clear the airways so that local listeners could indulge in"Dx-ing," listening to distant stations. On the way to school on the interurban I heard people bragging of their achievements. "I got KDKA in Pittsburgh last night." "At two o'clock this morning Salt Lake City came in real well."

A bicycle, along with radio and school, helped stretch awareness beyond the confines of a small farm. The bike, ordered from a Sears & Roebuck catalog, arrived by rail at the Buechel station, all disassembled inside a wooden crate. My face fell, for I had so wished to ride it home. Upon seeing my chagrin, the stationmaster, Mr. G. S. Carpenter, offered to assemble it right there on the station platform. From then on whenever I passed the station I remembered with gratitude Mr. Carpenter, a fixture for many years. When the Southern Railway built a station at Buechel he had been put in charge, although only twenty-one, and he stayed in charge for the next fifty-three years.

Mr. Carpenter used to recall how Buechel was when he opened the station in 1907: "Right down here on Six Mile Lane was Klondike Park, which was opened up by a fellow named Frank Bumann. He'd been a prospector in the Yukon and I remember him well. He wore a chain on his vest that had gold nuggets hanging from it."

While riding the bike south on Bardstown Road I used to pass Buechel's Tavern, opened by John Buechel shortly after the Civil War. The community took his name when he opened a post office in a corner of the tavern in 1883 and became the first postmaster. Drovers from all over that part of Kentucky stopped there overnight on their way to Louisville. They penned their stock in corrals out back and gathered in front of the tavern under the osage orange trees. To pass the time they would bet as to who could use the fewest blows to drive a nail into the ironlike wood of the trees. I often paused with the bike to examine the hundreds of rusty nail heads and wonder how many blows it had taken.

South of Buechel I would come to Fern Creek, where the first settlers had been James Guthrie and his wife, Eunice, a sister of John Paul Jones. The Guthries came to live there in 1778 when, in thanks for his Revolutionary War service, he was given a large tract of land stretching along what would eventually be known as Bardstown Road. Guthrie found the area full of Indians, and so for the sake of safety built his home of stone quarried from Cedar Creek. Because the house provided security it became a stopping place for Catholic priests and nuns on their way to and from Bardstown, which at the time was headquarters of the Catholic Church in Kentucky.

In the days that I biked through there, the most impressive thing in Fern Creek was the Nicholson Hotel, a long, two-story white frame structure, with a wide porch across the front and many trees in the yard. The hotel had been built by Noah Cartwright, who raised a company of men during the Civil War and went off to fight for the Union. The area saw some Blue-Gray skirmishes, but none sizeable enough to get into the history books.

In my childhood the hotel specialized in fried chicken and country ham, all you could eat, for fifty cents a meal. Jack Dempsey ate there; perhaps he was visiting Marvin Hart at the time. Babe Ruth once asked for a good place to eat and was sent to Nicholson's. Al Jolson ate there two days in a row.

If I rode the bike north of Buechel, toward Louisville, it was usually to Cherokee Park. How lovely, riding up and down hills, around curves and across bridges through a landscape heavy with great trees. It is painful for me to recall that on the afternoon of April 3, 1974, within a few minutes, a tornado detroyed two thousand of the trees. A forestry expert hired to supervise the replanting said, "No one alive today will live long enough to see Cherokee Park as it used to be."

The loveliness of Bashford Manor has also colored my impressions from childhood. In walking around those acres I felt as rich as I do today walking around the Notre Dame campus. When sick I looked from my bedroom window out toward the patchwork of pastures enclosed by white fences, with mares and foals grazing within those well-defined limits. Something in the view brought a poignancy that cannot be explained.

I never envied the owners of Bashford Manor, nor did I want the place for my own. Just knowing it was there was enough. I realize now that it had value because it was not trivial. It expressed an ideal. Its style and elegance were something to look up to. The grooms who worked there made less money, much less, than industrial workers, but they were spending their days surrounded by tranquility and loveliness, and so were more to be envied than felt sorry for. I learned when young that to be poor in a pleasant place is bearable. To be poor, or even rich, in a dreary, ugly setting must be painful and destructive.

Bashford Manor, the bicycle, and other distractions kept childhood from being unhappy as it might well have been, since the only thing I liked about school were the "free days"—Robert E. Lee's birthday, the pastor's feast day, and the holy days of the Church. Not even recess brought much relief. The kids swinging by their legs from the hitching rack and slamming each other over the head with school bags caused my head to spin. The quiet days on the farm were no preparation for this.

Suddenly, I had an obsessive desire for a typewriter. Never before or since have I wanted anything so much as the secondhand, portable Corona, with a $15 tag on it, displayed, of all places, in a bakery window. It was certainly improbable that a farm boy among middle-class city kids should be the first to own a typewriter. Sister Ermalinda was so impressed that she had me start a school paper. The first thing I wrote was an acrostic of Merry Christmas.

At a racetrack when a horse is slow in coming out of the starting gate they say he "dwelt." I certainly dwelt and did not begin "runnin' kind" until twenty. In the last two grades, though, there was a hint of hope. When Sister Ermalinda had me start the school paper and Sister Modesta put me in two plays I began to sense that I did some things better than most kids.

One September night, three weeks after my fourteenth birthday, Mother and I sat under the beech tree, both aware that in the morning I would be going away to boarding school to study for the priesthood. She must have realized that so much aloneness had prolonged childhood and that here I was stepping into boyhood having missed much of the give-and-take with other children. She said little that evening. Just as I was going into the house to go to bed she stopped me. "This is your last night at home. From now on when you come back you will only be visiting."

The next morning I went out into the chilly dawn to carve 9-11-28 into the giant beech tree. I must have sensed that September 11, 1928 would be one of the important days of my life, the day I left the nest.

Mother and I took the interurban to Louisville and went to Tenth and Broadway to board the Monon. The conductor was experienced enough to herd all of the boys going to Rensselaer, Indiana, into one car. Mother was wise enough to sit in the back of the coach and have me mingle with fellows who would be my friends for the next six years.

She was amused at the way the kids surprised some of the unoccupied men of southern Indiana. The boys filled paper cups with ice water, one cup in each hand, and stationed themselves at windows the length of the coach. When we rolled through sleepy towns, where men with nothing to do came down to the station to watch the train go through, the kid in the first window would spot an unoccupied fellow and let fly at him with two cups of water, and the others followed suit as the train rolled slowly past. Mother was delighted at the soaking given those "triflers," as she called them.

We took a taxi the two miles from Rensselaer station to the campus of Saint Joseph's. I can still picture the view that spread before us as we swung through the stone gateway—a round lake with an island, featuring a fountain in the center. Stretching just behind it was the fine old Main Building, a three-story red brick with Bedford rock trim, sitting on "a slight eminence," as the catalog put it.

A few nights ago I happened upon a rerun of *Brian's Song*, and there on the television screen was that very view. The film portrays the tragic friendship that developed between Brian Piccolo and Gale Sayers when they played on the Chicago Bears football team. (The Bears trained at Saint Joseph's each summer from 1944 until 1974.) In the opening sequence of the film that won five Emmys and a Peabody award, Sayers, played by Billy Dee Williams, is arriving at Saint Joseph's, passing through the stone gateway for the first time; there he will meet Brian Piccolo, played by James Caan.

Each time I see that scene with the round lake in the foreground I remember Gil Hodges, one of the great baseball players of his generation, and Gene Krupa, rated as the best drummer of his time. The year Hodges came to Saint Joseph's, sophomores were still hazing freshmen. When the sophs threw Gil into the lake he swam under water to the far side of the island before coming up for air. Since the sophs could not see him hiding behind the fountain, they took for granted he had never surfaced, and so began diving frantically to recover his body. As for Krupa, I was a young journalist when we met; he had been away from Saint Joseph's for more than a decade. He told me that as a freshman he had learned to swim in that lake.

The day Mother and I passed through the stone gateway the fame of Krupa, Hodges, Piccolo, and Sayers was far in the future. That September afternoon in 1928 the campus held scarcely three hundred students—in four years of high school and two of college—but to me, shy and scared, and straight from the farm, it all seemed overwhelming.

The way of doing things at Saint Joseph's was Central European. The school had been founded near the end of last century by German priests of the Society of the Precious Blood, and their traditions still held. The catalog said: "Those in charge of discipline strive to maintain the golden mean between excessive severity and pernicious laxity. . . . Idle, intractable, and vicious students will not be permitted to remain." The great advantage of this was the discipline of an ordered day. There were specific times for everything—sleeping, study hall, classes, recreation.

We began each morning in chapel with a prayer:

> Life is short and death is sure;
> The hour of death remains obscure.

Not a bad first-thought for the day. For teenagers, I suspect, those were mainly words, but recalled late in life they give direction to the day, for the meaning is felt down into the crevices of the soul.

During evenings in study hall I used to listen for the saddest sound in the world—the long wail of the night train. As I wrote in my diary, I saw those cars hurtling through the darkness "stitching the night like a golden thread." I envied the people in the brightly lit cars, coming from some place, going some place. Best of all they were unencumbered by the Latin ablative absolute, the Greek aorist, and the square of the hypotenuse that equals the sum of the square of the other two sides. I would lift the lid of my desk; under it was thumbtacked a calendar on which I checked off the days, always aware of how many were left until the start of Christmas vacation.

The hardest days followed Christmas. Those afternoons of dirty gray were part of the pangs of prep school. My heart ached, not so much to go home but to escape the dreary round of schooling for which I seemed ill fitted.

The greatest thrill of each school year came with a bright June morning when a pair of gray Percheron mares would pull away a haywagon stacked high with trunks. Later in the morning we crawled around and over the mountain of baggage inside the Rensselaer station, each searching for his trunk and eventually tying the baggage claim check onto it. With that act, three months of vacation began!

Latin and Greek were very big at Saint Joseph's and I was ineffective in both. We read Horace's odes, Virgil's *Aeneid*, Cicero's orations, Caesar's *Gallic Wars* and Xenophon's *Anabasis*.

How much do the classics mean to a high school student? Not much in any testable way, but there is a value beyond proof. So even though I did poorly in Latin and Greek the time was not wasted. The classics put me in touch with the Greek and Latin spirits—both worth brushing against, especially the Greek—and maybe some of the quality, the nobility of it, rubbed off. What we get by a spiritual osmosis seems more lasting than things memorized and passed in tests.

I feel the same way about teachers. What we get from them as people is more important in the long run than the subjects they teach. At Saint Joseph's Father Ildephone Rapp and Father Sylvester Ley had long-lasting influences on me.

Father Ley, in English composition, made me feel that I might eventually handle the language in an effective way. He was a great one for precision. For example, he might make the point that good style and good taste are not always one: "Some of your neckties are in good style, but they are not always in good taste." Or he might stress the distinction between habit and custom: "It is a custom to rise early here, but it never becomes a habit."

His was a generous spirit, much given to superlatives.

Father Rapp directed all of the plays, was in charge of public speaking, and taught a course called Expression. In Expression classes we heard our classmates deliver certain pieces time and again. Father Rapp sat through those repetitious recitations with apparent interest and good humor. He never seemed bored. After each he made comments with zest, precision, and kindness.

How often he must have heard Iago say:

> Who steals my purse steals trash; 'tis something, nothing;
> 'Twas mine, 'tis his, and has been slave to thousands. . . .

or

> This above all: to thine own self be true. . . .

Those classes had value. We sat listening to words well used. Some of the rhythms and some of the discernment of the writers must have seeped into our consciousness.

Father Rapp had great presence and a dignity that was almost measurable. Even from a distance he showed tensile strength. The way he walked, the movement of the hands, and everything he did seemed important. He made the most ordinary sentence sound like something worth saying.

I did well in Father Rapp's speech course and in the plays he directed and in Father Ley's writing courses, but that was the extent of my academic reach. Neither I, nor the teachers, nor my classmates would have believed that I was destined for the academic world.

Somewhere I have read that it is possible to have a vocation to study for the priesthood but not become a priest. Certainly the time at Saint Joseph's influenced my life in a way that evolved through the years. After graduating with a Junior College diploma I thought schooling had ended. Then something decisive happened. My life swerved to a new direction because of the two littlest words in the English language.

– 6 –

Starting Notre Dame

One summer morning when the Depression was hanging over the country like a dense gray fog, a phone call came from Sister Mary Gabriel Hayden, O.S.U. Through friends I had met her a year earlier, and although she had never taught me she was interested in the direction my life would take. Would I come to see her at a convent she was visiting in New Albany, Indiana?

At the convent door an elderly nun showed me to the parlor where I waited. It was typical of convent parlors in those days. The only pieces of furniture were an ancient oak rocker, a black horsehair chair, and a round mahogany table that held back copies of the *Sacred Heart Messenger*. All that hand-me-down furniture was beautifully kept. On the walls were an oleograph of the Sacred Heart and a photograph of Teresa of Lisieux, Sister Gabriel's favorite saint. The beige linoleum glistened and the whole room was enlivened with the smell of wax and polish.

Sister Gabriel, a small woman of elegance, entered and right off asked in a soft southern voice what I intended to do with myself. I said that there was the chance of a job in the shipping department of a hardware company.

"Oh, no!" she exclaimed. Those two little words sent my world spinning in a direction it has been going ever since.

"You should go to Notre Dame," she said.

She knew that I felt the need to be a journalist. I had done well on school publications in grade school, high school, and junior college. Once I had told her that when Charles Lindbergh came to Louisville in the *Spirit of Saint Louis*, in the summer of 1927, I went to Bowman Field to see him, but paid more attention to the newspaper reporters covering his speech than to Lindbergh himself.

Sister Mary Gabriel had received her M.A. in History at Notre Dame in the early 1930s. She spoke with admiration of a friend there, the head of the Department of Journalism, Dr. John Michael Cooney. He is a Kentuckian, she said, and stressed that several times.

I did not have to tell her that I lacked money; she knew that. Go to see the president of Notre Dame, Father John O'Hara, she urged. Tell him you want to be a journalist and are willing to work your way through college.

Because Sister Mary Gabriel told me to do it I went ahead and did it. First came the Monon trip from Louisville up the center of Indiana to Chicago and then the lurching ride on the South Shore. My first sight of South Bend was of a gigantic, red neon sign blinking the word "Bendix" in a dark rainy night.

At the South Shore station I asked a taxi driver to take me to a hotel, something cheap, and he did just that. He took me to the Lincoln Hotel, which I learned later, as a newpaperman, had a sleazy reputation.

The next morning, Monday, September 9, 1935, wherever I went around South Bend there was talk about Huey Long. "His bodyguards inserted sixty-one bullet holes into the fellow who shot him," said a barber.

On Michigan Street I boarded a streetcar for the swaying trip up Hill Street and Notre Dame Avenue to the end of the line, near where the Notre Dame post office now stands. Since this was a single-track system, with no turn-around, the motorman had to lower one trolley and raise another and move his equipment to the other end of the car for the return trip.

Bearing on the golden dome, I walked the length of the main quad; it looked then much as it does today. Father O'Hara occupied the office in the Main Building that all of the university's presidents have since occupied.

Eddie Boyle, the track star, was Father O'Hara's secretary; such arrangements were not unusual in those simpler times. Boyle asked what I wanted of Father O'Hara and when I told him he seemed amused; I thought for a moment that he would burst out laughing. Fortunately, he did not say that the president was out of town, or too busy, or that I needed an appointment. If he had, I probably would have gone straight back to Kentucky.

Father O'Hara, with biretta far back on his head and the cape of his cassock flipped back from his shoulders, sat behind his desk listening with focused intensity. I thought he would bore a hole right through me. He said nothing to me until after making a phone call and then announced in a terse sentence that I would be working for a scholar, Father Philip Moore, collating Latin manuscripts.

That was all there was to it. I had been in his office less than five minutes.

As I returned down the quad my inept Latin came in handy for the second time that morning. The strong bronze statue of Father Edward Sorin loomed above me, larger than life. From the Latin inscription on its base I learned this was the founder of the University of Notre Dame.

While I had come to these acres that morning on a chancy mission it was not nearly so chancy as the one that brought Father Sorin here. Later I learned from Sister Mary Gabriel, with her M.A. in history, of the series of Providential events that placed Notre Dame on this particular spot.

It all started when Chief Pokagon made a plea that a missionary be sent to Ste-Marie-des-Lacs. Missionaries had arrived in the area, where the river makes a bend to the south, as early as the seventeenth century. They soon neglected the region because the territory changed hands often in the wars fought by France, England, and Spain. For nearly a century priests visited the Indians only on rare occasions.

Chief Pokagon, displeased with the morality of many Indians, decided that his tribe needed spiritual guidance; so he rode a horse to Detroit, nearly 200 miles, to beg for a permanent mission. Falling down on his knees, he recited prayers in the Potawatomi tongue, prayers that survived fifty years since the last priest's visit. This so impressed a tough old missionary, Father Stephen Theodore Badin, the first priest ordained in the United States, that in 1831 he built a log chapel on a lake, the present site of Notre Dame.

Because of lack of funds Father Sorin had almost never left France. Providentially, a woman in LeMans donated a gold chain which was raffled off, and with this unexpected money Sorin and six religious brothers sailed from Le Havre.

In Vincennes, Indiana, Father Sorin told Bishop de la Hailandière that he wanted to start a school. The bishop offered him a piece of land where a log chapel stood near South Bend, some 200 miles north of Vincennes.

Looked at purely in human terms Notre Dame should have failed at its inception, Sister Mary Gabriel observed. What chance did it have when Father Sorin stood beside the log chapel and looked across a frozen lake in November of 1842? He was only twenty-eight, spoke little English, and had scarcely $600.

After leaving Father Sorin's statue I took the first of hundreds of walks that I would eventually take around the campus in the next fifty years. I walked, that early September, among the old brick buildings tinged with yellow and partly hidden by ivy, and marveled at leaded windows and slate roofs with their blue-gray cast. I failed to notice, though, how the old French section and the collegiate Gothic blend because of massed greenery of oak, maple, birch, sycamore, and pine.

The campus felt empty. Students would not arrive for another two weeks. Perhaps the only people living in the halls that morning were the bachelor professors—James Withey, Thomas Madden, Francis O'Malley, Joseph Ryan, Paul Byrne, Bowyer Campbell, and Paul Fenlon. These men, I would learn in time, encouraged tradition and deepened it. They met for tea or drinks in late afternoon, gave students good advice at any hour, and devoted their lives to Notre Dame. As Monsignor Philip Hughes would say, "They were not the kind you could order out of a catalog."

During my first days at Notre Dame I experienced loneliness as never before or since. The remembered pain is still with me a half-century later. I was assigned to Corby, a hall for juniors. (That was the last year that Corby housed students; from then on it would be a residence for Holy Cross priests.) The other juniors in the hall had been forming friendships for two years and were unaware that I was new. Had it not been for shyness I might more easily have found a place among them.

On the night of September 24 I came out onto Corby porch where some twenty fellows were gathering to listen to a broadcast of the Joe Louis–Max Baer fight. Since money was scarce in the Depression, few students owned radios and so that evening the hall rector turned up the volume of his and opened his window.

The rector, Father "Tuffy" Ryan, joked with the students while I sat on the railing at the dark end of the porch, remote from the lively silhouettes near the light. Even before the fight ended I walked toward the log chapel, continuing past it around the lake by the dark of the moon. (Had I known that in less than four years I would be getting married in that log chapel—standing on Father Badin's grave—I might have felt less lonely that night.)

The next morning, Vincent Murphy fell into step beside me in front of Father Corby's statue. Maybe he had been on the porch the night before and had sensed my loneliness. Our conversation on the way to breakfast in the dining hall somehow broke the dark spell.

Loneliness could not have lasted long because suddenly there was much to be done. Besides attending classes, I had to work in the afternoons for Father Moore. Within four months life was further complicated: On Tuesday, January 28, 1936, Professor Cooney detained me after class to say I should go to the *South Bend News-Times*, ask for George Scheuer, and say I would like to have the night job. When I went into the newsroom the headlines of the early afternoon edition told of the funeral of King George V. That is how I am sure of the date.

(Years later when an elderly man was taking my course in design I asked him, "Do you know what happened thirty-eight years ago today?" Of course he did not because it had not been the big day for him that it had been for me. "That was the day you gave me my first job," I said. (George Scheuer, after retiring from journalism, worked for a Master of Arts at Notre Dame and was graduated with it at age seventy.)

After starting night work on the *News-Times*, I faced the problem of getting into the hall at midnight. Lights went out and halls were locked at eleven o'clock. "Tuffy" Ryan, rector of Corby, and the following year, "Pop" Farley, rector of Sorin, gave me permission to come in late, but no key. Many nights in sub-zero temperature I stood on a hall porch waiting for a night watchman to make his rounds. The night watchmen, all old men, retirees from Studebaker or Bendix, were not inclined to go out too often on frigid nights.

While working for a scholar in the afternoon, I lived in the Middle Ages, and while working for a newspaper at night, I lived in the grim present. In that way I paid for some of my way through college. My sister, having graduated as a chemistry major, helped me by working in a doctor's lab and my father borrowed money on the farm, and that is how the rest got paid. What Sister Mary Gabriel had seen as a possibility eventually became a reality.

Athletics at Notre Dame were not for me. In growing up alone on a farm I had little chance to develop the competitive instinct that is at the heart of all sport. Still I had to reckon with a physical education requirement. For credits I could either kick a rugby football around Cartier Field with classmates or go to the Fieldhouse for fencing lessons. I chose fencing.

Pedro de Landero was coach. Although he started Notre Dame's fencing teams on the way to national recognition, his genius was not sufficient to lift me above mediocrity. The only things I learned were that Coach de Landero could disarm me with a flick of the foil and that fencing causes agonizing pains in the legs.

The best teachers that I had during those years at Notre Dame had one thing in common: a certain inner strength that came, perhaps, from a sense of vocation. Each seemed to be doing what he was meant to do; each was absorbed in his work and did not seem to be glancing around to see what "good deal" might beckon from afar.

The best ones helped develop some order in our minds, the first business of an education. An effective order is the stamp of a professional, and that they were. Good sense and good hearts kept them from adding to the fragmentation of the world.

By the way they gave a shape to their courses they brought assurance to those of us who were unsure. Instead of a labyrinth they offered a direction. We were spared the uneasy feeling that our teachers were "just winging it." We sensed that they knew where they were taking us and that we would arrive at our destination in good time.

The order that the effective ones created was neither artificial nor depressing. From the first minute it was evident that they had a way of getting a course off the ground, of charging the air with expectations. This is difficult, because students in large groups tend to be unduly influenced by the law of gravity. At the opening of each semester an inertia must be overcome.

This sounds as though every teacher in my student days was endowed with the touch of genius. Of course that was not the case. For instance, there was the alcoholic who had a few stiff drinks before setting out for class each morning. His meandering journey down the long walk that stretches from Lyons Hall to Howard Hall was carefully observed. Students crowded into the bay window above Lyons' main door to place bets as to whether he would pass through the right archway or the left archway when he reached Howard. It was honest roulette, because there was no way of knowing in advance through which arch his final lurch would take him.

Then there was the teacher who used "you see" at the end of many sentences and in the middle of some of them. How many times would he say "you see" in a fifty-minute class? Students wrote their bets on slips of paper and threw a nickle into the pot. The student who held the money and kept count did not bet, but, of course, everyone in the class also kept count. The winner collected about a dollar, which went a long way—it would buy two plates of spaghetti and two glasses of red wine at Rosie's, now called Sunny Italy.

A poor teacher is recognized at once, but it may take more time for a good one's best qualities to sink in. Our awareness of the best is often retrospective. The three Notre Dame teachers who meant much in my life I came to appreciate with the years. To express my admiration with more than glittering generalities I must tell of each in some detail.

– 7 –

A Gentleman of the Old School

One of the teachers who did most for me taught the first class I attended at Notre Dame. Dr. John Michael Cooney, in salt and pepper tweed, entered the room just as the bell rang that September morning in 1935.

"Let us pray for sense," he said. (In those days every class began with a prayer.)

A dozen students arose and stood there in the northwest corner of the old Notre Dame library. John Cackley, Jim Bacon, Paul Foley, and the rest of us prayed for sense. What an apt petition, especially for students.

After "Amen," the professor took the two steps up the podium and settled behind a tall desk, a perch that gave him a good view of the log chapel and of the lake beyond. Out of habit he tugged at his black bushy eyebrows, which contrasted with the white halo of hair encircling a bald head. He was not yet sixty, but to us at twenty he seemed ancient.

"Now for the Litany of the Saints."

From a red book of class records he called roll – Bock, Geary, Gillespie, Mulcahy, Riley – peering at each saint as though forever planting him in memory.

Gently he closed the book and began the semester in a soft southern voice: "All of you come from good people. How do I know? Because you are sitting here. Your parents have good values and are willing to make sacrifices for you."

Doctor Cooney saw it as his duty to our parents to teach us respect for the word. He set out to enlarge our awareness of the simple declarative sentence and promote the classical virtues of measure and restraint. Even before we turned in our first assignments he knew what our problems would be, for in teaching writing to generations of students he had observed that the weaknesses of each generation are much the same. He had long ago concluded that if at the Last Judgment we must account for every idle word, most of us will be busy late into the night.

I have been told that during one examination period he announced:

45

"Only ten minutes left. You can't write much in ten minutes, but you can cross out a great deal."

The advice he gave most often was: "Have something to say, say it, and be done with it!" He began that sentence with hands poised a foot apart, and brought them together with a resounding slap as he hit the last word.

In the fifty years since, I have not found better advice for a writer. Even now I hear the echo of that slap.

He considered it a matter of courtesy that a writer make himself understood. Gobbledygook is vulgar and reflects bad manners. He might have gone so far as to put clear writing on a moral basis: out of charity you ought not inflict on the reader unnecessary inconvenience. No undue pain.

The professor was gentle and gracious, except when a student turned in a piece of writing saturated with the sloppiness of a first draft. How impatient he was with the soggy. He liked to see a sentence definite enough to cast a shadow. "You'll never know how to write until you learn to rewrite!"

On one assignment Koehler, or Jordan, or Hurley wrote: "We took a ride in a horse and buggy."

The professor slapped his forehead. "Dunderhead! You can ride in a buggy, yes, but how can you ride in a horse!"

Sometimes he shook his head and sighed. "If you read student papers long enough, you get as dumb as they are."

He was from Kentucky and when he heard that I was too, he said: "The country people down there use the language better than many professors. They may not have so much schooling, and they may make some mistakes in grammar, but their sentences have more life in them. No jargon."

When he said that, I recalled hearing a farmer describe an ailment: "When I twist my neck a certain way it makes a poppin' sound, like a horse steppin' on a chicken." Many professors lack the ability to appeal to the senses the way that sentence does.

Leanness of prose was not enough for him; there had to be some life there, too. The directions on a can of soup are lean, he said, but where is the life? "Read more poetry and you will write better prose."

Professor Cooney's sensible advice about writing gave a direction to many lives. For example, Walter Wellesler Smith, of the class of 1927, said that as a student the person he most admired at Notre Dame was Doc Cooney. Since Red Smith was a sports writer, you might think he would have chosen Knute Rockne.

After being saturated with Professor Cooney's advice, Red Smith performed so well that he became known as the best sports writer ever, won a Pulitzer Prize, and had the satisfaction of knowing that all over the country English teachers read aloud his columns in class as examples of good writing. Red expressed one of Professor Cooney's attitudes when he said, "The English language, if handled with respect, scarcely ever poisons the user." He took to heart Doc's admonition that you don't know how to write until you learn to rewrite. He worked hard on every column. His wife said, "When he goes into his study and shuts the door, he can be heard calling upon the deity."

Professor Cooney promoted the classics because they remind us that ancient wisdom is still wise and makes us aware of the march of generations. Such insight, he felt, gives us a truer perspective. Whenever his own perspective became distorted he was the first to admit it. For instance, when visiting friends on a farm in Kentucky he stepped outside on a bright, sunny morning to see a colt running through the garden, sending vegetables flying in all directions. He rushed into the house to spread the bad news.

His host paused in the kitchen door, smiled, and said, "My, my, isn't he a pretty sight."

"Here I was all excited," said John Cooney, "And he was enjoying the beauty of it. He was right."

In the classroom he observed the twists and turns inside our simple psyches that distinguished one from the other. Realizing that this kind of difference is at the heart of style—for style is the reflection of character—he made sure that his advice went beyond dangling participles, split infinitives, and the comma fault. He saw through to the special weakness in each of us. Some were too dilatory, many too sports-minded, and a few wanted to write only armchair articles. John Cooney demanded that the dilatory make their deadlines, that the sports fans cover something in the arts, and that those who cherish their "think pieces" get out and dig.

He certainly had me scouted. Having been reared on a farm, I was accustomed to aloneness, preferring to blend into the woodwork and not bother anyone. He knew that to be a journalist I would have to learn to face into the winds of the world, and he decided to prepare me for it. So from his high perch in the classroom, whenever he saw a wedding party coming out of the log chapel he would send me to gather information and telephone it to the *News-Times* and the *Tribune*. The society editors always knew of the event before I called, and Professor Cooney knew that they knew, but he kept sending me anyway. I gained a great deal of experience in making a pest of myself; log chapel weddings were numerous during those Depression days because young couples could not afford anything very grand.

Doctor Cooney also had advice for the activists. He believed that it helps in a writer's development to bring some silence to the soul, and feeling that trees and water have a calming effect, he would suggest: "Go walk along the river down behind Saint Mary's. The noise of civilization will be far away, just a hum."

Some things in our characters were too basic to change and he took that into consideration, too. "Some people are sprinters and some are milers. The sprinter is capable of the brief, brilliant thing; the miler is good for the long grind. Learn which you are and live with it."

He realized that teaching should proceed slowly and that the press of time is so important in development. When a mother showed concern because her son was not doing as well in class as she would have liked, Doctor Cooney asked, "Has he grown much lately?"

"Why, he shot up a foot in the last year!"

"There now, you can't expect everything at once."

In those days newspapermen had the reputation for being heavy drinkers. The professor reminded his student journalists, "There is some advantage in that for you. If you don't drink, you will give a favorable impression in comparison."

Years later I came across this sentence in one of Montaigne's essays: "It is good to be born in very depraved times, for by comparison with others you are considered virtuous for a cheap price."

So many things have brought to mind John Cooney. I thought of him in Burma the day I heard the Buddhist admonition: "In life hold all things gently as you hold water in the hand." It caused me to recall a banquet for journalists at Notre Dame when Father Eugene Burke, C.S.C., told an anecdote about Doctor Cooney. While walking toward the lake on a summer afternoon, the priest had met the professor with a bathing suit under his arm.

"I hear the largest bank in South Bend failed this morning," said Father Burke with some excitement.

"Yes, I had money in it."

"Do you have anything left?"

The professor took some coins from his pocket.

"What are you going to do?" asked the priest with real concern.

"Right now I am going swimming."

John Cooney knew about holding things gently. Money, friendship, love, and life itself, hold gently like water in the hand. When you grasp you don't have anything.

Professor Cooney often spoke to me about Kentucky, especially of Bardstown where he had been a newspaper editor. It bothered him that so-called progress brings with it such clutter—filling stations, pennants flapping above used car lots, cinder-block buildings. He observed with a touch of sadness, "If you walk down some of the back streets, you can still catch a glimpse of how it was."

Like many southerners he was a fine storyteller. Everything reminded him of an anecdote. One day when he saw Johnny Mangan, the university chauffeur, drive along the road between the library and the lake, he was reminded of an exchange between the chauffeur and Frank Walker, the postmaster general of the United States.

Whenever Walker returned to his alma mater, Mangan was sent to the train station to meet him. On one such trip Mangan said, "I'll have to hurry up and get you out there, Frank. Have to pick up Chesterton. Take him for a ride every afternoon."

To tease the chauffeur, Frank Walker asked, "Who in the hell is Chesterton?"

"My God, Frank, don't you know? He's in the writin' business."

Professor Cooney could not abide a lack of common sense. During the First World War he was one of the 75,000 Four-Minute Men who agreed to give brief patriotic speeches in movie houses and in other places where the public gathered. He gave talks between shows at the Oliver Theater in South Bend until he was told to include in his talk something about how the Germans were poisoning wells at farms in Michigan.

"Right then I quit," he said. "I knew the Germans had more to do fighting a world war than to start poisoning wells in Michigan. I didn't want to become involved with somebody else's lack of sense."

He also thought it a lack of common sense when instruction in the German language was dropped by schools, and German books were removed from libraries, and Beethoven and Bach were scratched from the repertoire of orchestras.

If it is true that education is what remains after one has forgotten most of what was learned in school, I know what remains from my classes with Doctor Cooney: a regard for good sense.

When John M. Cooney died in the autumn of 1945 I learned of it by letter in New Delhi. A United States Army major crossed the verandah, pointed to the envelope and asked, "Bad news?"

I told him about a man who had held in high regard good manners, Kentucky bourbon, and common sense.

The major said that such gentlemen of the old school are of an endangered species. There will be no more to replace them.

Wherever Doc Cooney and Red Smith are, I hope they noticed that I rewrote this several times.

"Several! That's too indefinite a word," they will say with indignation.

Oh, well, *three* times; is that definite enough?

– 8 –

A Country Gentleman

Another fine teacher that I met that first day as a student at Notre Dame was John Towner Frederick. He walked into a well-worn classroom under the Dome and introduced himself to a dozen of us. Standing there, in the Indian summer sunlight, he spoke in a deep, grave voice about the art of the short story. Seven years earlier he had published *A Handbook of Short Story Writing*.

A slightly stooped posture, a slow way of moving, and a deliberate manner of speaking made him seem older than forty-two. Although he smiled readily, a hint of sadness softened his eyes. His long, angular face was set off by a trimmed mustache and spectacles with metallic frames. A loose-fitting black suit helped give him the look of a provincial parson or a small town newspaper editor. And an old-fashioned aura of courtesy infused everything he did. In a film he might have been cast as a country gentleman, which indeed he was.

The stories we wrote for him will never be filed under the heading of regional literature, John Frederick's abiding interest. Those I wrote have long disappeared, and only one clings to memory. It had to do with the sadness of "finishedness:" An aged actor, after the collapse of his career, fritters away his days at the racetrack, leaning on the rail, shouting to the horses lines from Shakespeare: "Gallop apace ye fiery-footed steeds. . . ."

Most of us sitting there at age twenty-one were unaware that John Frederick was that very age when he had started the *Midland*, a magazine devoted to regional writing. As an undergraduate at the University of Iowa he had come to believe that midwestern writers, if they told the truth about their region, had little chance in the big eastern magazines. They could not get published unless they made their stories conform to the eastern editors' ideas of the Midwest, a land of cowboys and Indians. Young Frederick felt that midwestern writers should have a chance to stay at home and develop a regional literature of their own, and he was willing to offer them the chance.

In 1915, without personal wealth or financial backing, he started the

Midland. It was one of the many "little magazines" founded in this country in a period that began just before the First World War and ended as the Great Depression deepened.

John T., as his friends called him, delayed publishing the first issue until 190 subscribers had sent $1.50 each, and he had on hand enough material to fill twelve issues. Subscriptions arrived as the result of a promotional flier explaining that the Midwest would receive proper attention only in the pages of a midwestern magazine.

In the early days, the *Midland* was provincial, but not in the limited sense of the word. It was provincial in the finest sense, exploring midwestern materials on the universal plane of literature. In its latter days it published as much material from other parts of the country as from the midwest, for Frederick had observed that writers in other parts were having just as much trouble staying honest as the midwesterners.

Although the *Midland* never had a large circulation, it did enjoy prestige. Another promotional flier quoted favorable things said about it in the pages of the *Literary Digest, Poetry*, the *Literary Review*, and the *Saturday Review of Literature*. Edward J. O'Brien, the short story anthologist, praised it highly year after year. In 1926, O'Brien in rating magazines as to the quality of their fiction gave the *Midland* 100 percent along with *Dial* and *Forum*. Below them came *Harper's*, the *Atlantic*, and *Scribner's*. Well down the list came *Redbook*, *McCall's*, and the *Saturday Evening Post*. No other magazines rated such a high proportion of stories in the O'Brien best-of-the-year collections for so many years.

H. L. Mencken once called the *Midland* "the most important literary magazine in America." A friendship between Frederick and Mencken developed at a time when Walter Lippmann said that Mencken was the most powerful influence on a whole generation of educated people.

Four of Frederick's own short stories appeared in Mencken's *Smart Set*. When, in 1920, Mencken tried to interest him in political writing, John Frederick replied that "the whole field of politics in America seems to me inconsequential."

When Frederick completed his first novel, *Druida*, Mencken suggested that he send the manuscript to Alfred Knopf, who published it and later published a second novel, *Green Bush*, both with midwestern farm settings. Collections of short stories, anthologies of literature, and textbooks on writing appeared at regular intervals through the years.

Because the *Midland* was getting so much favorable attention, many writers sent stories to it even though they might have done better financially by sending them to other magazines. John Frederick published some of the early writings of MacKinlay Kantor, Paul Engel, Phil Strong, James T. Farrell, Marquis Childs, Maxwell Anderson, Cleanth Brooks, Loren Eiseley, Howard Mumford Jones, Louis Kronenberger, Mark Van Doren, and Ruth Suckow.

Bylines of some Notre Dame men appeared in the magazine: Richard Sullivan, Harry Sylvester, Leo R. Ward, and Leo L. Ward. As collaborators, Frederick and Father Leo L. Ward published two texts, *Writing* in 1934 and *Reading for Writing* in 1937.

A book, *The Little Magazine*, said of Frederick: "Tact and charm drew to the editor many supporters." And it might have added, hard work and patience. For example, Frederick exchanged *eighty* letters with a young writer, August Derleth, who published two short stories in the *Midland* and eventually wrote more than a hundred novels.

Although the *Midland* was always printed in Iowa City, its editorial office moved about the country with the editor. It moved to Moorehead, Minnesota, in 1917 when Frederick received his M.A. from the University of Iowa and became chairman of the small English department at State Normal College. Two years later he resigned and moved his family to a wilderness in the northern end of Michigan's lower peninsula. There he and his father, both with a yearning for the pioneer's life, put together what money they had and made a down payment on 1,400 acres near Glennie in Alcona County. The land held two small lakes, large wooded sections, some pastureland, and two hundred acres ready for cultivation. The Fredericks cleared more woodland, raised cattle, sheep, and alfalfa, and built a large stone house with their own hands.

In the farmhouse, Frederick and his wife, Esther, who had been his assistant editor in Iowa City, read manuscripts by lamplight and planned the layout for the next issue. To pick up manuscripts and shipments of magazines at the post office, Frederick rode in a market wagon, pulled by a sorrel mare, across three miles of rough logging road.

After two years in Glennie the Fredericks were forced to admit that the future of the *Midland* was less than bright. Each year the magazine went into the red; each year the Fredericks made up the deficit from their own scant income. If the magazine was to survive John would have to return to teaching.

Back to the University of Iowa he went and introduced what was probably the first course in *contemporary* American literature ever taught in the United States. It is difficult to believe that early in this century English departments were hostile to courses in American literature, taking the attitude that no such subject existed. As late as 1928 American colleges offered as many courses in Scandinavian literature as in American, and twice as many in Italian and four times as many in French literature.

In Iowa City, in 1921, Frederick started the Saturday Luncheon Club. For five dollars a semester a student could attend five luncheons at a boardinghouse and hear lectures by such writers as Sherwood Anderson, Robert Frost, and Carl Sandburg. John T. told me that at about this time he and the artist Grant Wood had scouted around Iowa City for weeks searching out Victorian horsehair sofas and chairs to furnish a second-story room in a boardinghouse, a place for faculty and students to meet to discuss the arts.

After the last class each spring, John and Esther hurried back to the farm in Michigan. They preferred the life of pioneers, feeling it was a good one for their two sons to grow up in.

This went on until Frederick joined the faculty at the University of Pittsburgh for a year, and thereafter, starting in 1930, spent several years on the faculties of Northwestern and Notre Dame simultaneously, commuting twice weekly on the South Shore.

The first time Frederick visited Notre Dame was in the spring of 1928. In a letter dated May 4, he told a friend in Montana: "I spent the first three days of this week at Notre Dame, where I shared the apartment of Professor C. A. Phillips. . . . I gave one general lecture open to all members of the student body, addressed two class groups in which several classes had been combined, had a long session with the Scribbler's Club and met twenty or more boys in personal conferences in connection with their writing."

Years later Richard Sullivan, after having written several novels, spoke of that 1928 visit as one that gave him some of the encouragement he needed. He agreed with Loren Eiseley's observation that the *Midland* "helped to keep young writers active and interested when it was almost impossible to get attention elsewhere."

In the case of James T. Farrell it provided even more basic nourishment. In the last two years of the magazine's existence Farrell hung around its office in Chicago; he felt the need to talk with somebody who cared about the written word, and Esther Frederick, knowing the young writer was broke, sometimes took him to lunch.

Two years before I came to know John Frederick he went through the trauma of watching the *Midland* die. *Time* magazine ran a photograph of him with the caption: "Ratings, high. Funds, low."

Artistically the magazine was successful; financially it was a failure.

Year after year Frederick reached deep into his own pocket to keep it alive, until the Depression, when the debt grew at the rate of a thousand dollars a year. He chipped away at the $5,000 debt for several years after the magazine was only a memory.

What it meant to him to discontinue the *Midland* may be guessed from a sentence in the final editorial, in June 1933: "For nearly twenty years I have given to it money and time taken from my work as teacher and farmer, from my reading, from my family life; and although the money and the time have been alike sometimes needed and hard to spare, my personal rewards have been great."

After graduating from Notre Dame I kept in touch with John Frederick through his weekly half-hour radio broadcast, "Of Men and Books," over the CBS radio network, from 1937 until 1944. His national reputation as critic grew as he commented on current books and interviewed such authors as Aldous Huxley, Archibald MacLeish, Thomas Mann, Franz Werfel, Sigrid Undset, Eric Maria Remarque, John Dos Passos, Robert Frost, and Stephen Vincent Benet.

Years later the producer of that radio show told me he was amazed at how John Frederick always got the show off the air on the exact second. When I told this to John he said he used a system later used by Fulton Sheen on television. The trick is to prepare the last minute, word for word, something that has in it the feeling of a strong ending. Then when the director gives the signal that there is one minute left, go into the prepared part and the audience thinks that it all just happened that way.

That exactness, that dependability was so like John. He never missed a deadline and was never late for an appointment. He always seemed to have lots of time.

In many ways John Frederick gave readers the benefit of his cultivated taste. When the *Chicago Sun* started, in 1941, he began a weekly column in the book supplement. At the same time he took over the monthly book department of *Rotarian*, a department handled for years by William Lyons Phelps.

During the war, he devoted most of his time to farming. As he said, "The things I was equipped to teach were not particularly needful in a war program." At Glennie he pitched into the job of raising cattle with the same dedication he had put into editing, teaching, and writing.

When I joined the Notre Dame faculty, at the end of the war, Professor Thomas Stritch and I shared an office in the Main Building. John T. came to the office many days to confer with his students about reports they had written after having read the works of F. Scott Fitzgerald, William Faulkner, Ernest Hemingway, or Willa Cather. I overheard his comments and they became a part of my education.

At that time Frederick and Stritch were planning courses in American Studies for students who wanted to make a living in journalism. Their aim was to teach students how to write, to give them something to write about, and to train them in the techniques of publication. Courses in American Studies should give students something useful to write about, they said. Listening to them plan the program was another part of my education.

John T. helped me develop as a writer during a writers' conference organized by Professor Louis Hasley, in 1949. Frederick, John Nims, Richard Sullivan, and Jessamyn West gave talks daily for a week in the conference room of the Rockne Memorial. In the summer of 1950, Caroline Gordon and J. F. Powers held forth along with John Frederick, for another week. The conference for writers continued for two more summers, but I could not attend them because I was recalled to the military service when the war started in Korea.

When I returned to the campus, John T. and I began taking walks together. We got along well because we were both eternal country boys.

The *New Republic* once said: "The *Midland* specializes in quiet." That could have been said about its editor, too. Many of our hours together were quiet, for we shared silence without uneasiness.

It was the quiet and the solitude, I think, that drew John to farming. Cities were not for him. Milton Reigelman, in writing about how Frederick failed to fit into city life, said: "He was more at home on his Glennie farm or in the Iowa City *Midland* office that looked out on huge elm trees down the slope to the Iowa River. Paul Engel recalls how harried and different Frederick looked when he first saw him in the Chicago office, which gave out on concrete and asphalt."

One day while walking around the lake, I asked John T. what more than anything else had influenced his childhood. He said that he valued the hardships of growing up on a farm in Iowa. To get to school he rode a horse each day in all kinds of weather across five miles of back roads.

He added that his mother's brother, Judge Horace M. Towner, had also meant a great deal to him. The judge read aloud to his nephew and had him tutored in Greek by the Congregational minister in Corning, Iowa, and taught German by a high school teacher. Eventually the uncle urged the boy to attend the University of Iowa, where the judge was a part-time member of the law faculty. The judge was eventually elected to the United

States Congress and later was appointed governor of Puerto Rico.

Since the judge did not provide money for John's education, after two years the young man had to leave college to work in Prescott, Iowa as a high school principal and athletic coach. It was good for him, he felt, for he grew in maturity. Upon returning to the university he was brilliant in literary criticism and student debate; he was voted president of the senior class and elected to Phi Beta Kappa.

When John Frederick reached age sixty-five, Notre Dame asked him to delay retirement and stay for a few years as chairman of the Department of English. He continued in that position until 1962. Just before leaving, he spoke to the faculty about their debt to students: "I feel more keenly than ever just how much they deserve of us. They deserve, simply, our best; and even that best is not going to be good enough."

Esther had died a decade or so earlier and John had remarried. He and his second wife, Lucy, moved to her farm near Iowa City. From it he commuted to the University of Iowa to teach. Life had come full circle.

In a letter dated June 12, 1970, he wrote to me: "The fact is, Ed, that my final semester of teaching proved to be one too many. I had two good and responsive classes; but as the semester progressed I became increasingly and painfully tired, and had all I could do to keep up with papers and preparation, while feeling all the time I was giving my students less than they deserved. I'm only now beginning to emerge from the acute fatigue and beginning part of the time to feel something approaching what I hope may prove to be par for whatever time remains for me."

In the time that remained, he brought out two books: *The Darkened Sky*, a study of how religion is reflected in early American novels, and a biography of William Henry Hudson.

My guess is that some of his most pleasant hours in later life were spent in conversation with a young teacher, Milton A. Reigelman, who later wrote: "Despite frequent ill health over the past few years, Frederick has been willing to talk with me for long hours about *Midland*." Reigelman's book, *The Midland: A Venture in Literary Regionalism*, was published by the University of Iowa Press a few months after John's death.

John Towner Frederick died January 31, 1975, the day before his eighty-second birthday. The news reached me on a writing assignment in Korea. I put the letter in my pocket and walked from the village out into the quiet countryside.

I recalled little off-beat events that seemed small when they happened but now showed significance. For instance, John was sitting next to a colleague on the South Shore when Carl Sandburg boarded the train just west of Michigan City. Sandburg grasped John's hand and pumped, not letting go while telling Professor Guth how long he and John had known each other. Sandburg was unaware that the hand he grasped so roughly was throbbing with an infection. In not flinching and in not mentioning the pain, John Frederick reflected his approach to life: Accept your share and never feel sorry for yourself; just take for granted that adversity comes with the territory.

While climbing a Korean hill, I remembered our quiet walks. How delighted he had been with an anecdote I passed along to him: Frank Sheed had told me that one day he and Monsignor Ronald Knox were walking to the train station at Durham when they passed a brass band. Knox said, "Of course good music is better than bad music. But the best music is inferior to silence."

I remembered our last hour together. John T. had returned to the campus for a meeting of the Library Council and we talked in the lobby of the Morris Inn after dinner. He told me that he had gone to one of the smaller buildings on the farm to read a manuscript he had completed and after finishing it had started a fire in a coal stove to feed the pages to the flames one by one.

It may have been the manuscript of *The End of the Iron Age*, a science-fiction book. If so, it is just as well that the man who promoted regional literature all of his life did not in his last days publish science fiction. It would have struck a wrong note.

More than a half-century has passed since a courteous man stood in a classroom under the Dome and quietly spoke of things young writers needed to hear. He wanted us to use words "so true and simple that they pose no obstacle to the flow of thought and feeling from mind to mind."

Benjamin Appel used words just that way when, upon hearing of John Frederick's death, he wrote: "I remember the magazine and the editor with the kind of glow that only a good man can radiate across time."

– 9 –

A Genius for Friendship

Professor Paul Fenlon taught a class in contemporary American writers the first semester I attended Notre Dame. Covering the material in the course was not nearly so important for me as becoming aware of the man. He, like Professors Cooney and Frederick, was truly a gentleman.

During my senior year I lived in room 330 Sorin and Fenlon's room was around the corner and down the hall in the northwest tower. Although I often saw him bounding up the stairway I never came to know him well until I joined the faculty a decade later.

Paul Fenlon took up residence in Sorin, at age twenty, during the First World War. As student, teacher, and retired professor he lived there for sixty-four years.

The gentleness of his youthful upbringing left a stamp on him that the abrasions of later life could not erase. His boyhood was idyllic in the old Victorian house with a cupola and tower, where he was born July 31, 1896, in Blairsville, Pennsylvania. The long, lazy afternoons on the family tennis court and unhurried trips by buggy to an aunt's place in the country reflected gentler times.

When young Fenlon came to Notre Dame a sentence in the college catalog influenced his life more than it did the lives of most of his classmates: "These are the years during which the beautiful and the abiding friendships of after life are formed and cultivated."

Rarely does a man reach his eighties with so many abiding friendships dating from his youth. He kept in close touch with Clarence (Pat) Manion, George Shuster, Paul Byrne, and others. "He has a genius for friendship," said George Shuster.

Friends knocking at Professor Fenlon's door were always interrupting the conversation one might be having. From things said during those visits it became evident that he not only cherished old friends but had a lively interest in all of their friends and their relatives, too.

For example, when I was visiting Paul one afternoon, a husky, handsome young man, wearing an ND monogram, came to Sorin tower to complain of a toothache and ask if Professor Fenlon would get him an appointment with a dentist. In an aside the professor explained, "This boy's father was in the class of '39." He went on to enquire in some detail about the young man's four brothers and three sisters. In another aside he said, "His father and his brother, Bob — the class of '73 — flew up here from Indianapolis a few weeks ago. A single-engine plane. Took me up into Michigan. I was scared to death."

On another occasion, Father Dan O'Neil came in asking if he could do anything. Professor Fenlon said, "I lost my Infant of Prague statue. My father carried it for years. It's worn smooth from handling. I dropped it when I was getting into bed last night."

Father O'Neil got down on his knees to look under the bed. Professor Fenlon said, "Here, use Charley Phillips' famous Alpine walking stick. He's been dead since 1933. He used it when he was writing that book about his beloved Poland."

When Father O'Neil left, Professor Fenlon said, "He comes in nearly every day at noon if for no other reason than to see if I'm still living. I taught him as a junior. His friendship has been wonderful."

This harvest of friendships began in a matter of minutes after young Fenlon and his father stepped off the streetcar at Father Sorin's statue in September of 1915. As they walked toward the golden dome, Notre Dame had a more rural look to it than it has today: barns, pigpens, and cultivated fields came up close to the main campus; the trees were smaller, and most roads and paths were gravel or dirt.

From the steps of the Main Building, the president of the university, Father John W. Cavanaugh, greeted the Fenlons and with that Paul's first friendship at Notre Dame began. The priest's courtesy and charm so impressed the elder Fenlon that he said he was glad he had decided to send his son to Notre Dame instead of to Georgetown, the only other school considered.

Father Cavanaugh led the Fenlons into the Main Building and turned right into the east wing, known then as Brownson Hall. Paul's cousin, an alumnus from Woodstock, Illinois, had told him, "You'll never be a true Notre Dame man if you don't live in Brownson Hall." Paul took one look at the many rows of desks in the study hall and at the rows of beds in the dormitory and whispered to his father, "This is not for me." So his father put up the extra money that his son might have a private room in Corby

Hall. Professor Fenlon recalled that anyone living in Brownson could get room, board, and tuition for $400 a year.

A student got his money's worth in discipline, Professor Fenlon used to say. The catalog in 1915 said: "The Faculty maintains that an education which gives little attention to the development of the moral part of a youth's character is pernicious, and that it is impossible to bring about this development where students are granted absolute relaxation from all Faculty government while outside the classroom."

The day began with a prefect ringing a cowbell at 6:30. If the student was a little slow in getting up, the chances are the foot of the bed was lifted into the air several inches and let drop to the floor. At 6:50 there was morning prayer in chapel and at 7 o'clock breakfast.

"The trouble was," said Professor Fenlon, "that the boys in college got the same treatment as those damn little minims and preps. They were grade school and high school kids. Father Burns cut out the minims and the first two years of the preps. A good thing!

"The boys won't believe it when I tell them now, but it's true, that at seven each evening we went to chapel for evening prayers and from then on there was absolute quiet in the halls. All lights out at ten o'clock! After several years, lights were extended to eleven and that was a big thing.

"After lights out we would go to the bathroom to study. They were on in there all night. Everybody had candles in his room. Wonder we didn't burn the place down. We painted our transoms so no light would show to a prefect in the hall. See my transom, it's still painted."

As the catalog said: "The quiet and concentration of mind that are needed for college work are not obtained except where discipline exists." With a sigh, Professor Fenlon recalled those quiet days, while listening to students thump and bump on the floor above, shout down the corridor, and turn up stereo sets to decibels that sent acid rock cutting through Sorin like a buzz saw through soft pine.

Less noise and less social life were the big differences between his student days and the latter part of his life. The catalog made the point about Notre Dame having a social life of low profile: "The campus includes more than a square mile of park, and students are expected to take their recreation on the campus rather than loitering about the city. College life lasts only four years as a rule and the special charm of it lies in the points wherein it differs from the life of the city rather than in the points wherein it resembles that life. These are the years during which young men dream dreams and see visions."

Paul Fenlon told me about his first class day at Notre Dame. The course, history, was taught by Professor James Hines. Before saying a word to the class, Professor Hines held a piece of chalk at arm's length and dropped it to the floor. Deliberately, he picked it up, held it out again, and dropped it. With great solemnity he picked up the chalk once more and dropped it. Then he said in husky tones: "Just so, gentlemen, does history repeat itself."

During another class, a little later in the morning, Father Burke said, "Close the door, we can't compete with that." Professor Fenlon explained, "It was Rockne bellowing away, teaching chemistry across the hall. That ended when Jess Harper left during the war. Then Father Cavanaugh appointed Rock head football coach. I often heard him say that he did that with some trepidation. He feared Rock was too young for the job."

Rockne's mentor in those days was Father Julius Nieuwland, who practically lived in Science Hall conducting experiments with synthetic rubber, which eventually brought him honors from all over the world. Young Fenlon was fascinated by the small sad-faced priest, but not because of his research. "He used to sit at the head table. I watched him every night. He would eat one bowl of cereal and then leave the table."

The events of those early days remained clear in Paul Fenlon's memory because he recalled them often. Old grads would come by the tower room on alumni weekend, or at commencement, or before or after football games and leaf through his collection of yearbooks. Each photograph evoked memories, and as Professor Fenlon turned the pages he would think out loud:

"That's George Haller. He was our brain. Our valedictorian. Comes back to see me. He was what we called a 'Lifer.' He went through the minims, through prep, and through four years of college—a Lifer. He was a professor of law at Detroit College of Law.

"F. X. Dinsney. He was in '23, the last student to take Greek and Latin for four years. Rock used to say, 'That's one athlete I don't have to worry about. Any track man who takes Greek and Latin, I don't have to worry about.'"

The Alumni Directory also showed signs of use. The professor was not happy with it though: "Joe Mulligan was here the other day. We spent the weekend looking through this. So many of them never filled out the forms for this."

When young Fenlon was graduated in June of 1919, Father Joseph Burke, the dean of studies, asked him if he would care to stay on and teach in the Department of English. "My father wanted me to get out. He said, 'Did you ever hear of a teacher *doing* anything!' I answered, 'Dad, look at

Woodrow Wilson!' He was an ardent Democrat, and so he had no answer for that."

The elder Fenlon won, but his victory was brief. Paul's uncle got him a job at the First National of Chicago, and the new graduate took a room in a boardinghouse in Hyde Park. Five mornings a week, from August to May, he went to work at the bank in the Loop.

"I hated every minute of it!" said Paul Fenlon with feeling. On weekends he came on the South Shore to the place he felt most at home, the Notre Dame campus. There was an extra bond when his sisters, Sarah and Mercedes, were students at Saint Mary's. During these visits Father Burke could see that the young man was facing up to a job with no real sense of vocation. So he again offered Paul a position teaching English.

When Fenlon returned to Sorin Hall in 1920 two of the first young teachers he became friends with were George Shuster and Clarence Manion. Both left Notre Dame, in time, but both kept in touch with Paul. Shuster became managing editor of *Commonweal*, State Commissioner of Bavaria, and president of Hunter College. Manion served as dean of the law school and then went into political broadcasting and private law practice in South Bend. Shuster, after receiving the Laetare Medal in 1960, returned to Notre Dame as advisor to the president, and the three old friends, Shuster, Manion, and Fenlon, were reunited.

Paul Fenlon often recalled that day in 1920 when a big blond fellow moved into Sorin. "He introduced himself as Manion. Said he had graduated from St. Mary's College in Kentucky a year earlier and had lived in Washington Hall for the past year. He couldn't sleep there. Too much noise all night long. The ghost. That's when the legend of the ghost of Washington Hall started."

Professor Fenlon recalled with pleasure the many adventures he and Pat Manion had together. For example, one day during Prohibition when Gilbert Keith Chesterton was giving a series of lectures in Washington Hall, the president of the university, Father Charles O'Donnell, called Fenlon and Manion to his office. "Chesterton has expressed a desire to see an American speakeasy," the president said. "I know of no one more capable of helping him than you two gentlemen."

As Fenlon recalled, "Pat had an old Essex. In it we took Chesterton around to three or four speakeasies. Alby's was one. It must have been a sight. Here was an enormous man with a great Inverness cape, pince-nez spectacles with a ribbon flowing from them, and a gigantic hat. When we walked into a place people began to leave."

Manion and Fenlon and two other professors, Steve Ronay and Charley Phillips, decided to give a party for Chesterton, to be held in Phillips' room, the second-floor tower room on the northeast corner.

"Steve Ronay got the bootleg beer and Manion and I went to town in the Essex to get a tub of ice at one o'clock in the morning. The party wasn't until that night. Pop Farley was prefect of Sorin and so that he wouldn't see it we stored the ice under Charley Phillips' bed. He claimed that ice under his bed gave him a backache."

Chesterton was a gigantic man and getting him up to the second floor of Sorin was no easy task. When he was finally settled in Charley Phillips' great chair, with a stein of beer in his hand, Manion whispered to Steve Ronay, "We got him up here, but how in the hell are we going to get him down."

"Charley was deaf," said Professor Fenlon. "So Chesterton had to speak up. He had a high squeaky voice. Whenever he said something funny he would lift up his feet and click his heels together. He smoked cigarette after cigarette and let the ashes fall so that they filtered down into the folds of his vest. With all that beer he never got up and went to the bathroom. But when he stood up to go home all those ashes came tumbling out of the folds. It was like an eruption of Vesuvius."

By now dawn was near. Steve Ronay and John Frederick volunteered to drive Chesterton to his house on Pokagon Street. Getting him through the narrow door of Ronay's Ford took some pushing. Harder still was getting him out at the other end. Mrs. Chesterton was waiting up and was furious. She told Ronay in no uncertain terms that Mr. Chesterton was always in bed by midnight.

Paul Fenlon often recalled the first period of great growth at Notre Dame: "In the mid-twenties Father Irving said to me, 'Paul, we'll never allow the enrollment to go beyond 3,000.'" It is three times that now.

"The Four Horsemen and Rock rode to fame in the twenties and brought Notre Dame fame. There are lots of them who never wanted to admit that, but that's the truth.

"During the Second World War the Navy took over. Only two dorms were left for Notre Dame students. The Navy offered Notre Dame eighteen million for the place. Wanted to make an Annapolis of the Midwest. They liked the lakes and our infirmary—'sick bay' they called it. Pepper O'Donnell was president. He said something like, 'I'd rather give my blood than sell Notre Dame.'

"I thought I'd lose my room in Sorin. Two distinguished Navy men, with the scrambled eggs on their visors, came to my door. 'This is the last room we're looking at,' they said. 'Have you lived here long?' I said, 'Since 1917.' They said, 'This old hall, you'll be glad to know, won't do for us.' They pointed to the high ceiling and said whoever built this wasn't practical. They ended the conversation by saying, 'Your heads are awful.' They saw the look on my face and explained, 'The rest rooms.'"

This anecdote prompted Professor Fenlon to recall that even though he nearly lost his place in Sorin during the Second World War, it was the First World War that got him in there ahead of schedule. Only upperclassmen were accepted in Sorin and so Fenlon, a sophomore, was still in Corby when the United States declared war in April of 1917. Father Cavanaugh announced that any senior who enlisted might leave the campus immediately and be assured of his diploma. Those who were not too sure of their diplomas hurried to the recruiting office and left enough empty space for Fenlon to move into Sorin early.

His room in the last years of his life was on the first floor, in the tower nearest Sacred Heart Church. It featured an eighteen-foot ceiling. Pat Manion said, "If you turned it over on its side, you'd have a suite." Photographs covered the walls, the mantelpiece, the bureau, the desk. They ranged from faded sepia to bright Kodachrome.

Professor Fenlon would begin the tour of his gallery with the pictures of his mother, father, and two sisters, all deceased. He paused, seeming to go far away. After a few moments he continued. "Here's John Cavanaugh the Second. Taken when we were at Manions for Thanksgiving in 1947. . . . Kerndt Healy. He died in '60. . . . These four on horseback are the O'Neils from Cleveland. They run a large trucking firm. Leaseways. You see them on the road all the time. . . . The Art Careys. Art graduated in the famous class of '35. Comes here every football game. They've had five children graduate from Notre Dame and St. Mary's."

He would point to a woodcut. "Paul Beichner made this of Sorin. It's one of the few things I'll take with me, if I move. . . . And here is my beloved Breadloaf. I spent two summers there in Middlebury. . . . Charley O'Donnell wrote this poem. I had it framed. George Shuster recited it the day he received the Laetare Medal. See it begins:

> So well I love these woods I half believe
> There is an intimate fellowship we share."

A tiny chip of gold, set against black velvet, and displayed in an elegant gold frame seemed to have a place of honor. "This is a chip from the dome.

Jimmy, the little gnome who used to run the cafeteria, gave it to me." He pointed to a handsome page of Gregorian chant and explained how he came to own it. "This will go to Dan O'Neil." Also on the wall a poem written by Pat Manion at the time of his graduation. "The original copy. See, it's signed and dated, June 13, 1922. This will go to Marilyn." On the bureau stood a thin gold watch set into a circular wooden medallion. "My uncle gave this to me when I graduated from Blairsville High School in 1915."

From the three long windows in his tower Professor Fenlon could look out on three favorite views. The left window frames the church steeple; the right, a cluster of trees on the main quad, and the center, the golden dome. With a spring in his steps and his tall, wiry way of walking he visited other favorite spots on campus. "The grotto is one of the best scenes. I go there nearly every day." He liked to stand on the porch of the Main Building and look down the long path past the statue of the Sacred Heart toward Sorin's statue. It was where Father Cavanaugh had stood that September morning in 1915 when young Fenlon and his father walked toward him between the long rows of trees.

Of his lifetime at Notre Dame the years that Professor Fenlon remembered with most pleasure were the 1930s. He said he made more friends in those days than at any other time. "I had a theory that the odd-numbered years had the better classes. In the class of '31 were some of the best friends I ever made. Jerry Crowley was from Chicago then; he didn't move to South Bend until later. There was Bob Baer, Phil Angsten, Donald O'Toole. In '33 there were Chick Sheedy and Bill Dreux. In '35 were John Neesen and Gene O'Brien, a football player who didn't associate with football players—a cousin of Jerry Crowley's. In that class was Bill Miller. He taught us to play bridge. He was something of a semi-professional. He later ran for vice-president on the ticket with Barry Goldwater."

It was in the thirties that he met a student from Nashville, Tom Stritch. Their friendship grew with each decade. Right up to the end, Professors Fenlon and Stritch dined together a good many evenings a year.

Also during the thirties Paul Fenlon enjoyed a growing friendship with Professors T. Bowyer Campbell, Paul Byrne, and Tom Madden. He remembered with pleasure their afternoon teas. "T. Bowyer lived in the tower of Morrissey Hall. Fourth floor. Every Monday we went there for tea. Always arrived at exactly 4:30. He made a ritual of it. He thought tea bags were atrocious."

Tom Madden died in 1962. Professor Fenlon kept in touch with T. Bowyer Campbell and Paul Byrne after they lived in retirement in the East.

Another friend from the thirties was Joseph Ryan. When Professor Ryan left the campus in 1974, Fenlon became the last of a long tradition of bachelor professors living in student halls. Ryan lived out his days in Chicago with his brother, Quin Ryan, a well-known sportscaster of the thirties.

The decade that Professor Fenlon remembered with least delight was the one just before his retirement. "The older I grew, the fewer students I came to know. When you get older they think you are older than you really are." In June of 1962 he retired from teaching the Victorian novel, American fiction and the short story. For several years after that he worked in the Main Building helping George Shuster with some alumni matters.

When I asked if he could think of any other life he might have enjoyed more, his answer was an instant and definite, "Never!" Without hesitation he continued, "I was happy here from the first day that I came as a student. I never wanted to change schools. The only period of my life that I didn't enjoy was that half year in the bank. No, I have never wanted to leave here."

When he died, the last of the bachelor dons, on November 7, 1980, he still did not leave. He rests in the cemetery at the western edge of the campus among the priests and the brothers.

– 10 –

Into the World

At five o'clock Sunday afternoon, June 6, 1937, we emerged from the Fieldhouse, diplomas in hand. We were going forth to witness, as Shakespeare says in *Lear*, "the rise and fall of great ones that ebb and flow with the moon." We were ready to make the golden journey in search of the Holy Grail.

The next morning the state editor of the *News-Times*, Tom Philipson, sent me and Harry Elmore, the photographer, to Culver Military Academy, forty miles away, to cover commencement exercises. All I remember of that Monday is having a long talk with a movie producer whose son was in the Culver graduating class. Jean Harlow had just died and was to be buried on Wednesday; that gave direction to the conversation. The producer said that in the summer of 1929, Arthur Landau, an agent, was at the Hal Roach Studios where Laurel and Hardy were making a movie. Stan Laurel called Landau's attention to a blonde girl who had appeared as an extra in several Laurel and Hardy comedies. The agent got the girl a film test for *Hell's Angels*, being produced by Howard Hughes, and that film made her a star.

During those early days in newspaper work the advice that I found most useful was Doctor Cooney's admonition: "Have something to say; say it, and be done with it!" There were some uneasy occasions, though, when I had to learn from my own mistakes.

For instance, I was sent to interview Thurman Arnold, much in the news as Roosevelt's "Trust Buster." Arnold had written a bestseller, *The Folklore of Capitalism*. When I met him in the home of a South Bend judge the first thing he said was, "I suppose you have read my book?" I had not.

The look on Thurman Arnold's face told me that he knew I was unprepared to conduct an intelligent interview. "Tonight I am speaking at the lawyers' banquet here in town," he said, "why don't you come and cover that." So I did. That was the last time I went on an interview without doing my homework.

Each newspaper has its own peculiarities which the beginner must learn and abide by. For example, on the *News-Times* we never wrote the words *yesterday*, *today*, and *tomorrow*, but named the day of the week instead. That was because some stories that ran in the late edition one day might be carried in the early edition the next day. Once when I used the word *today* in a story the managing editor, Pi Warren, said, "The Bible says that Jesus Christ is the same yesterday, today, and tomorrow, but on this paper he is the same Monday, Tuesday, and Wednesday."

Although nearly half a century has passed, the sights seen on assignments are clear in mind. For instance, I remember the little man in a hunting cap and sheepskin coat sprawled in front of an open garage door. The tiny hole in his right temple, rimmed with purple, bled very little that bitter cold morning. The rifle, a cheap one, had been bought just for this one shot. The price tag was still tied to the trigger guard. The little man was just too sad to go on.

I came to hate automobiles when going to wrecks night after night. Most were evidently the result of crazy driving. I thought of Shakespeare's character Punch, who said, "What fools these mortals be." The photographer and I often arrived at the scene before the police. One night I pulled a dying man from the wreckage in the ditch. A photograph of my efforts appeared in the paper the next day. The police displayed the picture on their bulletin board with the penciled admonition: How Not to Take a Man out of a Car.

As a young reporter I was exposed to a lot of human nature. One thing I learned was that people can be noble when faced with troubles not of their own making. Such disasters as floods, tornadoes, and explosions bring out the best in them. They get so busy helping others that they forget to gossip, backbite, and bicker. Once the rubble is cleared they return to being themselves.

No green reporter ever enjoyed being a newspaperman more than I did. With a starting salary of sixteen dollars a week I felt wealthy. Even a small amount of money had buying power in the Depression. I recall getting a full tray of food at Smith's Cafeteria for fifty-four cents and a tweed suit at Max Adler's for thirteen dollars. No one on the *News-Times* made much money, but the morale was high. Fortunately, we knew at the time that we were enjoying life; too often we do not realize that until years later.

The shadow of approaching war, however, fell across those days. When the Nazis absorbed Austria, Pi Warren said to me, "Soon I'm going to look out that window and wave to you as you go marching down Colfax." He repeated that when the British capitulated to Hitler at Munich and the prime minister spoke of "peace in our time."

Along about my birthday, August 17, 1937, Mary and I met in the South Bend Public Library. What a fitting place to meet; we had both spent much of our lives in libraries. I could call it a happy chance except that I no longer believe in chance. Since growing old I am aware of the Providential. As Anatole France said: "Chance is the pseudonym God uses when He does not want to sign His name."

Forty-five years later a young woman who was writing a magazine article about Mary asked why I had been attracted to her and why we had married. I could give the young writer reasons that sound good on paper, but the real reason is beyond my saying. I can say she was pretty, lively, intelligent, charming, but that would not be the real answer, because I knew other young women with those qualities and yet did not consider marrying them. In such really important matters the true answer is a mystery.

Our actions in really important matters, like the choice of a vocation, should spring from a deep inner imperative that will not be denied and cannot be explained. For instance, if someone asked why I am a writer instead of a cost accountant I could give surface reasons but would know in my heart that I was attempting to convey what I cannot say. In our lives the intrinsic is the unutterable.

During our courting days our dates were determined by what press passes were available at the newspaper; all unmarried men on the staff used that system. If there were tickets for a dog show, we went to the dog show; if the advance man for the circus was generous with "Annie Oakleys," we set off in a lively group for the big top; if someone was covering the opening of a country fair, that assignment was turned into a date. One night a small town had a street dance to celebrate the opening of a new main drag. Several of us went there on a date. The opening sentence for my story was: "They danced beneath the harvest moon Monday night in Walkerton."

Our own lack of money caused no great concern, but the lack of money in the bank account of the *News-Times* did cast a shadow across our lives. It was evident that the paper's days were numbered. Amos 'n' Andy struck the final blow.

The owner of the paper, Joe Stevenson, was something of a big spender. He owed money at the bank, but each year when the loan came due, the bank president would say just pay the interest and let the rest ride. That was all well and good until Freeman Gosden and Charles Correll, Amos 'n' Andy, decided to come to South Bend for a football game. The bank president asked them to attend a party at his house and when they agreed he set about planning a gigantic affair. Joe Stevenson knew the two radio personalities from his vacations in Florida and so he too invited them to a party. They promised to drop by for a few minutes before hurrying on to the bank president's party. At Stevenson's they stayed on and on, and never did get to the party they were supposed to attend. The next time the loan came due the bank president wanted the money right now. And there went the *News-Times*!

There was a farewell party in the newsroom after the presses ran for the last time the day after Christmas, 1938. Although I was no longer on the staff I returned to South Bend to attend the party and to write a piece for the last edition, an interview with an elderly woman who said that she was losing a friend, because she had been reading the paper since girlhood.

I was not on the staff at the end because several months earlier Tom Barry, the director of public information at Notre Dame, had phoned to say that since the *News-Times* was about to become merely a memory, I ought to apply for an opening that was available on the *Chicago Herald-Examiner*. Had the *News-Times* not folded I would have stayed on and my life would probably have been much different. I would have stayed because Mary was in South Bend and besides I liked the town, it was not too large for me. Chicago, "the city of the Big Shoulders," always made me feel a stranger.

The first day at the *Herald-Examiner* I passed a door with Pulaski's name on it. It pleased me to think that I was working on the same paper with the cartoonist who had influenced my childhood. I always regret that I passed his door often but never stopped to tell him how much he had meant to me. Had I been assigned to interview him I would have done so readily, but I could not bring myself to make a social visit. As Carrie used to say, "too backward."

The person I best remember from those Chicago days is Oscar Nelson, who came often to the office late at night. The guard would stop him in the vestibule and phone in the announcement, "Somebody out here who wants to see somebody, anybody, in the sports department." One night Warren Brown, the sports editor, introduced me to the old man with great deference: "This is Battling Nelson, the greatest Lightweight Champion of the World that ever was." He did it in a way remindful of the time an old Negro groom introduced me to a great racehorse. He swung open the stall door slowly and said softly, almost with awe, "Man o' War, hisself."

Although I was not in the sports department I often went out to the vestibule to talk with Battling Nelson. His voice, thin and reedy, came through badly battered features, something that looked more like a condition than a face. I spoke of Marvin Hart and Nelson said that they had been in their prime together.

One night the old fighter brought his scrapbook. There he was with President Theodore Roosevelt and the King of Sweden. Yellow clippings told of one of the classic fights of all time when Tex Rickard promoted a title bout between Joe Gans and Battling Nelson, at Goldfield, Nevada, in 1908. His 132 professional fights—59 wins, 19 losses, and 54 draws—made him look older than his fifty-six years. Yet he must have been in good condition, because he lived until he was seventy-two. In the scrapbook was a story of how the city of San Francisco honored Nelson for the thousands of dollars he had donated to help the victims of the 1906 earthquake. The man who had been so generous with his money was now spending his days in a seedy hotel. I asked Warren Brown, "Why does he come up here so often? Does he need money?"

"He could use some," said Brown. "But he has a greater need. Somebody like him can't stand to feel forgotten. He comes around to let us know he is still around."

Late one evening Father Sylvester Ley, my old mentor from Saint Joseph's, and Father Paul Speckbaugh, a young priest I had never met, came to the place I was staying near the Water Tower. The hallway in which I greeted them was overcast, but did not seem so when graced with Father Speckbaugh, who stood tall and thin with a face full of good will and intelligent thoughts.

The two priests were in Chicago to ask if I might be interested in coming to Saint Joseph's to start an alumni publication, develop a news service, and teach some writing. The junior college had begun expanding to a four-year undergraduate program and needed all the help it could get.

A couple of years earlier Father Ley had come to Notre Dame to ask if I might be interested in such a job. I had told him then that I needed a couple of years of experience in journalism, but that I would take his offer seriously enough to enroll for two courses in education at the University of Louisville in the summer of 1936.

I asked the two priests that night in Chicago when they wanted me to start. At the beginning of the second semester, February 1, they said. So on January 31, 1939, I drove to Rensselaer through a blizzard in an ancient Hudson Terraplane.

Brother John Marling helped me unload and settle in. As prefect of study hall and of dormitory he had been a campus character during my student days. As a child he had suffered a paralysis and so his right arm and leg were underdeveloped. In spite of this disability, perhaps because of it, he drove himself to become an exceptional competitor in billiards and in ping pong. His skill drew the admiration of high school and college students through the years; no one could recall seeing him defeated.

It was only natural that he should develop a false sense of invincibility. In the classrooms at Saint Joseph's I had learned about the Greeks' belief in *hubris*, the pride that precedes the fall, and now I was about to witness it.

Not long after I settled in at Saint Joseph's, Willie Mosconi came to the campus as part of his tour for Brunswick, the manufacturer of billiard tables. It has been said that no man has ever dominated his field the way Mosconi has dominated his. In straight pool he once had a run of 526 balls in succession. He did not do that well the day he played on our lumpy tables, but he did have Brother John standing around waiting most of the afternoon for a chance to shoot. That was the day John Marling learned what it means to be *really good*. He left the room so dejected that a high school kid called after him, "Don't feel so bad, Bro. It was like me fighting Joe Louis."

All of this, however, was in the future that afternoon when John Marling helped me unload the Terraplane and settle into a room in the fine old Main Building, which was later destroyed by fire. Certainly neither of us could foresee that in less than three years he would speak a sentence—give a one-sentence piece of information—that would send my whole world spinning. Just as Sister Mary Gabriel Hayden had done a few years earlier.

One of the first things I was asked to do at Saint Joseph's was to raise money for a new fieldhouse. My assistant was Brother Cletus Scheuer, cousin of George Scheuer, the newspaperman who had given me my first job. I will always remember Brother Cletus for his unusual expressions: "He was grinning like a mule eatin' sweetbriars. . . . I didn't know him from Adam's off ox. . . . That headline was set in type big enough to scare a stallion. . . . They were jumpin' around like cinch-bugs on a sheaf of wheat."

One day Father Paul Speckbaugh invited me to dine with Frank Sheed, who would eventually publish my first book. During dinner Father Paul spoke of how much he admired the work that Sheed and his wife, Maisie Ward, were doing in publishing. However, part of the time that evening was spent in teasing me, the kind of joshing that future grooms get as the wedding day approaches.

On Easter Monday, April 10, 1939, Mary and I were married in the log chapel at Notre Dame. Father Aloys Dirksen, the president at Saint Joseph's, performed the ceremony. For our honeymoon we drove the 101 miles from South Bend to Rensselaer and settled down in a rented frame cottage. Mary was soon turning orange crates into bookshelves.

In time we bought a Dutch Colonial house which Mary loved very much. Whenever she was away for a day or more, immediately upon her return home she ran through all the rooms as though taking possession of them once more.

In those days the Catholic Church liked to repeat that when a couple marries the "two should become one." Right off we knew that if the two are really individuals, then trying to be one will surely cause some warping. So from the beginning we lived in three worlds—she has her world, I have mine, and we have a world together. That means that some of our interests, activities, and friendships are separate and some are combined. Neither of us ever tries to use the other as a crutch. So far it has worked.

We felt at home from the beginning in the small town aura of Rensselaer. We enjoyed such characters as Jim Jonas, Squee Merritt, Wadrow Warner, and Lefty Clark.

Lefty Clark, the editor of the newspaper, was being urged to run for county treasurer. He balked a long time, but when he finally gave in he limited his campaign tactic to handing out cards that said: "If you vote for me that'll make two." He won, of course.

Jim Jonas ran a saloon. He had wallboard delivered, but before the carpenter arrived a farmer with muddy boots walked across it. Wadrow Warner said not to clean off the mud; just nail up the beaverboard panels so that the footprints go up one wall, cross the ceiling and come down the other side. And so it was done.

Squee Merritt had a car with a short gearshift in the middle of the floor. When he came out of the saloon one night he lifted his leg into the car and the gearshift ran up his pants leg. He began groping for the gearshift and complaining, "While I was in there somebody stole part of this car."

For some reason or other I saw little of Father Paul Speckbaugh that spring. Our close friendship seemed to begin at noon on Memorial Day of 1939 when I was walking past the side door of Gaspar Hall just as he stepped out into what was truly a broad day. The air was balmy enough for the windows to be open, and through them came the hectic voice of a radio announcer trying to pierce through the "varooming" noise of cars racing in Indianapolis.

Father Paul pointed to the book I was carrying and asked the name of it. *The Green Pastures*, I said. That pleased him. He was pleased when anyone showed an interest in drama of any kind. Next to his religion, I suspect that the theater occupied more space in his heart than anything else.

Paul Speckbaugh was a frail man of tremendous energy. Besides directing plays, he served as chairman of the Department of English, was moderator of several student clubs and faculty advisor for the student literary quarterly. He taught Shakespeare, Chaucer, and creative writing and contributed his poems to several magazines.

His interests were wide. In one conversation he might praise the liturgical art of Eric Gill, discuss the latest issue of *Books on Trial*, and speak of a current Broadway play starring George M. Cohan or Helen Hayes. His talk moved with ease from cookery to metaphysics, making you sense how important and interesting each subject is.

Often I came to his study in 206 Gaspar Hall to find it crowded with students, sitting around on the floor—English majors, pre-meds, athletes, bookworms, and goof-offs. Somehow he brought a semblance of order out of all the chaos that burdened them.

For one thing, his enthusiasm rubbed off. How delighted he was to see students work on publications, paint pictures, play musical instruments, and take part in stage productions. He wanted to see them in some activity that liberates, that frees from narrowness, a part of liberal education. His stress was not on *doing* but on *becoming* a certain kind of person, one who develops a soul that is worth saving.

Father Paul was not against the specialist. He was all for the accountant, the chemist, and the biologist, but he disliked seeing anyone specialize too early in life. He firmly believed that everyone needs some familiarity with arts and letters, for he saw them as ways of letting God into the world.

Paul Speckbaugh "lived" arts and letters. He saw them, as he saw religion, as something that should permeate daily living. He believed, for example, that an interest in the arts ought to influence the appearance of the room in which you spent most of your time. As for letters, he felt that an interest in good writing needs to show in all forms of writing and often quoted Bernard DeVoto: "Good writing is good writing even in a report of the Geodetic Survey."

How delighted I was, upon returning to Saint Joseph's in 1978 to give the Father Paul Speckbaugh Memorial Lecture, to find that his former study was the central office of the CORE curriculum. The young professors who have developed the curriculum—which puts together bits and pieces of studies into larger meanings—did not know that they occupied the room in which Paul Speckbaugh had influenced so many students, but their choice was very fitting. In the college catalog I read that CORE curriculum emphasizes becoming "a self worth being." I never heard Father Paul use those words, but that idea was a dominant theme in his life. Because of the CORE curriculum, Saint Joseph's had much national publicity in 1984, receiving applause in books, newspapers, and magazines. Somehow, I feel sure, the spirit of that curriculum can be tracked back to Paul Speckbaugh.

One Sunday noon in 1941 I went to the campus to talk with the president about the fieldhouse dedication, set for the following evening. After that I went to Father Paul's study to ask advice about a magazine piece I was writing. He was pointing out a way to improve the structure when the door burst open. Brother John Marling stood there panting. A wild look filled his eyes as he announced: "They are bombing Pearl Harbor!"

– 11 –

Off to War

The plaintive wail of the night train, the one I used to listen to in study hall, sounded especially cheerless October 5, 1942. On the station platform at Rensselaer, thirty men clasped an assortment of overnight bags. How long will we serve? The question haunted us as the Monon chuffed southward toward Indianapolis. Such a feeling of uncertainty may be war's heaviest burden.

During the next eight months I endured the rigors of basic training at Camp Croft, South Carolina, and Officer Candidate School, at Fort Benning, Georgia. After being commissioned I wrote field manuals for the Infantry School at Fort Benning, and Dan Dowling, the political cartoonist for the *Herald Tribune* syndicate, drew the illustrations.

Mary was working for a doctor in Rensselaer. A small town was a good place for a young wife in wartime; each evening the war-wives met to tell of letters received from all parts of the world, to listen to newscasts, and wonder how long it would last. As the psychiatrists say, "They provided a support system for each other."

After a year at the Infantry School I noticed a sign on the bulletin board asking for volunteers to run mule-trains through Burma to supply Merrill's Marauders. Here was my chance to go to Fort Riley, Kansas, to take Cavalry School classes with the high-sounding name of Officers' Animal Pack Transportation Course.

Twenty of us gathered at Fort Riley—polo players, jockeys, cowboys, horse trainers, and ranchers. Our month's training started the morning of August 28, 1944, in a shadowy riding hall. There we were confronted by a sergeant as gnarled and tough as an old grape arbor; he had a weathered look that went all the way through to his soul. I don't recall his name; everybody called him Sergeant Muleshoe. Since none of us officers had been in the Army for more than two years, Muleshoe must have figured us for recruits whose bunk-tags were still swinging. He might well have said, "I used more ink signing pay vouchers than you drunk GI coffee."

We were clustered around Muleshoe in the center of the riding hall when the mules were led in, an impressive parade of lithe, lean creatures. They switched their sassy tails, tossed their heads, and minced with the grace of professional dancers. Muleshoe explained that the safest place around a mule is close in to him. When he starts to kick throw yourself against him, never jump back. If you throw yourself against a kicking mule all he can do is shove you, but if you step back he can really tee off on you. You must accept this on faith alone, because when a mule starts to kick every instinct in your body screams to jump back.

During a class in animal management, the lecture was often interrupted by a clop, clop, clop from the back of the room as a groom, who resembled Uncle Dick, lead in a strawberry roan, D824, Reno Hindoo. By looking at Reno Hindoo and some anatomical charts we learned about the inside and the outside of a horse.

Equitation was our favorite class. Everyone knew how to ride before coming to the Cavalry School, but now we had to ride cavalry style, known as the forward seat.

The final exam consisted of three parts. First we went into a room full of feed to judge it, noting for instance, that the oats were so mildewed they would give a horse colic and the alfalfa held so much dust it might cause heaves. Next we entered a room full of horses to judge them. Reno Kismet was sickle-hocked; Red Currant was Roman-nosed and blind in the left eye, and French Girl was goose-rumped and cow-hocked. Only Dot Kilty approached perfection. Finally, we had to shoe a horse. I drew Big Chief, a massive black gelding. As soon as I picked up his off hind leg he started pumping it back and forth like the driving rod on a locomotive, while I pulled off a shoe and trimmed the hoof to a shape God never meant it to be. The air was heavy with the acrid smell of scorched hoof as I drove the nails at an angle that may have left Big Chief lame for life.

Anyway, I was graduated on September 23. The general who gave the commencement address began, "Gentlemen, great adventure awaits you!" That sentence was to be repeated time and again, months later, in the jungles of Burma.

A gold seal and yellow ribbons endowed our diplomas. Years later I looked at mine with a certain sadness when the Army football team brought its mascot, a mule, to Notre Dame. The truck delivering the mascot parked at the north end of the stadium, across the street from my office in O'Shaughnessy Hall. There was a great to-do, I am told, about getting the mule off the truck; his eyes rolled white and his nostrils flared, as he slammed himself back on his haunches, breaking a halter shank and threatening a cheerleader. Nobody called me. It proved that our educational system does not use its manpower efficiently. There I was, perhaps the only university professor in the history of American education to hold a diploma that indicates that he knows how to communicate with mules, but nobody called me.

While I studied the mystery of mules at Fort Riley, Mary and I lived in nearby Manhattan, Kansas. Each night I practiced tying knots on bedposts—butterfly, square, bowline, and a dozen others. I feared that overseas I might be expected to teach enlisted men the intricacies of the squaw hitch and single diamond and show them how to throw a Phillips cargo and basket hitch. Training manuals explained how to do this, but we would not be allowed to take them overseas because the Cavalry School needed the few of them left in the world. So Mary made drawings; few women in history have drawn as many pictures of mules as she has.

From the time of graduation from Cavalry School until my overseas orders arrived about ten days passed. Mary and I cherished each day as a gift beyond price, while haunted by the uneasiness of uncertainty. At noon on the day I was to leave for the West Coast the postman delivered a letter from Father Speckbaugh. It was in the spirit of a farewell note, saying that I should not abandon writing, because I have a feeling for significant detail, for the fragment that suggests the whole. A few years earlier when I wondered if I ought to quit writing, since I found it so difficult, he had said, "Maybe that is an indication that you ought to write," and quoted Thomas Mann: "The writer is someone who finds writing more difficult than other people."

A few minutes after Mary and I had read the letter, a Western Union boy rode up on a bicycle to deliver a telegram. It said that the previous evening, Sunday, October 9, 1944, an automobile had killed Paul Speckbaugh as he walked from the college campus to Rensselaer.

How heavyhearted we felt at six o'clock when I boarded a westbound train on a trip that would extend to India, Burma, China, and Ceylon. An hour later Mary took an eastbound trains on the way to a Solemn Requiem Mass in the chapel at Saint Joseph's.

Another shock awaited me up ahead. After a few days in California the mule skinners boarded a troopship for a month's voyage to India, eight days by train from Bombay to Assam, and a three-day trip by truck down the Ledo Road.

At dusk on Christmas Eve we reached our destination, a jungle clearing near Myitkyina, Burma. When I reported to the headquarters of the Field Replacement Depot, a recording of Bing Crosby's "Silent Night" was

playing on a record player sitting atop an empty ammunition box in front
of the tent. A disheveled major, reeking of bourbon, squinted at my orders
and read them with moving lips. By the light of a candle his face went a
little off-center and he paused, as though trying to decide how best to say it.

"Lieutenant, we don't really need you."

Christmas Eve on the other side of the world and they don't need me!

"We don't use mule-trains anymore. Air drop. Fly in low. Kick out
the stuff by parachute."

With slurred speech the drunken major assured me that something
would turn up. A week later he sent me to Myitkyina to report to the
headquarters of Northern Combat Area Command. There I was assigned
to help ride herd on fifty-five war correspondents on the first convoy across
the Ledo Road.

The first convoy attracted so many correspondents because the Ledo
Road was considered necessary for driving the Japanese out of northern
Burma. When Japanese troops captured Rangoon, in March 1942, they
raced northward to take the Burma Road and cut the last land route of
supply to China. The only way the United States could continue to supply
China was to fly equipment across the Hump, backbone of the Himalayas.
The problem then was to cut a new land route across northern Burma to
link India with China.

A detachment of American engineers turned tea plantations and mat-
ted jungle into bivouac areas. With a few bulldozers and some sorry British
lorries they pushed the road up into the Patkais. Indian laborers were im-
ported and brought with them headaches galore. Each of India's seventy-
five languages and dialects was represented. Eating habits, dictated by custom
and religion, made it necessary for the Quartermaster Corps to stock dozens
of different rations. The caste system demanded strict segregation of certain groups. Self-feeders refused to eat food prepared by another lest the
cook become his brother and claim all of the possessions of the man who
ate the food. So thousands of fires blinked in the jungle each night as individuals prepared meals. Some laborers would work only at certain altitudes.
The turnover was discouraging.

During the monsoon, 200 inches of rain fell in four months. The
engineers endured untold hardships. Wet all the time, they slept in water-
logged tents, bamboo lean-tos, and jungle hammocks. Tractors tumbled over
steep banks. Pack animals bogged down, broke legs, and slid off cliffs on
Pagsau Pass. Landslides buried bulldozers. Long purple leeches caused wounds
that festered. Sometimes Japanese bullets ricocheted off the blade of the

lead bulldozer. In spite of all, the road moved ahead a mile a day.

By the time I got the new assignment many correspondents were already in Myitkyina: Theodore White, of *Time*; Fred Friendly, *CBI Roundup*; Hal Isaacs, *Newsweek*; Tillman Durdin, *New York Times*.

Everybody was getting itchy to be on the way. The convoy could not start, though, because the Japanese held the area between Namhkam and the China border. To ease tensions I began conducting Cook's tours. The first was a flight over the front lines, because correspondents said they would like to do stories describing an air drop. Our C-47, loaded with American, Indian, British, Australian and Chinese war correspondents, flew over the area where Americans of Mars Brigade and Chinese troops were fighting to push the Japanese from the Burma Road.

As we circled the area, cargo plane after cargo plane flew in low over a sandbar and dozens of bright parachutes flowered in their wake, floating down bearing food and ammunition. Soon the sandbar looked as though it had been struck by a snowstorm of divers colors.

The Japanese took a notion to fire on us. Just as the pilot said, "We've been hit," the copilot spotted an unidentified fighter zooming up the valley. We ducked into an adjoining valley, flying low over a river with mountains high on each side.

Five minutes after we had left the area, a cargo plane was shot down, not by the Japanese but by the Chinese. An American liaison officer had warned them to hold their fire when cargo planes came in low for a drop, but the Chinese had a way of disregarding instructions.

On January 22 the convoy began to move. Vehicles of all sizes, 113 of them, crossed the Irrawaddy at Myitkyina on a pontoon bridge said to be the longest in the world. Some trucks carried Chinese combat troops, some American engineers, and most had artillery pieces hitched behind. In jeep 13 Lieutenant Walter Kerns and I lurched along with our driver, Sergeant Bud Celella, a nephew of Jimmy Durante. Kerns represented Service of Supply and I represented Combat Command. Our war correspondents occupied thirty-three jeeps, for which Kerns and I were responsible.

The odor of decaying bodies still hung heavy in the air as we descended into the Shweli River valley, where the town of Namhkam still smouldered. An officer stopped us and said: "The Japs are on the road up ahead, and in the hills to the right. They see every move you make. They're got artillery. They forced our artillery out of position twice yesterday. Don't know how long you'll have to stay here."

To eat our rations, Lieutenant Kerns and I sat behind a pile of rubble that protected us from a sniper working across the road. A soldier, deciding to take a bath in a stream thirty feet away, had hardly stripped when a sniper's rifle cracked. A bullet dug into the soft bank a few feet from him. Without taking time to collect his clothes he dove into our sheltered spot.

As artillery thunder rolled that night along the Shweli valley, I came upon a sergeant seated on a heap of rubble beneath the skeleton of a house. He hovered over a candle, while beneath his grimy fingers were a pencil, a piece of crumpled paper, and a ruler. At his elbow were two booklets for homemakers. He leafed through them picking out the fireplace that struck his fancy, the bathroom that suited him, and the open stairway he had long dreamed of. The incongruity was amusing and sad.

Dr. Gordon Seagrave and his nurses returned to his hospital in Namhkam the day we reached there. He was now a Lieutenant Colonel in the U.S. Army, but had been family doctor to the natives for twenty-two years. When the Japanese overran Burma in 1942 he and his nurses fled with Stilwell. From his experience he wrote a best-seller, *Burma Surgeon.*

The good news of his return ran through the hills. Tribesmen dressed in their brightest, infiltrated enemy lines bearing jungle hen, wild boar, greens, garlic, onions, rice. A Kachin *manau* dance came as the climax of the celebration. Since the Japanese allowed no *manau* during the occupation, the natives were primed for this one. Seagrave told me that the dance is "a religious, sexual, alcoholic trance."

Two hundred men and women formed a long line, grasping each other at the waist and started a movement similar to a snake dance at college. All the men bore swords and had rifles or muzzle-loading shotguns strapped to their backs. As the tempo of pipes, cymbals, gongs, and drums throbbed with increasing vigor, the mongoloid features grew more sullen.

Suddenly, three war correspondents burst into the clearing. They had downed just enough rum to think it was great sport to sway with the dancers. Doc Seagrave grabbed me by the shoulder, breathing brimstone. "Get those fellows out of there!" he ordered. "A Kachin in a trance is apt to kill anyone who interferes." With hesitancy I tugged at the correspondents while the Kachins, none too gently, tried to pull me into the dance.

The next morning I took several jeeps of correspondents forward to witness the final fight to link the Ledo with the Burma Road. Suddenly we saw the Chinese troops, pointed toward the village of Pinghai, firing beyond it. They were doing the best fighting of their careers, but they were firing on their own troops. The clash was between Chinese who had spent two years fighting from their homeland westward into Burma and the

American-trained Chinese who had spent those years fighting eastward from India across Burma toward China.

While Chinese infantrymen fought each other, tanks chased the Japanese out of Pinghai. The correspondents, moving down the hill to see the mop up, bunched together as though on an Easter parade. One burst of machine-gun fire would cut down the lot of them. Remembering my infantry training, I asked them to scatter, but soon they were back in a knot tighter than before.

We met General Sun Li Jen, commander of the First Chinese Army, which had just entered Burma. In a clearing he served us rum, peanuts, and fried cakes. I got into a conversation with a young Chinese officer who spoke English with almost a midwestern accent, but he said he had never been out of China until just now.

He asked me what university I had attended.

"Did you ever hear of Notre Dame?" I asked.

The Chinese officer leaned back on the teak log and sang "Cheer, cheer for old Notre Dame," never missing a word or a note.

The only casualty among my group of correspondents was Fred Friendly, who suffered a badly damaged hand when in a wreck with a wild Chinese driver. On our last night in Namhkam the doctors at Seagrave's hospital put the hand back together. Friendly wanted to continue on with the convoy, but the medics insisted that he fly back to India.

Thirty years later, when attending a reception at Notre Dame that announced the publication of one of Father Hesburgh's books, a publisher from New York happened to mention the name of his friend Fred Friendly. When I told him about the accident in Burma the publisher said, "I have often noticed that something had happened to one of his hands, but until now never knew what it was."

Shortly after leaving Namhkam, the Ledo Road tied into the Burma Road near the China border, and we rolled on toward Kunming, 566 miles away. Each day we marveled at the doggedness that had built the Burma Road. From October 1937 until early in 1939 some 200,000 coolies had literally scratched out the road with their hands. The only machinery used were a few drills to plant dynamite.

In the Salween River gorge, photographers asked me to bunch up the trucks so that they could get a good shot of them coming across the Salween bridge. If there was one thing I had learned in Infantry School it was: Keep plenty of interval between vehicles so that damage from bombings or strafings may be minimal.

General Lewis Pick, the man in charge of building the Ledo, was at the head of the convoy. I stopped his jeep at the bridge and presented my opening argument in favor of bunching up the trucks. Before I could get a reply, the convoy was well bunched. Pick did not seem to mind; he loved a good press.

Then a siren sounded. American antiaircraft men, stationed at the bridge, jumped to their guns. The officer in charge said, "Thirty-one Jap planes headed this way. What a target! This convoy all bunched up in the gorge. What a target!"

I felt suddenly sick.

After what seemed a century, but was less than an hour, an all-clear sounded. Why the Japanese did not strike I never heard. Tokyo Rose, in her broadcast that night, reported that Japanese planes had destroyed a good number of trucks in the Salween gorge. I was so happy the report was false I could have kissed that girl for her lies.

All the way to Kunming one celebration followed another—rice wine, much food, and long speeches. In Kunming, parades, concerts, operas, and parties galore soon grew tiresome. Finis Farr, Bert Parks, and I decided to fly back to Burma. Captain Farr had written the script for eighty weeks for "Mr. District Attorney," a popular radio show. Now he was teamed with Lieutenant Bert Parks, who as a network announcer had been the straight man on "The Eddie Cantor Show." (After the war he would play the lead in *Music Man* on Broadway and become a tradition as master of ceremonies at the Miss America contest.) During the war Farr and Parks traveled the Far East making recordings for a Sunday night radio show in the States called "Yanks in the Orient."

Why we were so anxious to fly the Hump to get back to Burma, I don't remember. Each day the operations officer at the airport told us that the weather over the Himalayas was too severe. On February 10 he said that weather or no weather they had to fly that night. Did we want to chance it? We did. The sergeant gave us parachutes and told us what to do in the event we had to bail out. We climbed into a C-54 and settled into bucket seats.

A yellow-haired kid who looked like a high school sophomore came aboard and said he was the pilot. I thought it was part of a joke—pilots sometimes decide to give their passengers a scare by acting drunk or wearing glasses as thick as the bottom of wine bottles.

"Don't let him fool you," I told Parks and Farr. "The pilot will board just before takeoff."

When we began to taxi down the runway the kid was at the controls. Sleet tapped at the windows. Off we went across the Hump, the graveyard of 379 planes.

– 12 –

History as Written

After the night flight across the Hump, we landed in Myitkyina to learn that headquarters of Northern Combat Area Command had moved a hundred miles southward to Bhamo. Farr, Parks, and I hitched a ride on the plane General Dan I. Sultan had inherited when he took over the job as theater commander from General Stilwell.

Now that my assignment as escort officer for war correspondents had come to an end, I wondered what would happen to an unfrocked mule-skinner. Before the morning was out an officer in G-1 told me to start gathering material for the combat history of upper Burma.

"Where do you want to go to write it?" he asked.

"Anywhere, just so it is quiet," I said, meaning I would like a tent by myself somewhere in the rubble of Bhamo. Glory be, the officer in personnel sent me to a deserted Buddhist monastery on the Irrawaddy River. The monks had fled during the battle of Bhamo, and their building, like the town, was a wreck. A teakwood frame, however, still stood, and the U.S. Army enclosed it with yards of burlap and topped it with a corrugated metal roof.

My first visitor was George Weller, war correspondent for the *Chicago Daily-News*. A big man with voice and intellect to match, he had a way of making whatever he said interesting. When he heard I was from Notre Dame he asked if I read the *Review of Politics*. I told him that the quarterly had started after my time on campus and that I had not yet seen a copy. He mentioned the names of Waldemar Gurian, Frank O'Malley, Matthew Fitzsimons, and Father Thomas McAvoy, men I would come to know after the war. "I think highly of the *Review of Politics*," George Weller said, "even if it did give my book a bad review."

Life in the monastery was not dull. Rats, for one thing, kept me alert. I made sure the netting was tucked around my bed at night to keep out mosquitos and scampering rats. Snakes were something else to avoid. One day a war correspondent came to my room carrying a small snake, saying,

"I just whacked this fellow to death." It was a krait, the most deadly snake in Burma.

That evening I went to the rear of the monastery where statues of the Buddha lined the courtyard. GIs had put up a hoop and were shooting baskets. A tired sergeant started to sink down into the tangle of vines at the edge of the court. Just joking, I said, "Look out! You'll sit on a cobra." He paused momentarily, just long enough for a cobra to bestir itself and go slithering the length of the courtyard.

When living under primitive conditions the craving for the simple pleasures of life can become very real. One night, for instance, Bert Parks burst into the monastery announcing that down the road a unit of engineers had "a freezer full of ice cream!" His eyes were aglow. Although the monsoon fell in torrents, and miles of deep mud stretched between us and the ice cream, we managed to get there. We commented on how here we were two grown men, somewhat sophisticated and thirty years old, acting like kids.

I spent my days exploring the combat strategy that had been used in Burma: Stilwell was to advance from India, with Chinese and American infantrymen, and take Myitkyina. Meanwhile, the British 14th Army was to stab at the heart of Burma with Mandalay as its objective. Another British unit was to proceed down the Mayu Peninsula. In the midst of this, General Charles Orde Wingate was to land glider troops behind enemy lines. Meanwhile, a Chinese force would be coming toward Burma from China. The Japanese were supposed to get caught and be destroyed in the midst of all these moving forces.

The American combat unit was officially named the 5307th Composite Unit (Provisional). Its code name was Galahad. When Brigadier General Frank Merrill was put in command, the correspondent of *Time-Life*, James Shepley, started calling the unit Merrill's Marauders and the name stuck.

The Marauders were volunteers from American troops stationed in Guadalcanal, New Guinea, Trinidad, Puerto Rico, and the United States. As Fred Eldridge said of them, "They were a tough bunch, mad at the world." The morale of the volunteers started low and never rose to great heights. A lack of furloughs, a British training camp, and a misunderstanding about the number of missions to be accomplished caused much bitterness.

While the Marauders were training, Stilwell's American-trained Chinese began the reconquest of Burma, moving well until meeting the first Japanese. Then they dug in and refused to fight. Stilwell went into the jungle to give the Chinese officer a tongue lashing. Legend has it that Vinegar Joe personally led a Chinese platoon, a lieutenant's job, against an enemy position just to shame the Orientals into action.

The Marauders left Ledo on February 9, 1944, and from the start the going was rough. They made wide, sweeping arches through jungles and mountains, avoiding the road and returning to it only to make surprise penetrations behind enemy lines. Acting as an anvil, they held while the Chinese coming down the road hammered the Japanese caught between.

Deep in the jungle the Marauders started on their run around left end, one that had to be a scoring play or the campaigns of northern Burma were doomed. They had to capture Mitkyina, a rail, river, and road terminus.

By now the Marauders were at low ebb physically and mentally. They had lost 700 men killed, wounded, or sick. Malaria, dysentery, typhus, monsoons, insects, monotony, and poor rations were taking their toll.

A Kachin guide led the Marauders over a secret trail. Two days from Myitkyina a snake bit him and it looked as though he might die. Two American officers slashed the swollen foot and sucked the blood. The guide completed the assignment astride Colonel Hunter's horse. He did such a good job that Japanese working on the airstrip at Myitkyina were unaware of how many eyes were on them when the Americans were out there hiding in the tall grass.

The Mauraders took the airstrip easily on May 17, but taking the town was another matter. Two confused Chinese units, mistaking each other as the enemy, inflicted heavy casualties on their fellow soldiers. This gave the Japanese time to bring up fresh troops.

For lack of seasoned troops the siege lasted two and a half months. Of the 3,000 Marauders who had started into Burma only 1,310 reached Myitkyina. The replacements were green Chinese troops and GI truck drivers, cooks, and warehouse men, some of whom were handed a machine gun even though they had never before touched one. Eventually, some American combat troops landed at Bombay and were flown to Myitkyina. They captured the town on August 3.

Just as I was getting well settled into the Buddhist monastery, writing all of this in longhand, a message came saying that Lord Louis Mountbatten, the Supreme Allied Commander of South East Asia, wanted to talk with me in Kandy, Ceylon. The message failed to say what about.

Never have I seen a more beautiful land than Ceylon. That emerald, set in the Bay of Bengal off the southern tip of India, is rich in forests and tropical plants, all more benign than the jungle I had come to know. An old Icelandic map shows the biblical Paradise fitting snugly into Ceylon.

Arab traders called it "Serendib," from which comes the word *serendipity*, an unexpected happy experience. When that comely country became a republic, in 1972, the name was changed to Sri Lanka, "the resplendent land."

Mountbatten said that I had arrived early and suggested that I take one of his cars and a chauffeur to see the sights of Ceylon. We would be having lunch he said, in the King of England's Ceylon palace five days hence.

Handsome Mountbatten came down the palace stairway in a breezy mood, with sixteen ribbons on his chest and knickknacks all over his shoulders. These were not armchair decorations adorning Queen Victoria's great-grandson, cousin of the Czar and relation of the King of England. Early in the war he had commanded the destroyer HMS *Kelly* and made Germans fear it in two oceans. Four times his ships were bombed or blown up from under him. Later, as chief of commandos, he planned and took part in surprise landings at Dieppe, Saint Nazaire, and North Africa.

At lunch Mountbatten said that he wanted me to write the story of Chinese and American combat in Burma so that he might incorporate it in his report on South East Asia Command. It must tell the truth, even when the truth embarrassed, for history should not be all sugar and honey.

He told of an incident in Europe that would probably not appear in combat history but, he felt, should: At Brest, the RAF made the blunder of bombing ships of the British fleet. Mountbatten gave the order that any plane attacking the fleet should be shot down. He was asked to revoke the order but refused. He reasoned that a ship costs more than a plane, and so it is foolish for a ship to sit and take it while a plane makes mistakes.

Mountbatten told of another piece of bungling that had cost him equipment: He asked for a shipment of tanks, but somebody in an armchair in Washington said, "There must be a mistake in this order. Tanks can't be used over there. This must be for Europe." So the tanks went to Europe.

Encouraged by Mountbatten's apparent love of truth in history, I asked, "How about our troubles with the Chinese troops?"

He hesitated, thought a moment, and said that the report would not need to go into American problems with the Chinese troops, because it might cause the Chinese to lose face. After all, Mountbatten said, "Chinese officers aren't even asked questions in Staff School, because if they do not know the answer they lose face."

I asked Mountbatten for a deadline. He set September 1, four months away. The project, however, became very hurry-hurry when Chiang Kai-shek heard we were doing a report for the British, and so he wanted one for the Chinese.

I was transferred from the monastery in Bhamo to India-Burma Theater Headquarters in New Delhi and Lieutenant Paul Geren was assigned to work on the project with me. One of the nicest things that happened to me in the war was getting to know Paul Geren, a scholarly young man with a doctorate in economics from Harvard. When the Japanese attacked Burma he was a professor in Rangoon. To do his part in the emergency he hurried to northern Burma to join Doc Seagrave's medical unit and so, in time, became a part of Stilwell's walk out of Burma.

The first general I worked with in New Delhi was Frank Merrill. He was a warm, cheerful man who saw the writing of history as an exercise in public relations.

General John P. Willey, who commanded the Mars Brigade, in Burma, was not interested in public relations; he was even willing to call attention to his own mistakes. Although he had been chief of staff at Myitkyina, he said, "We must put down about Myitkyina just the way it was. It is not a pleasant story. It's embarrassing. But we must write it the way it was. Maybe others will read and not make the same mistakes. The biggest lesson we learned at Myitkyina is that you can't use green troops and get by with it."

I was surprised to have General Willey tell me that the theater commander had ordered him to cut the Burma Road and that he had refused to do so. "I wanted to cut it here," he said, pointing to a map. "Had I been given permission, I would have done it because I could approach the road without exposing men too much. But General Sultan said cut it here and I didn't do it because I would have lost too many crossing the wide open approaches to the road."

General Sultan read the manuscript and wondered why we had been so hard on the Chinese. Also ease up on the British, he said. So we began making adjustments here and there. For example, the Chinese and the British disagreed over the capture of Mogaung. Each claimed the credit. It is difficult to imagine why anyone should care about getting credit for taking such a remote village. So in the report to Chiang we said that the Chinese had taken it in; in the one to Mountbatten, the British captured it. In our report to our own War Department we admitted that we did not know who had captured Mogaung.

While living in New Delhi I began to realize that the sun was really setting on the British Empire. This was impressed on me while attending the trial of members of the INA (India National Army) in the Red Fort at Delhi. The British brought three Indian officers to trial on charges of treason, murder, and abetted murder. At the fall of Singapore British officers had surrendered their Indian Troops to the Japanese. Many of those prisoners of war had formed an Indian National Army to side with the Japanese and fight for the freedom of India.

In the tacky courtroom sat eight British judges. In front of them sat three Indian officers. They had a cocky attitude not expected from men on trial for their lives. Most of the onlookers were well-saried Indian girls who had brought their knitting with them.

The defense had not a leg to stand on. The officers were guilty and everyone knew it. At an earlier time, and in another place, they would have drawn the death penalty. All of us felt, though, that the British would not dare impose that sentence. Protest riots were flaring out all over India.

When the Indian officers were set free everyone realized how much the Empire was on the run. Just after the verdict, friends of the defendants whisked them into Delhi, where a parade formed and the three officers, with garlands of marigolds about their necks, began to live the life of celebrities.

I doubt that anyone in the Red Fort that day would have thought the Empire would dissolve as fast as it did. Just two years later, August 15, 1947, Mary and I were moving into our home near Notre Dame when a copy of the *South Bend Tribune* was delivered to the door. The lead story said that Mountbatten, the last viceroy, had officiated at a ceremony giving India its freedom. There were also stories of the appalling violence as Hindus and Moslems tried to destroy each other.

Soon after the Japanese surrendered, in August 1945, I realized that army life in peacetime is not for me. The war had been a pep pill that induced nervous stimulation, but a feeling of uneasiness followed. Still I had to keep at the history for another five months.

– 13 –

Back to Notre Dame

Bert Parks, having recovered from an illness, was about to leave New Delhi. We were having our last breakfast together in Central Vista when Noor Mohammed handed me an envelope: "Letter for sahib. Not from memsahib." The return address, University of Notre Dame, surprised me. I had been away from the campus for eight years; how did the university know where to find me on the other side of the world? The contents, only three or four sentences, asked if I would be interested in joining the faculty. Things were done with more simplicity in those days.

I handed the letter to Parks, but did not say what my answer would be. A decade later, when he was host of a network game show on television, one of the contestants was Jim Kelleher. When Kelleher said he was a student at Notre Dame, Parks asked, "Did Ed Fischer ever join the faculty?" Kelleher replied, "I'm in one of his classes this semester."

I did not join the faculty right away. From India I wrote to Mary saying I felt a certain loyalty to Saint Joseph's and would return there. She made the trip from Rensselaer to South Bend to give my decision to Father Howard Kenna, dean of studies. As they sat on a park bench in front of the Main Building, Father Kenna told her that if ever I changed my mind to let him know.

Through the years I have learned that when you are supposed to do something you had better go ahead and do it; if you don't everything goes haywire. Everything went wrong that year at Saint Joseph's. In the spring of 1947 I told Father Kenna I had changed my mind.

On Saturday, June 7, 1947, I came to South Bend to attend the tenth reunion of my class, but I never reached the campus. When I stopped at the *South Bend Tribune* to see old newspaper friends, one of them said, "Clare Booth Luce is giving the commencement address at Saint Mary's this morning. I'm going to interview her before that. Come along."

After the interview in Sister Madeleva's study, I went to visit Doctor John M. Cooney's daughter, Catherine Anne. As Mrs. Daniel O'Grady she still lived in the gracious old home on LaMonte Terrace. She said that when her father was nearing retirement, not long before his death, he had told the university administration that he would like to have me teach his courses. Although there was a stack of applications for the position, the university had followed the professor's wish and offered it to me. I would never have applied, feeling that Notre Dame's standards were out of my league.

Catherine Anne inquired about Mary and our six-month-old son, Paul. Where would we be living? I said that a house for sale would be difficult to find. Houses, cars, and even clothes were scarce after the war; for several years production had been directed toward the military. The former Knute Rockne home is for sale, Catherine Anne told me. When she gave the address as Saint Vincent Street, near the campus, I decided to investigate; I always preferred living within walking distance of work.

Near noon I entered the Dutch Colonial, two-story, white frame house, and fifteen minutes later agreed to buy it. The owner said, "You were so nice about this that I am going to knock $500 off the price." I had given the place such a cursory look that when time came to get a mortgage loan and I was asked if the garage was for one or two cars, I didn't even know if there was a garage.

When I went to see Father Kenna a week later he must have said to himself, "Oh my, here comes another young teacher wanting to know where he might put his family." I assured him right off that I had bought a house and he brightened.

"My problem is different," I said. "Where might I stable a saddle horse that I bought in Kentucky?"

He brightened still more, pleased to meet a problem he had never confronted. "That should not be too much trouble," he said. "See Brother Nilus at the university farm."

I went to the farmhouse on Bulla road, the brick building now called Wilson Commons, a social hall for women graduate students. I asked, "Brother, might I keep my horse in your stable?"

He gave it some thought and then answered with a prolonged, "Nooooo." After more consideration he explained, "If I did it for you, I'd have to do it for *everybody*."

Eventually I took the horse to the former Studebaker Farm on Ironwood Road.

I well remember the first faculty meeting in September 1947. Father Kenna said, "If anyone approaches you to change the grades of an athlete, don't discuss it. Just tell me."

He said that the university had spent $5 million the previous year, but the budget had been for only $4 million. (The budget for 1987 is $176 million.) I was not exactly a beginner, having been out of college for ten years working as journalist, college teacher, and army officer—my starting salary was $3,600.

I had been teaching for only six weeks when Mary and I suffered through the darkest night of our lives. At seven o'clock on Friday evening, November 7, 1947, two neighbors came by the house to ask me to go with them to a pep rally in the Fieldhouse. It would be a highly charged evening, they said, because Army would be playing at Notre Dame the next day, the final game in a series that stretched back several decades. They were right, it was an hour full of bands, cheers, and fiery speeches.

When I returned home a neighbor, Dale Drinkwater, was waiting in the front yard. Even in the darkness I could sense his shock and sadness.

"Mary has taken Paul to the hospital," he said.

"Is he dead?" I asked.

There was no reason to ask that; he had not been ill. Like all crib deaths it was sudden and without warning.

Four months later, March 4, John was born. Because of a coincidence, Jim Costin heralded the event in his sports column in the *Tribune*: That March 4 would have been Rockne's sixtieth birthday.

When I began teaching, the department's office was in the gritty confines of a Navy building left over from the war. At Thanksgiving, Tom Stritch, head of the department, acquired the office that had originally been Father Sorin's. It was at the end of the corridor that stretches from the front door of the Main Building. The office's high windows looked out on what seemed a French village—the old convent and five small brick buildings were grouped along the curve of a dirt road. The scene is now one of parking lots.

Stritch and I and Jim Withey shared the large, high-ceiling room. The first time that I saw Withey he was his usual dapper self: a hound's tooth tweed jacket, gray flannel trousers, highly polished brown loafers, and a blue bow tie full of polka dots. He was a slight man who moved with a gliding motion, with right shoulder higher than left. There was a grace in his movements that made you wonder if he was about to pirouette.

I was sitting at my desk when he approached his at the other end of the room. He ignored me, just rummaged through his papers, peering at them through thick lenses, with an intent, annoyed look on his face. I said nothing. After all, I was the new kid on the block; he should make the first move, or so I thought. Besides, I was still the boy from Buechel who usually spoke only when spoken to.

This happened several times. Finally, one afternoon Jim asked me a question and from that minute our friendship grew. I know now my instincts were true; had I rushed toward him with outstretched hand, acting the part of a hail-fellow-well-met, he would have graded me as "One of those!" and the blooming friendship would have been highly improbable.

Withey was as mercurial and as capricious as the climate of northern Indiana, swinging from effervescent to grim on short notice. Within an hour he could be talkative, silent, enthusiastic, critical, reflective, and carping.

His interest in sports was zero, or zip, as sportscasters say. He would try to see how far he could get into the week without learning how the football team had fared in Saturday's game.

Jim was a great lover of nature. Winter landscape is the best, he thought, because articulation of bare branches pleased him more than the soft fullness of greenery. He preferred days with a gray cast, for then colors show best. His idea of a wonderful night was to stretch out on his back in the middle of a pitch-dark field with a telescope and a bottle of gin.

As one of the bachelor dons he lived in Walsh Hall, preferring Walsh because of its ugliness. "It is better to be inside looking out than on the outside looking at it," he said.

I learned much about teaching technique from him. He impressed on me the importance of the first day of class. He had disdain for teachers who use the first day as a throwaway: calling roll, making cute remarks, and then letting the students go early. "If you *get* them the first week, you won't lose them," Jim said, "but if you don't get them then, just write off the semester."

He believed that the first class should be used to set the tone for the semester. On that day, students are full of good intentions. That is the time to impress them with the difficulties that lie ahead and pray that those defective in character will hurry to the departmental office to ask for a drop slip. "But, of course, they never do," Jim added. He never suffered fools gladly. If he found a student especially annoying he would put the problem child far off to one side of the room and then direct his own vision to the other side of the room for the rest of the semester.

No one on this campus ever taught writing better. In his fight against "sludge," that heavy jargon called gobbledygook, he covered student papers with splotches of red ink. One of them said, "It looks as though he severed an artery while reading this." I remember a doll-faced nun standing outside of Jim's classroom peering at a red-stained paper and trying the read his admonitions through misty eyes.

I thought about Jim Withey several years ago when Professor Stephen Rogers gave the commencement address at the end of a summer session at Notre Dame. He recalled how he had resented it when a dean told him and several other new teachers that they would of necessity be examples to their students. The idea burned Rogers "like a hot rivet in the hand," and he wanted to get rid of it at once.

"What frightened me," he said, "was the dean's word 'example.' It has an unmistakable moral tone. How could any person who was conscious of his own failings set himself up as a moral example?"

After the passing of twenty years Rogers admitted that the dean had a point. Teaching is a moral activity. "My colleagues and I," he said, "had to be examples for our students as our teachers had been for us, and their teachers for them, back as long as there have been people willing to learn and people presumptuous enough to try to teach them. We cannot help it."

Withey made me aware, that first year at Notre Dame, that teaching is an art; just knowing something is not enough. I found myself recalling the best teachers I had known and observing my new colleagues.

All the best teachers seemed to realize that the deepest things reach young people not through preachment but through a sort of osmosis. To put it another way, students "catch" attitudes, for a virus of the spirit is as contagious as the Hong Kong flu. Withey's protégé, Tom Stritch, so believes in contagion of the spirit that he has, through a half-century of teaching, urged students to "take teachers," whenever possible, rather than take courses.

Since Withey believed that students learn more by imitation than either they or their teachers realize, he spoke to me about "that hat." As a young professor I affected a hat that had lost its will to live. Professor Withey suggested that I bury it, observing that what we wear is not wholly a personal matter: we are somebody else's environment.

"Other people have to look to you," he said, peering at me as though squinting at an offending glare. "It is like owning property; you have to keep it up for the neighbors' sake, if not for your own."

Withey, like all good teachers, helped develop some order in young minds, the first business of an education. An effective order is the stamp of a professional and that is what good teachers always are. Good sense and good hearts keep them from adding to the fragmentation of the world.

By the way effective teachers give a shape to their courses they bring assurance to the unsure. Instead of the labyrinthine, they offer a direction. A student needs to feel that the teacher knows where he is taking the class and that they will arrive at their destinations in good time.

The order that effective teachers create is neither artificial nor depressing. From the first minute it is evident that they have a way of getting a course off the ground, of charging the air with expectations. This is difficult because students in large groups tend to be unduly influenced by the law of gravity. Inertia must be overcome.

Every professor who sticks in my memory had a way of endowing things with importance, an importance that was there all along but needed to be brought to the surface so that the rest of us might see. That is the art of teaching.

Being artists, the teachers who are most effective have style. Someone described style in writing as a series of small surprises—not big jolts, but small surprises. Good teachers have that ability, they say things and make fresh observations that bear a personal stamp. Each is an original.

The teachers I remember best made me feel I was leading a more quickened life than the ordinary. As W. H. Auden wrote: "I have met in my life two persons, one a man and the other a woman, who convinced me that they were persons of sanctity. Utterly different in character, upbringing, and interests as they were, their effect on me was the same. In their presence I felt myself to be ten times as intelligent, ten times as nice, ten times as good-looking as I really am."

Withey, like all good teachers, was uneasy in the presence of banality. He could not abide it. Fortunately he did not live to hear, "Have a nice day," or hear "hopefully" at the start of so many sentences. He would have groaned at the mindless use of "the bottom line," and "a ballpark figure," and "between a rock and a hard place." As I said earlier he avoided jargon, favoring words that are as common as bread. The vulgarity of the latest fad found no place in his life.

Any movement aimed at "showing the world" also held no attraction for him. He was more interested in understanding life than in making judgments on it. He seemed endowed with enough of the grace of acceptance that he did not seek revenge on the world.

Like all admirable teachers he felt that at any given time a university should be the mountain peak of a culture where the best of the past is cherished and the best of the present is encouraged. Out of that belief teachers can give students a vision of life well lived, where the first-rate is cherished above the third-rate. In this environment the young, evolving out of darkness, may begin to care about a life of the mind. Some may even realize that it can be exhilarating.

It was a lively experience working with Jim in 1951 when the two of us drew detailed plans for our classroom in the new home for the College of Arts and Letters, a classroom that would become known as 361 O'Shaughnessy. The architect responded to our drawings almost by return mail, assuring us we would get everything requested excepting northern exposure, for he had fit our space into the south end of the building.

Since Withey could not abide glare, the request for nothern light had been his idea. Southern light is hardest on the eyes, he used to say. When we saw that glare was inevitable, he and Stritch and I agreed that teachers should face into it and not have students distracted by such annoyance.

During his first class in room 361, in the fall of 1953, Professor Withey spent so much time shading his eyes that his instruction lacked its usual panache. He was not flitting about the room with the birdlike movements that students had come to expect of him. Later that morning he told Father Charles Sheedy, then dean of Arts and Letters, that he was considering painting the windows blue. No, said the dean, don't start cluttering up the building just yet, it's too new. With unaccustomed grace Withey accepted this, perhaps sensing that *hubris* would somehow take care of that decision, and so it did.

Father Sheedy always included room 361 in his tour for distinguished visitors, for in the days of its glory it was the most impressive room in the building. Especially magnificent were twenty-five large oak desks with a typewriter, drawing board, and T square for each; they were especially suited to the courses taught there, writing and design. Marshall Field and Company must have had something to do with the desks, because the firm sent a photographer from Chicago to take pictures of the room. Those desks and the long golden rows of bookshelves, storing cabinets, and magazine racks were the pride of Angela, the maid who kept them glowing with bar wax. There was a blackboard, wash basin, electric clock, green lectern, tall stool with red seat, and a rack with a dozen red coat hangers. As a final touch of elegance Tom Stritch hung an impressionistic painting of the crucifixion, a gift from Cardinal Stritch. Except for the annoying glare, room 361 in those days was a many-splendored thing.

At that time we still had classes on Saturday morning even during football season. On one such Saturday Professor Withey was holding his own against the distractions—the stadium could be seen from our southern exposure—and was coping with the unwanted light when Father Sheedy entered with a visitor. It was Admiral Turner Joy, whose name had appeared in news reports each day during the Korean conflict as he tried with small success to arrange peace terms with the North Koreans. Now he was in charge of the Naval Academy at Annapolis and had come to Notre Dame for the Navy game.

The admiral paused in the classroom door, put his hands to his eyes and exclaimed, "What a glare!"

Professor Withey pointed a finger at Dean Sheedy, "See, an old navy man who has been looking over glaring water for years can't stand it. How do you expect me to?"

That weekend before the last notes of the "Victory March" could shake down the thunder from the sky, Jim Withey had painted the windows blue.

The next visitor that Dean Sheedy brought was Irene Dunne. He said, "Miss Dunne, I would like to have you meet Professor Withey, one of the best teachers of writing in the United States."

"That is indeed top billing," said the actress.

Father Sheedy was right. In room 361 Withey continued promoting a prose style as clear and as hard as glass. He taught students to take chunks of facts, bits of personal experience, and the chaos of their emotions and shape it all into a piece of writing that somehow justified their existence.

Just before the end of one of the summer sessions, Jim Withey told his students, most of them religious, that when they write they must keep in mind that eighty-five percent of the people in this world are donkeys. This was not original with him, for in the pages of *The Sweet Science*, A. J. Liebling says that an old prizefighter, Al Thoma, used to observe, "The masses are asses."

That evening several nuns returned to the classroom 361 and applied scissors to construction paper. The next morning at the start of the final class, there they sat—nineteen nuns, two brothers, a priest, and a layman— waiting for Professor Withey. Eighty-five percent of them had long donkey ears pasted to the sides of their heads.

Other strange things happened in room 361. One day while I was teaching, the door flew open and there stood another visitor, Father Gilbert Hartke, chairman of the drama department at Catholic University. The former actor, dressed in the ample white robes of his order, threw up his right arm in dramatic gesture and moaned in a voice of doom, "You will suffer eternal damnation for this!"

Eyes bugged out all over the room. The students did not recognize Father Hartke and certainly they did not realize that he was playing a role of Savonarola when he explained that such luxury can only lead to dire results. Some never did catch on to his sophisticated japery; long after he had continued his procession down the hall they had difficulty with their concentration.

One morning I came across Edwin O'Connor standing at the door of the Department of English, just across the hall from room 361. He said he was looking for Frank O'Malley.

I told him, "I never saw Frank O'Malley up here. In fact, I don't believe there is a Frank O'Malley. Just a rumor in the blood."

"Race memory, maybe. Part of the collective unconscious," said O'Connor going along with my foolishness.

I invited him into the classroom to talk to the students. He told them that whenever he developed a writer's block in Boston he came out to his alma mater and just drifted around the place, meeting with the likes of O'Malley and Stritch. The title for his latest novel, he said, had dawned on him while sitting in the lobby of the Morris Inn: *The Last Hurrah*.

Not long afterward, Budd Schulberg was a guest of 361. The night before, he had received an award at the Bengal Bouts in recognition of what his writing had done for the sport of boxing. He said he was pleased because all of his life he had been handing awards to others, and now, at last, he had received one himself.

Upon leaving the classroom, Schulberg went to the airport to fly to New York. That night he gathered with friends to listen to the Academy Award ceremonies from Hollywood. His movie *On the Waterfront* received eight Oscars.

Arthur Mayer, at age seventy-five came to room 361 to give a lecture about film. He had worked in Hollywood for fifty years, and now in retirement was finding inactivity anything but congenial. It was evident during his talk that he was a "natural" as a teacher. At the end of the hour I said, "Arthur, you should get a job teaching." Even as I said it I thought of how foolish it must sound: Here at Notre Dame teachers retire at sixty-five and I am urging a man of seventy-five to begin a career in the classroom.

Some months later a letter came from Mayer saying he had taken my advice and was now teaching at Dartmouth, Stanford, and the University of Southern California. He and Lillie commuted back and forth to take advantage of the best weather on each side of the continent.

At age eighty-eight he was still teaching when *The New Yorker* ran a profile (December 9, 1974) about him, stressing his teaching career and not his film career. A motion picture documentary, *Arthur and Lillie*, told of the rapport he and his wife had with students. It was entered for an Academy Award, and although it did not win, it was shown nationally several times on PBS television.

Room 361 became the setting for an educational film, *The War on Gobbledygook*. Since it was simpler for me to go to California than to bring a film crew to Notre Dame, the classroom became a set on a sound stage. When the designer asked how the classroom was furnished I said, "You had better just put in some of those chairs with one large arm on each, the kind found in most classrooms. If you put in twenty-five executive-type desks, the audience will laugh, saying. 'That's Hollywood for you. Can't even present an honest classroom.'"

A decade later, it seemed that an actor, Jason Miller, might help solve my recurring problem in 361, just as Admiral Turner Joy had helped Jim Withey solve his. Jim's problem was glare, mine was heat. That room had the climate of the equator at high noon. Winter was the worst. I would walk up Notre Dame Avenue with the west wind coming in low over the golf course, penetrating the thickest of Harris tweeds, and enter a classroom with a climate that called for cotton seersucker. After each complaint somebody with a clipboard and a monkeywrench came in, mumbled over the radiator, and left, assuring me that there was no possible solution.

It was hot in there the afternoon Jason Miller spoke to Professor Stritch's class. Although he came as the author of the play *That Championship Season*, he was also at the time playing the role of a young priest in the movie *The Exorcist*. That very week *Newsweek* carried as its cover a close-up of Jason Miller, in priestly garb, thrusting a crucifix at the world.

By the end of the class hour Miller had broken out in a heat rash so severe that he considered seeing a doctor. I used the occasion to observe, "He defied the hot hinges of hell in *The Exorcist*, but the heat brought him down in this classroom. How can the rest of us be expected to stand it?"

I avoided mentioning that Miller had been wearing a woolen turtleneck during the lecture.

Ill health made Jim Withey's presence in that classroom an on-and-off affair. When it came to ailments he was a Renaissance man, not specializing in any one but acquiring them all. I still flinch when I recall how he took shots; he would flourish a needle in the office and jab it through his trousers into his thigh.

He became something of a legend at Saint Joseph's hospital. One of the stories told about him had to do with the time a patient died while sharing the room with Jim. When the nurse eventually made her appointed rounds, Jim looked at his watch and announced, "He's been dead an hour and eight minutes."

"Why didn't you call me?" asked the nurse with some concern.

"What could you have done?" asked Jim.

Long after Jim's death in 1967, I heard Professor Elizabeth Christman say of one of the younger members of the faculty, "If I had children I would like to have her teach them."

I thought of Jim Withey.

What a fitting test for a teacher: would you put your children under his influence? Such a test goes beyond the subject matter of the course, beyond conferences attended, beyond articles published and committees served. It goes deeper than the usual academic concerns. It makes a judgment on the spirit.

Top photos: Ed, ages three, fifteen and nine. Bottom left: with Aunt Linda; right: mother under the big beech tree.

Rev. John Farley, C.S.C.   Rev. John Ryan, C.S.C.   Rev. John O'Hara, C.S.C.

Press Club, 1936. Bottom row: Cackley, Johnson, Fitzsimons, McHugh, Riley. Top row: Reilly, Hurley, Hutchins, Fennelly, McClain, Fischer, Rev. McViney.

Rev. Philip Moore, C.S.C.   T. Bowyer Campbell   Francis J. O'Malley

Right: John M. Cooney.
Below left: John T. Frederick;
right: Richard Sullivan and John
Frederick in 1951.

Paul Fenlon, left, and friends from early photo album.

Joseph Ryan and Paul Fenlon on the steps of Sorin Hall.

Top row: Mary Fischer engagement photo; cub reporter with Gene Krupa. Middle section: sons Tom and John Fischer on Lewis Carroll statue; Mary in 1942; Bertha Fischer. Bottom: Edward Fischer, Sr., with grandsons.

Class in design in room 361 O'Shaughnessy.

James Withey and
Thomas Stritch

Saint Mary's Lake is the set for a student film.

Sister Madeleva, C.S.C.

Marion McCandless

Pieta in Sacred Heart Church
and sculptor Ivan Mestrovic.

Above: Richard Sullivan.
Left: Joe Boland.

Above: Ann Blyth and cowboy Ed in a 1965 film promoting film appreciation.

Below: Ben Gilbert, Rolland Tooke, Alvin Toffler, and Ed Fischer at Salzburg Seminar in American Studies, 1963.

Mary and Ed arrive in
Majorca, 1977, on
vacation.

Bel-Air, in the Irish hunt country of the Wicklow hills, provided a
quiet place to write *Everybody Steals from God.*

The Notre Dame class of 1937 at their forty-fifth reunion, 1982.

– 14 –

In the Classroom

When I was a student at Notre Dame a track man came into Sorin Hall one afternoon looking dejected. He had just competed against Jesse Owens.

"I picked the wrong time in history to be a runner," he said. Had he competed several years earlier or had he been able to delay his career for several years, he would have looked better in the record books. To run against Jesse Owens was to be eclipsed.

I felt the same way when I began teaching writing in Jim Withey's time. It was hard to look good against his high standard. Whenever I walked into a classroom to start a course my heart went out to the students sitting there, in part because they had been assigned to my section instead of Withey's, but mainly because writing is such an onerous line of trade. The students may have heard amateurs exclaim that writing is fun, but professionals know it is akin to scraping a thumbnail across a rough brick.

On the first day of class I knew that I could teach these students how to gather material, organize it, and avoid gobbledygook, but that only God could give them the grace to bring a piece of writing alive. I was aware that at the end of the semester they would be only three months older; not many days of maturing, considering that a writer is formed by the press of time.

On a March morning, years ago, I asked a farmer if he would have his trotting horse ready to race at the county fair in September. "Yes," he drawled, "but we'll have to put in a lot of sloow miles first." How many of these students have the patience to put in a lot of "sloow miles" is something else I wondered about the first day of class.

The most important thing a teacher of writing can do is help a student develop some clarity of thought. Clear writing cannot come from hazy thinking. Even if one writes idiocy it must be idiocy clearly conceived and presented in a way the reader understands.

I speak of clarity of communication, not correctness of thought pertaining to politics, economics, or scientific theory. For example, theologians may hold opposing views, yet each should be able to present his in a clear, well-organized way; if he is truly blessed his writing will even be interesting.

A good piece of writing is haunted by the presence of the writer. Or call it a climate. It is an atmosphere that might be wry, or solemn, or lively — the weather of the soul. In all the vast acreage of bureaucratic gobbledygook there is no presence, no climate, only the void that preceded creation.

To grow as a writer a beginner needs professional humility. That means admitting that the first draft is sorry and the second not much better. People who think that whatever they do is wonderful just because they do it may be authors, but not writers. Anyone publishing a book is an author, but not necessarily a writer.

Some of Dylan Thomas' poetry went through a hundred drafts. In a Frost sonnet the last six lines were written fifty years after the octave. Even the careful Henry James began revising his novels toward the end of his life.

I was never favorably impressed when a student said, "I stayed up all night writing this." The piece was almost sure to be a mess. Had he started weeks earlier so as to allow days to elapse between rewrites, he might have put enough distance between himself and the work to detect cloudy spots and inanities. He needed to rewrite until the whole piece had the feeling of inevitability about it. While the discerning reader would then give him credit, I must admit that others might find it all looks too easy, for many readers admire jargon and are impressed only with things they really don't understand.

"Be definite!" are the two words I used most often as a teacher. A writer needs a concern for the definite because everything in the world is saturated with it. There is no such thing as a generalized flower; it is a tulip, or a violet, or something else just as specific. No two snowflakes and no two fingerprints are identical. Everything in creation has its own particularity.

The senses are "the gateways to the soul," as William Blake said. A writer uses the senses to reach the soul, while avoiding glittering generalities along the way. "She is sad" is an observation born of the senses, but it has lost definiteness. Homer wrote, "She knows the saltiness of tears," and summoned the sense of taste. "She sighs" appeals to the sense of hearing. "A tear formed on her eyelid" appeals to sight.

There is no guarantee, though, that definiteness will bring distinction to a piece of writing. It may come bearing its share of poor taste. For instance, a newspaperman early in this century began a story: "The trap door sprung at 6:05 this morning and Johnnie Magee, dressed in a tight-fitting black suit and wearing a thick noose around his neck, danced all the way to his Maker." As you might have guessed the headline read: "Jerked to Jesus."

In a final exam a student was plenty definite but lacked good sense when writing: "Dante stood with one foot in the grave of the Middle Ages and with the other saluted the rising sun of the Renaissance."

When John Kennedy was wondering what he would say at his Inaugural, and how he would say it, he asked Theodore Sorensen to try to learn the secret of Lincoln's Gettysburg Address. Sorensen studied the speech and decided that it is powerful because "Lincoln never used a two- or three-syllable word when a one-syllable word would do, and never used two or three words where one word would do."

Eric Hoffer also believed in making every word count. He gave the University of California at Berkeley an endowment that would yield $500 a year to be given as a prize for a 500-word essay. A dollar a word. "There was an outcry from the students and some of the faculty," Hoffer said. " 'What can one say in 500 words!' My answer was that there is not an idea that cannot be expressed in 200 words, and the prize allows words enough for two and a half ideas."

That a sentence should never be more difficult than the thought it holds is something else I harped on. If it must be reread because the thought is so new or subtle, that is all right. If reread because of cloudiness, it steals the reader's time, the worst theft of all. Of course, in all of this keep in mind Einstein's admonition: "Everything should be made as simple as possible, but not simpler."

A teacher needs to encourage students to develop a taste for the language by reading those who write with grace. And it is good to listen to those who use words well. Not all people with schooling galore use words well. The official organ of the Academy of Arts and Sciences, *Daedalus*, offers this paragraph to a waiting world:

> The concept of sociocultural levels is a heuristic means of analyzing developmental sequences and internal structures. The approach seeks hierarchies both of organization and of sequence—the autonomous nuclear family, extended families of various types superimposed upon the nuclear family, or a multicommunity state unifying hitherto independent settlements.

A young writer hanging around such prose can be ruined for life. At the start of the semester I had students make a collection of such horrors.

I suggested that they turn to advertisements, listen to the evening news, read newspapers, make notes at lectures, tune in talk shows, riffle through government reports, and especially look into their textbooks—all sources rich in the abuse of language.

I used to have the students translate these horrors into the English language. They grappled long and hard with a note that the principal of a Houston high school sent to parents announcing a special meeting:

> Our school's cross-graded, multi-ethnic, individualized learning program is designed to enhance the concept of an open-ended learning program with emphasis on a continuum of multi-ethnic, academically enriched learning, using the identified intellectually gifted child as the agent or director of his own learning. Major emphasis is on cross-graded, multi-ethnic learning with the main objective being to learn respect for the uniqueness of a person.

My students decided this means: "We are planning a program for students of all races which we hope will encourage the brighter ones to move ahead at their own speed. Grading will be geared to the learning level of the student. In this way we hope to teach and grade each student according to ability to learn."

At this point in the course I gave the students good sentences and ask them to distort them into gobbledygook. It helped beginners see how silly such mumbo-jumbo really is. Once they began to laugh at it, they had a hard time taking it seriously. They translated clear sentences, such as this one, into something a bureaucrat could feel proud of: "Each department head must see that he and each employee under him gets his vacation."

Stretch those fifteen words into at least thirty or forty words, I said. After a certain amount of grinning and mumbling to themselves students would read aloud something that sounded like this: "It is the responsibility of each and every department head to properly arrange the affairs of his organization in such a manner that each employee, including himself, will receive the full vacation to which he is duly entitled."

After getting them to laugh at gobbledygook, the next step was to get them laughing at cliches. A good device is to have students line up three cliches in such a way that the result will take on the mood of Oriental wisdom, a do-it-yourself Confucianism.

> He who eats crow
> While making mountains out of molehills
> Ends with grit in his craw.

He who keeps dragging his heels
While jumping at conclusions
Ends as a basket case.

He who rocks the boat
When taking the bull by the horns
Will always put the cart before the horse.

When the students are appalled by gobbledygook, and amused at cliches, the time has come to ask them to consider what is causing the destruction of language. They soon see that nonlanguage is being written for any of three reasons—inability, deception, self-promotion.

Some people are unable to write with clarity because direct, clear, forceful expression comes from a clear, uncluttered mind. A murky mind cannot give birth to clear prose any more than a water buffalo can produce a thoroughbred. Making ideas come into sharp focus is real work. Simple is hard.

Some people are unclear because they want to deceive. Especially when running for reelection. George Orwell said, "The great enemy of clear language is insincerity."

Perhaps most gobbledygook is a form of self-promotion. When a bureaucrat asked his secretary what she thought of his report, she said, "I think it is hard to read." He said, "It ought to be hard to read, I worked hard compiling it." For him writing is a form of showing off and he believes that vagueness is a form of profundity.

The next step was to get students to care about structure. A good piece of writing says things worth saying within a framework of effective design: the beginning gets attention in the right way, the middle develops ideas in good order, and the ending has the feeling of a good place to get off.

Even a complex piece of good writing has a simplicity found in organic things. All parts work together with nothing existing for itself alone—no cute remarks, no show-off comment. It has the rightness that graces the body of a well-proportioned animal, as a Greek philosopher said.

"Should I be a writer?" is one of the most uncomfortable questions a teacher is asked. Since the ability to write is a gift, it comes under the heading of vocation. A vocation is not something settled on after weighing various job opportunities. Such conscious choice is only for the uncommitted.

My advice to students has been: If you can *not* write, don't. But if you *must* write, then you must.

I always thought it ironic that Professor Withey never became a writer, not even an author. He lacked the need to write. Since he suffered no such compulsion his words survive only in red ink on yellowing student papers tucked away in hidden places.

I introduced film studies at Notre Dame and eventually helped pioneer them throughout this country and abroad. Tom Stritch and Jim Withey encouraged me all the way. How I prepared myself for that new development is answered in a later chapter.

Film studies at one point became so popular in schools at every level that I felt uneasy; it was like being caught in a fad, something I try to avoid.

At the height of the film fad I was having lunch with an elderly Jesuit, Father John LaFarge, when he asked, "Professor, do students still write poetry?" I felt embarrassed for the old man, his question was so out of touch with the times. Students no longer care about poetry, I said, all they want to do is make films.

Were someone to ask that question today, I could answer that poetry is alive and well at universities. At least at this writing, but by Tuesday, who knows? One learns while teaching that subjects rise and fall in popularity with a movement not unlike the tides of the sea and the phases of the moon.

My course, Film as Insight, was popular to the point of embarrassment. When students slept in the hallway overnight to be near the front of the line to register for the class, I cringed. Although the auditorium in the Architecture building could hold eighty chairs, if everybody held his breath and nobody blinked, the demand for the course went far beyond that number.

I would screen a film, the students would write a review, and then we would discuss it at some length. We looked at productions made in the United States, Canada, England, Sweden, France, and Italy. On our list were feature films of every genre, short subjects, and documentaries. Quality was the one thing they had in common.

I began by saying that a film of quality should be given as much respect in a university as a play, or a novel, or a poem of quality. In those days a sign in the public library read, "Literature Mirrors Man"; I pointed out that it might just as well read "Movies Mirror Man"—at least the best ones do. The best films, like the best of literature, tell how it is to be human under certain circumstances and allow us to live beyond what our own living might be. They allow us to run our fingers across the texture of life and explain us to ourselves in the realms of thought and feeling and action. To observe how the filmmaker does this we studied the technique, for the artist uses technique to reveal meaning.

Any film that speaks truly of the human experience is of some value to the spirit. Because of this, a young monk approached me after I had given a talk in Louisville to ask that I come to the Trappist monastery, the Abbey of Gethsemani in Kentucky, to talk about films and show a few that have value for the inner self. Three times I went there to lecture; on one occasion Mary went along and she, too, gave a lecture to the Trappists.

In a course called Motion Picture Production, students sometimes made individual films in 8mm and at times worked as a group on a 16mm production, something sufficiently professional to be shown beyond the campus confines.

We made our first film, *Shake Down the Thunder*, in the spring of 1953. It told how the "Victory March" had been written in the basement of Sorin Hall and from such humble beginnings had gone on to echo around the world.

The movie opened with Jack Shea, a student, hurrying across campus to Sorin Hall to see his brother, Mike. Since the time was supposed to be early in this century, we used a soft-focus lens, a certain film stock, and the right kind of lighting to get the diffuse, flat look of early motion pictures. We tried for an exaggerated style of acting to imitate performances in old movies. It was supposed to look as though we were using film from the archives.

In those opening scenes Jack was intent on getting Mike to put music to words he had written for a school song. Mike, the more scholarly, was busy with studies. Jack finally led his brother to a beat-up piano in the Sorin rec room where Mike picked out note by note, giving life to the scribbled line, "Cheer, cheer for old Notre Dame. . . ."

In the following sequence the Shea brothers were in the music teacher's room, trying to get Professor Peterson to make musical arrangements for every instrument so that the band might play their song at the next football game. Mort Kelly and Edward Giacomini played Jack and Mike Shea. Professor Cecil Birder was cast in the role of the music teacher.

Suddenly, on the screen, the gate in the green fence of old Cartier Field burst open. The band came blaring through, waking up the echoes with a discordant "volley cheer on high." To get just the right touches of discord, Robert O'Brien and some of his bandsmen spent an evening recording on tape in the old audio-visual room on the second floor of the Main Building. It was such a warm May night, in that spring of '53, that the windows in the studio were open, as were those in Washington Hall, just next door, where Frank Lloyd Wright was trying to give a lecture. What an impression of our band he must have taken away with him!

After those opening sequences, the film told of improbable places the "Victory March" was heard during the Second World War. The first, a dramatization of something I had experienced, was set in Burma in 1945.

I told in an earlier chapter how a Chinese officer leaned back on the teak log and sang the "Victory March", without missing a word, without cracking a note. For the dramatization of this we rowed to an island in the lake, the one nearest the log chapel, where the tangle was dense enough to resemble a Burmese jungle. Lawrence Lee, professor of engineering, played the Chinese officer and I played myself.

The next sequence was located in China. At Tientsin, at the end of the war, thousands of United States Marines landed to disarm Japanese soldiers. Local Chinese craftsmen saw this as a chance to unload the miniature violins they had been carving during the long years of war. Of course they needed to demonstrate the virtues of those tiny instruments, and so they played the "Victory March."

For this sequence Robert Zier and Wilfred Beauchamp and their helpers created a Chinese marketplace behind the Main Building, where there was still a charming cluster of buildings — an old convent, an antiquated gymnasium, and several tiny shops that I described earlier. These were so well camouflaged with Chinese signs that when the movie was shown at a meeting of university film producers everyone thought we had bought some footage shot in China and had inserted it for long shots.

James Lewis Casaday, director of theater in the South Bend school system, loaned us a few dozen Chinese costumes. Every person coming toward the camera was an Oriental; everyone going away from it was Caucasian. The cameraman, Everett Warren, selected his angles so well that when the movie was shown on television it was difficult to detect how much we were faking.

In this sequence a jeep, driven by Lester Halsema, playing the role of an American army officer, eased through the chaos of milling throngs and tote poles and carts. The officer paused in front of a merchant to dicker over the price of a tiny violin. The merchant demonstrated the glory of the instrument with a squeaky, "Send a volley cheer on high, shake down the thunder from the sky."

The next sequence was set in Lodz, Poland. It was based on a letter sent to the president of Notre Dame after the war; in it a British army officer described an experience he had had in a prisoner of war camp in 1945. British prisoners in the stalag at Lodz somehow came into possession of a hand-cranked phonograph, with its morning-glory horn, and a stack of records. They were allowed to have a concert for one hour each evening, providing they played nothing patriotic. Don't open or close with "God Save the King," or anything like that, the German commandant warned. So the prisoners decided that their opening and closing theme would be the "Victory March."

This we filmed on the second floor of Father Lange's gymnasium. A few metal beds and lots of gloomy empty space gave the place the dreary look of a POW barracks. The role of Captain Trevor E. Hughes, of the British 51st Highland Division, was played by Professor Stritch, because he could imitate an English accent.

Father Carl Hager, C.S.C., wrote variations on the "Victory March" theme for background music. O'Brien's musicians played different variations to set the mood for Burmese jungle, or Chinese market, or POW camp.

In collecting material for the script we had other anecdotes which, for lack of time and money, we made no attempt to dramatize. For example, according to the Navy film *Appointment in Tokyo*, United States Marines sang the "Victory March" when landing on a South Pacific island. A national magazine reported that troops of the 36th Division sang that song during the landing at Salerno.

Coach Frank Leahy told me that whenever he heard the song that the Shea brothers had written, he remembered a small island in the Pacific: "During the war I was in charge of recreation for submarine crews on Myrtle Island. One day the natives invited us to the village for a program of songs and dances. After they had finished their native songs, they said they wanted to sing something they had heard on the radio. You can guess what it was."

While their song went on and on around the world, what were the Shea brothers doing? Jack, who wrote the words, went into business and politics. Mike, who wrote the music, was ordained a Jesuit.

The next film we made as a group was *Life without Germs*, the story of the development of LOBUND. The script called for James A. Reyniers to appear as student and as professor. By then, the spring of 1955, he was a quarter of a century beyond student days and had the look of a fading matinee idol. Fortunately, a student in the course, Charles Klee, had the black hair, dark complexion and Mediterranean good looks needed to play the young Reyniers.

Our great problem, one we had not foreseen, was filming Professor Reyniers himself in his office. As a lecturer he was most able, confident, and persuasive, but as soon as a camera began to roll he tightened up. Even when he said his lines well enough, he wanted to try again, and so we went through many retakes.

During lectures I had seen him draw animals on a blackboard with deftness. In the script I called for him to do some drawing. He refused to try. We had to make an animation of two rats—one normal and one germ-free—and cut it into the film.

While the animations are on the screen Reyniers says: "Suppose we take a specific, known germ. Let's call it germ B, and put it inside the normal animal. We can't study the exact reaction to this germ because it will gang up with other germs. So we can't tell just what is going on. But suppose we put germ B inside the germ-free animal. Now we know whatever reaction the animal shows is being caused by germ B."

Quick cuts of various scientists at work appear on the screen as Reyniers explains: "Germ free life can be helpful in solving health problems. Scientists have come to Notre Dame to work on experiments in cancer . . . virus infection . . . tooth decay . . . radiation sickness . . . heart disease."

The last time that I talked with Reyniers was in August 1957 on a flight to Detroit. By coincidence I was holding on my lap a print of *Life without Germs*, taking it to be shown at a national meeting of the University Film Producers Association. It was eventually used on television in this country and was screened for groups of scientists in many foreign countries. Eastman Kodak added it to the collection of exceptional films produced at a university.

More than a quarter of a century later the film still holds up, said Dr. Morris Pollard, director of LOBUND. Because of its historic value, Pollard showed it in June 1984 to some 300 specialists in germ-free life when they gathered at Notre Dame from all over the world.

The film about how the "Victory March" got around the world has also had a long life. Shortly after completion it was shown on television and then went on the alumni circuit for several years.

I was puzzled in 1981 when people began saying that they had seen me on television. Then I learned that I was in the one-hour film *Wake Up the Echoes*, the history of football at Notre Dame made by NFL Productions. The director has inserted a few frames from *Shake Down the Thunder*. The fleeting sequence shows Larry Lee and me on an island in the lake, making believe we are in a jungle in Burma, and Larry, as the Chinese officer, is singing the "Victory March."

Whenever anyone asked what I taught and I said, "writing, film, and design," the next question was, "Design? What kind of design?" I would exlain that design is a visual language and like any language is used in many ways. For instance, the Russian language, once learned, may be used to write a report, a novel, or a love letter; the language of design may be used in paintings, automobiles, buildings, and in a million other things.

In the classroom we limited our designs to things that could be developed atop the large desks in room 361 O'Shaughnessy. After lecturing about the characteristics of good design—unity, variety, harmony, balance—I had students create book jackets, brochures, magazines, advertisements, record albums, and such.

Out of regard for the Chinese proverb: "I hear and I forget; I see and I remember; I do and I understand," I used ninety percent of the time for student work. We gave ourselves to synthesis because so much of education is given to analysis. In much of our schooling we try to appreciate something that someone else has done, but in design we did things for someone else to appreciate. It was wonderful for morale.

I developed the course from one taught by Bernard Cullen, a Notre Dame alumnus who used to teach at the Chicago Art Institute. When I joined the faculty I took his course and then enlarged upon what I had learned through graduate work in art at Indiana University South Bend and at Notre Dame.

Dean Sheedy asked me to give a talk to the Arts and Letters advisory council when the membership included a film director, an actress, a museum curator, and a dozen other professionals in the arts. I was to explain the way I taught writing, and so I focused on the written word and did not mention my course in design.

After the talk, a member of the council introduced himself as Virgil Exner, Sr., vice-president in charge of styling for the Chrysler Corporation. "I don't know anything about writing," he said, "but almost everything you said about it I am saying all day long to my young designers." I told him that after a course in design some students write better. He said he could understand that.

Design is an all-inclusive subject—no matter where the eye falls it falls upon design, either God-made or man-made. What God created is first-rate, but what is made by people sometimes falls short: for instance, the approaches to our cities with all the fast-food eateries, filling stations, motor lodges, their shouting signs and awful architecture—chaos strung out across the miles. If at semester's end my students could still drive without flinching through Roseland, north of Notre Dame, the course had failed them.

The omnipresence of design came into the conversation when I was working on a film script for NASA. A professor in Nieuwland Science Hall and I were leafing through a textbook and I happened to remark that I could use the illustrations to teach a course in design.

The scientist, Frank d'Alelio, paused, looked puzzled, and refused to continue with the script until I had explained in some detail how a course in art could make use of a book of science. His interest was personal, for at that moment his daughter was studying art in Italy. He had seen scant relationship between his work and hers, and perhaps she had seen none.

Yet each was concerned with design. He searched for design within the depths of polymers; she worked to create design with pigments on canvas. No matter what the specialty—polymers, mountains, genes—scientists discover superb design imbued with the same characteristics that creative people work so hard to get into their own projects.

Every course in a university catalog is to some extent about design. Either it explores God's design or considers something designed by one of God's creatures. When an artist wants to create something he is stuck with getting into it the same characteristics of good design that suffuse all of creation. That was the theme of my book *Everybody Steals from God*.

All of these pages about my classes in writing, film, and design make it sound as though I did all of the teaching and none of the learning. New learning did reach me, though, through association with remarkable people. Many of them came along, but to keep it simple I will limit this to four remarkable spirits—a nun, an artist, a broadcaster, and a writer. Different though they were one from another, they were enough alike in their professionalism to give me the desire to be professional. Now they are all gone; their shadows no longer fall upon the earth, but that diverse foursome still haunts me.

– 15 –

A Woman for All Seasons

With back straight and chin high, Sister Madeleva sat poised in a Windsor chair. She was making the point, as I interviewed her for a magazine article, that no matter what milieu you create, it reflects your inner self.

"Do you want to know about me?" she asked right off. "Take a look at my office. And look around this room, too; it has been my study for nearly twenty-five years. They will tell you much about me. They 'look' like me."

Both rooms showed definite character, reflecting warmth and elegance. Each echoed the Tudor-Gothic motif of LeMans Hall.

Sister Madeleva's office revealed the variety of her acquaintances. There stood rows of autographed books written by her friends: Mortimer Adler, Bernard DeVoto, Charles DuBos, Christopher Fry, Romano Guardini, C. S. Lewis, Phyllis McGinley, Walter Kerr, Joyce Kilmer, the Maritains, François Mauriac, the Sheeds, the Trapps, Sigrid Undset, Evelyn Waugh, and W. B. Yeats.

A collection of Scriptures stood next to volumes about birds and wildflowers. Books about fund-raising, public relations, and the financial reports of U.S. Steel, Esso, and Sears were juxtaposed with the Great Books of the Western World.

The room adjoining the office had been her study and conference room since 1934, the year she was appointed president of Saint Mary's College. Its north wall was taken up by a fireplace and bookshelves crowded with volumes of poetry from Beowulf to Eliot. Opposite, windows framed the front lawn of LeMans. The east wall featured three large maps of Sister Madeleva's favorite places, London, Oxford, and Paris. The west wall held photographs of Chartres, two rare icons, and prints of Giotto, Fra Angelico, and Botticelli.

Because of its accumulations, she called this room "the old curiosity shop." A medieval bellows leaned against a bookcase. A large handbell, which had called generations of students to their studies, served as a doorstop.

There were cowbells from a farm in Vermont, elephant bells from India, and camel bells from Nazareth. The mantel held a delicate baroque statue of Our Lady, an ancient ivory chalice, and a crucifix of enamel and copper, a gift of Clare Luce.

One corner was crowded with a fine collection of canes, walking sticks, and hiking sticks—blackthorn, red birch, and hawthorn—gifts sent by alumnae from all over the world. Her favorite stick she carried when walking around campus in search of fringed gentians, towhees, and other evidences of God's hand.

As for furniture, two chairs upholstered in soft, red velvet brocade were the most evident things in the room. "Fit for an abbess or a prioress," said Sister Madeleva. She preferred one of the four Windsor chairs. In the center of the room the conference table displayed under glass a reproduction of a medieval almanac showing the months of the year, the signs of the zodiac, the tree of life, Adam and Eve, and the Nativity.

Everything about the room spoke of a discrimination that preferred the elegant and the exotic. To use an old-fashioned expression, it reflected "a lady of breeding." A woman for all seasons.

It was in this study that I had first met Sister Madeleva, June 7, 1947, a day I mentioned earlier. That morning she introduced me to Clare Boothe Luce, who was at Saint Mary's to give the commencement address. I recall little of the conversation, except that I contributed scarcely anything to it.

Clare Luce, recalling an earlier visit to the campus, said that she had been trying to decide which of many requests for speeches to accept and had sought the advice of Fulton Sheen, who urged without hesitation, "Go to Sister Madeleva."

I was to learn in time that Sister Madeleva never let a conversation go on for long without some reference to God, and so it was that morning. As time neared to join the academic procession, she stood, a regal figure, in the window looking at the lowering sky above the trees and observed that God has permitted man to direct many things, but has reserved for Himself the direction of the weather.

The morning that I met her she was two weeks beyond her sixtieth birthday but appeared much younger. I would learn through the years that special occasions had a rejuvenating effect on her. I remember how young she looked in November of 1955 when Helen Hayes put a trowel of mortar on the cornerstone of the Fine Arts Center. Even a small occasion gave her a lift; for example, when she had a tea party for me in Stapleton Lounge to observe the publication of a book, I overheard an elderly nun whisper to another, "Just look at her! She looks fifty years younger!"

Sister Madeleva enjoyed the company of men. She wrote near the end of her life: "The presence of 7,000 college men on our horizon contributes subtly and, I am sure, very constructively to our world."

Through the years hundreds of Notre Dame students sought her out with their problems. She could be severe with them, if necessary, for her character was not without steely elements. I was never around when the velvet glove was off, but those who have felt the steel tell me it could be unnerving.

I doubt that Sister Madeleva showed the steel unless she believed it was worth showing. The only time that I was aware of her determination being in conflict with another's, I was on her side. This may sound strange because her conflict was with Marion McCandless, a woman I loved.

One afternoon in April of 1950, Marion and I met at the front door of LeMans Hall. It was the day after her seventieth birthday, she said. She was still a substantial woman, with the bearing of a Victorian lady and with the bright, dancing eyes of a young girl. Although she was beginning to have trouble walking, she insisted that I leave the car parked at LeMans and that we go on foot to the old auditorium known as Angela Hall.

Marion McCandless, of the class of 1900, was executive director of the alumnae association for many years. She knew Saint Mary's graduates who dated back to the Civil War. Sister Madeleva was aware that she knew them and that is where the conflict began.

As Marion and I walked toward the old convent buildings clustered high above a bend in the Saint Joseph's River, she spoke of the southern planters who had sent daughters to Saint Mary's and sons to Notre Dame for safekeeping during the Civil War. As we approached Bertrand Hall it reminded her of a great to-do caused by the girls from the South when they became incensed over something and ripped up their petticoats to make a Confederate flag, which they waved in defiance from the hall porch.

"The first person to tell me about that was Fannie Fitzpatrick," said Marion. "She is still alive. More than a hundred!"

Fannie often recalled the 1865 commencement, when General William Tecumseh Sherman and his staff came to Saint Mary's. The general, in delivering the commencement address, thanked the Sisters of the Holy Cross for their hospitality, recalling that while he was marching through Georgia, his wife and children had lived at Saint Mary's.

"Fannie remembered the occasion well," said Marion, "because she gave a piano recital in honor of the general. The piano she played had an ebony case with mother-of-pearl keys and a spray of wild roses inlaid in mother-of-pearl above the keyboard."

Michael Fitzpatrick was so proud of his daughter's performance that he arranged with Mother Angela to have the piano shipped to his farm near Lockport, Illinios. It was still in the living room when—six months after my conversation with Marion—Fannie Fitzpatrick died at age 102.

Just as we reached Angela Hall I said, "You ought to write this down!"

"I've been writing it all morning," said Marion with a hint of annoyance in her voice. "Sister Madeleva is seeing to that!"

Although Marion did not want to write about those things, she seemed to enjoy talking about them, and so I asked some questions about the Civil War years. This brought to her memory Edwin Booth, whose brother assassinated President Lincoln. Edwin and a Saint Mary's girl, Mary McVicker, were much in love.

"Whenever the actor came to the campus," Marion said, "a nun had to be present in the parlor at all times. Mary, who was born into a theatrical family, wanted to be on the stage and she also wanted to marry Edwin Booth. They must have felt too uncomfortable with the chaperone around, because Mary withdrew from school before graduation. She married Booth, but neither her marriage nor her career was successful."

That theatrical romance led Marion to a recollection of the romance between another Saint Mary's woman, Ellen Quinlan, and a Notre Dame man, James O'Neill.

"As a married couple they later traveled up and down the land together," said Marion. "James O'Neill was one of the great tragedians of his day. His Monte Cristo will always remain a classic of the American stage. But the greatest contribution the O'Neills made to the theater was to give it their son, Eugene."

Marion told me that one of Ellen Quinlan's classmates, Ella Nirdlinger of Fort Wayne, became the mother of the drama critic, George Jean Nathan. Another classmate, Irene Frizzell, later known on the stage as Irene Fenwick, married Lionel Barrymore.

I wondered aloud why such a strong theatrical tradition thrived in the remoteness of northern Indiana. Marion explained that actresses and actors used to travel so much. The legitimate stage and vaudeville, before the coming of movies, kept them living out of a trunk. So they found it convenient to file their children in a boarding school.

Later in the afternoon, when I told Sister Madeleva that I was glad she was getting Marion to write things down, she said, "I have been badgering her for a long time to write her memories of the alumnae. This morning I asked her if she had heard the excellent lecture last night and she said, 'No! I haven't the time. I am working on that book you told me to write!'

"Her excuse has been that she doesn't know how to write a book, and seventy is too late to learn. I keep telling her you learn to write a book by writing it." (Sister Madeleva practiced what she preached; she wrote an autobiography, *My First Seventy Years*.)

Marion's book, *Family Portraits*, was published in 1952. Although she lived to be ninety-two, I doubt that she committed to paper any other memories, unless Sister Madeleva badgered her.

To get back to Sister Madeleva and her friendship with Notre Dame students, one who visited her often was Tom Dooley. He came to the tea dances, a tradition for two decades, and played the piano from three to five on Saturday afternoons. Afterward he would loom, tall and angular, in Sister Madeleva's office. His problem was whether he should be a professional musician or a medical doctor.

After he became known all over the world as Dr. Tom Dooley he still returned to South Bend at every opportunity to visit Sister Madeleva. A news photographer caught them rushing forward, arms extended, to greet each other. The very design of the photo says so much.

Although I never talked with Sister Madeleva in my student days, I saw her quite often between September of 1953 and June of 1956. During that time I crossed the highway three times a week to teach in the afternoon at Saint Mary's the same course in writing that I had taught in the morning at Notre Dame. When we met in the corridor, or along one of the paths, she would ask a question and usually answer it herself. Never was the conversation trivial.

One day she asked what I thought of modern art. Immediately she told an anecdote about a woman who looked over a little girl's shoulder and said, "Oh, you are drawing a pink elephant. I never saw a *pink* elephant!" The little girl answered simply, "Isn't that too bad."

She continued: "We have to re-learn to see things with the eyes of childhood. As Matisse said, 'To look at everything as if you saw it for the first time takes courage.' People sometimes look at pictures and say, 'That doesn't look like anything that ever existed.' But it did exist, it existed in the mind of the artist."

In speaking about the old masters she said she often remembered something one of the presidents of Notre Dame said years ago: "If you stand before a masterpiece and it says nothing to you, don't make the mistake of thinking it has nothing to say. At first you will have to take on faith in the judgment of the ages that this is a work of art and that it has something for you. If you find it negligible, don't think the defect lies in the work. The defect lies in yourself."

One day in the great hall of LeMans I met a Saint Mary's student sputtering with indignation. She was coming from Sister Madeleva's office, where she had gone for an interview for the school paper only to be told by the secretary that Sister was not to be disturbed: "She is reading poetry."

The child was almost shrill as she told of the incident. "Reading poetry!" She could have accepted almost any other excuse.

A day later when the girl reporter began the interview, Sister Madeleva said, "Now sit up straight and act as though you are asking for a $5,000 a year job" (an exceptional starting salary in the 1950s).

Knowing how much she wanted to write poetry, read it, and teach it, I wondered how heavily the trivia of administration weighed on her spirit. She admitted in a piece of writing to "the constant restive desire amounting to an imperative need to write, with no time, no leisure, no freedom from the pressure of persons and things." She spoke of "the inner nauseas of the half-finished."

Insomnia was the solution for a time. She would use a sleepless night to write a sonnet. Exhaustion, of course, was inevitable.

When she was a student at Berkeley—where she was the first nun ever to receive a doctorate—Henry Seidel Canby told her: "Whatever you may do in creative writing, you will return eventually, I think, to poetry." He was right. Although she published several books of prose, including an autobiography, I believe her ten books of verse meant most to her.

Consider all of the frustrations embedded in this simple sentence: "During her twenty-seven years as president the enrollment of the college grew from under three hundred to more than a thousand." Imagine the agony she felt in facing all of those committee meetings, clashes in personality, building plans, curriculum revisions, public relations problems, fund-raising drives, speeches, and those long trips that subjected her to socked-in airports, dreary hotels, and slipshod restaurants. She, the daughter of August Wolff, must often have thought of the German word *Zerrissenheit*, that fierce inner sense of being lacerated.

An old professor who had similar problems said: "I have always been complaining that my work was constantly interrupted, until I slowly discovered that my interruptions were my work." Maybe in time Sister Madeleva also discovered that the interruptions were her work. Or maybe she stayed with the job because it was what nuns called an "obedience." She took that word seriously, and so Saint Mary's grew and prospered.

I believe the happiest time of her life was her student days at Oxford. She traveled around England and the Continent with spirit flying high. She wrote of the "copious graciousness, the spontaneous hospitality, the indigenous charm." Civility and quality always set her head spinning.

When *Life* magazine did a picture story about Sister Madeleva, in June of 1957, it quoted her as saying: "We have gone two million dollars in debt, but it is a good debt because it is for beauty." She was referring to the debt incurred when the Sisters of Holy Cross built a Fine Arts Center on the Saint Mary's campus.

Since *Life* had not enlarged on that quote, I asked her to do so. With zest she explained that since Beauty—along with Goodness and Truth—is an attribute of God, the Catholic Church must concern herself with it. She recalled that Eric Gill has written, "Take care of goodness and truth, and beauty will take care of herself," but felt inclined to rearrange that sentence to read, "Take care of beauty, and goodness and truth will take care of themselves."

The Fine Arts Center is worth sacrifices, she said, because in it students will come face to face with beauty as found in the dance, drama, music, and all of the fine arts. Through familiarity with things of quality they might develop discernment. Most important of all, she said, the arts can help open students' eyes to see God in the world around them.

"God is reflected in the world, you know, but we need to have our eyes opened to see Him. If the Center helps students see God, it is worth everything we spend on it. I don't know of any money lying around idle that can do as much good as this money we have spent that we haven't got."

Sister Madeleva had given me a tour of the Fine Arts Center in the spring of 1956. Workmen hurried about the place trying to get it ready for the first commencement a few weeks hence. As Sister Madeleva and I wandered through the vastness she explained that the auditorium is continental in style, meaning that there is no center aisle and the rows of seats are set so far apart that they can be entered with ease from either side aisle.

Her commentary was filled with facts and figures: The auditorium seats an audience of 1,350. The stage is fifty by one hundred feet. The orchestra pit holds forty musicians. Under the stage are rooms for wardrobe, dressing, makeup, and the green room.

From O'Laughlin Auditorium we went to the Little Theatre, which seats 285, and looked into a few of the rooms in which would be taught music, voice, ceramics, sculpture, art history, and painting. Our tour ended with a visit to the art gallery, and music/art library, and a suite, with kitchen and lounge, where visiting lecturers and performers would be entertained.

The workmen had O'Laughlin ready for the first commencement on a bright June day in 1956. Attending those exercises was my last official act as a part-time member of the Saint Mary's faculty. After that I crossed Highway 31 with less frequency and did not see Sister Madeleva again until January of 1958, when we met in the auditorium during a rehearsal of Ruth Page's Chicago Opera Ballet.

Standing there in the semidarkness, as beautiful bodies moved through beautiful patterns, Sister Madeleva spoke with satisfaction of the things that happened during the first eighteen months of O'Laughlin's use.

The NBC Opera Company had come there three times. During the last visit the company had presented a thirteen-day festival, holding workshops for students in stagecraft, set designing, and costuming. Raymond Massey and Agnes Moorehead had starred in Norman Corwin's *The Rivalry*. Elizabeth Schwartzkopf and Hilda Gueden had presented concerts. So had the Budapest String Quartet. The José Greco Dancers had also performed. Sister spoke of how helpful Helen Hayes and Maurice Evans had been. She was pleased that Robert Speaight had directed the students in *Midsummer Night's Dream* and was about to return to stage *Twelfth Night*.

Each year I saw less and less of Sister Madeleva. By 1960 we were meeting only at airports. I recall the night we dined in the restaurant at Newark airport and I felt embarrassed when ordering something "well done" after she had ordered hers "rare." She said, "Last week in a restaurant in Dallas they warned me against saying, 'rare.' They said, 'Here they won't even kill it!' "

She was so quotable. Always direct and clear. No jargon. Those who knew her well still quote her: "I like to go to Marshall Field's just to see how many things there are in the world that I don't need."

"When some people look at the horizon they see the sunset; others see the toll road."

When the toll road was being built, in 1955, just behind the college, she sighed, "Soon we won't be able to remember when it wasn't there."

When a student asked her what books to read to become a writer, she said, "The Bible, the Oxford Dictionary, and seed catalogs."

When a nun complained that with so many students walking across a certain carpet they would soon wear it out, Sister Madeleva said, "Let us not canonize the carpet."

When someone complained about students walking on the grass, she said, "Of what do we have more?"

After she left the presidency in 1961 I saw Sister Madeleva very seldom. Word of her death came to me by long-distance call one night when I was out of town. While at Cardinal Cushing College in Boston she had suffered a severe pain and after tests at New England Baptist Hospital underwent surgery for a nonmalignant condition. A post-operative complication set in and caused her death. It was so sudden that you might say she was active for all of her seventy-seven years. As Caroline Gordon Tate said in a telegram on the day of the funeral: "The harness-maker's daughter died in harness."

Upon returning home I walked to Saint Mary's to search out Sister Madeleva's grave. It is difficult to find, for it has no preferential place. I came upon it between two trees on the eastern edge of the community cemetery.

The girl who had been born Mary Evaline Wolff, on May 24, 1887, in Cumberland, Wisconsin, died as Sister Madeleva, C.S.C., on July 25, 1964, and now rests among old friends.

– 16 –

While the Light Was Good

Whenever I enter Ivan Mestrovic's former studio I can still see the Master sitting beneath the window at the northwest end. Being a chain smoker, he would thrust a cigarette into his mouth and I would cringe as the flaming match threatened his wiry beard.

The first afternoon that I went to see him, in the autumn of 1956, he was working on *Christ and the Samaritan Woman at Jacob's Well*. In black beret and clay-stained gray smock he set a pace at age seventy-three that younger men might find exhausting.

After extending a hand as rough as corduroy, he turned to lead the way to the back, where the building now joins the Snite Museum of Art. En route we maneuvered between the unfinished projects of his eight students, all especially selected by the Master. In his tiny office he lowered himself very thoroughly onto a creaking chair and regarded me with great, sad eyes.

Three years earlier Father Hesburgh had told Ivan Mestrovic that the university would build a studio for him if he would leave Syracuse University and come live out his days at Notre Dame. Soon thereafter I watched from my window in O'Shaughnessy Hall as buff bricks and limestone trim evolved into a long narrow building with a steep slate roof. The design, Tudor-Gothic, echoed the motif of the nearby Arts and Letters building completed a year earlier.

After the studio was finished, in 1955, Olga Kestercanek Mestrovic delivered her husband there at nine each morning, except on Sunday. In a black overcoat that reached nearly to his ankles he walked the two dozen steps from road to building as though his feet hurt. At lunch time Olga drove him home and after he had had a short siesta returned him to the studio to work as long as the light held.

His high regard for light was impressed on me at the end of each interview. I would ask, "When might we meet again?" and he would squint at the skylight and answer, "Tomorrow the light should be good until four-thirty. After that." While the light was good he fulfilled his destiny, which did not include talking with me.

During October and November of 1956 I researched Ivan Mestrovic's life in some detail in the university library and interviewed him four times in his studio and twice in his home at 214 East Pokagon, almost across the street from where G. K. Chesterton had lived while lecturing at Notre Dame.

Ivan Mestrovic was born into poverty, August 15, 1883, in the tiny village of Vrpolje. His father, Mate Mestrovic, had been seeking work in the Sava valley of Croatia in the northern part of what is now Yugoslavia. A few months later Mate returned his family to his home village of Otavice. There Ivan grew up.

Among the boy's earliest memories were those of tending sheep and goats on the western slopes of the Dinaric Alps, in Dalmatia, a few miles from the Adriatic Sea. Once, while describing the severe landscape, dotted with the ruins of castles and monasteries, he paused for such a long time that I thought he had forgotten me.

Ivan's father, a stone mason, taught the boy the basic techniques of a sculptor. The elder Mestrovic also stimulated his son's interest by taking him to study carvings in the cathedrals at Sibenik, Trogir, and Split. Mestrovic recalled his father's ballads about the struggle between Croat and Serb, and spoke of his mother's Bible stories and her tales of holy people. "Is that why so much of your work is about heroes and saints?" I asked. The Master responded with a shrug, as much as to say that his interest was in art and not in my pop psychology.

During lonely hours on the mountain the shepherd began carving from wood and soft limestone the first of his heroes and saints. His parents, sensing something special about the boy, encouraged him. The peasants of the village of Otavice thought it unfortunate that he was unlike other children, so withdrawn and lacking interest in the kind of play and work that filled the hours of most young people.

Ivan's early education was a family affair. His father, the only man in the village who could read, had a few volumes of epic poetry and the Bible. The boy read the books over and over, steeping himself still more in the themes of patriotism and religion.

He did not learn to write until, in his early teens, he was apprenticed to a master marble-worker who made altars and tombstones in the town of Split, on the Dalmatian Riviera. Word got around that there was an apprentice in the marble-worker's shop in Split who showed great talent.

An old man in Vienna heard about Ivan and offered to pay for his education if he would come to Vienna to study. The plan collapsed when the old man learned how expensive an education could be, and Ivan was left stranded in Vienna.

It was a frightening experience for a sixteen-year-old peasant boy to be alone in a big city, lacking money, and not knowing the German language. A kindly Czech family gave him a place to stay while he learned German and carved statues. A Professor Otto Koenig was induced to give Mestrovic some lessons to prepare him for the academy. They had hardly begun when the holidays intervened and the boy went home to Otavice. Upon returning to Vienna he got another jolt—Professor Koenig had disappeared.

To make some money Ivan sold statues in the streets. Just as the statues and money were about gone, and it seemed he would have to return to Dalmatia to work out his life as a peasant farmer, Edmund Helmer, assistant director of the Academy of Vienna, offered Ivan admission to the Academy without the usual examinations. The young man insisted on taking the examinations and passed brilliantly.

The Viennese artists and critics soon were aware of the Croatian's work and attended his exhibits with interest. From Vienna, Mestrovic went to Rome to study the work of Michelangelo and then to Paris to open a studio. He became a close friend to Rodin, who was so impressed with the young man's work that he said, "Mestrovic is the greatest phenomenon among the sculptors." When Prince Djordje, the brother of Yugolsav's King Alexander, asked Rodin who would take his place, the aging artist replied, "Don't worry. Your Mestrovic is greater than I."

Young Ivan admired Rodin's work. Yet in his friendship with the great French sculptor he always felt uneasy; the old man was too much of a rake to suit the artist from the Dinaric Alps.

In Paris, Mestrovic began making plans for the Temple of Kossovo. At this point in our interview he began speaking of various blood feuds. His political emotions were rooted in his boyhood. He recalled time-out-of-mind hatreds between Serb and Croat and how both agreed in their disdain of the Ottoman and the Austro-Hungarian empires. Mestrovic's dream was that the Temple of Kossovo would stand as a shrine on the battlefield of Kossovo, a memorial to the Slavic heroes who died in 1389 fighting vainly to defend their land against the Turks.

Mestrovic made a wooden model of the proposed temple and began to turn out sculptures larger than life-size of the heroes and the widows of Kossovo. The work spoke of a people who wanted to be free. Soon it was being exhibited all over Europe.

The Turks no longer ruled Mestrovic's people, now it was the Austro-Hungarian Empire, so unacceptable that when Mestrovic was asked to do figures for the facade of the crown prince's palace he refused for patriotic reasons. When asked to show pieces in the Austro-Hungarian pavilion at an international exhibit in Rome, he again refused. Instead, he arranged to have a Croatian-Serbian pavilion built at the exhibit and there he showed his work. After winning first prize his position as an outstanding artist on the Continent was assured.

When three of his statues were selected for purchase by the Belvedere Museum, Archduke Franz Ferdinand canceled the order, feeling the works embodied too much Yugoslav nationalism. The publicity surrounding this incident did more for the Yugoslav cause than had the works gone to the Belvedere.

On the day the Archduke was assassinated at Sarajevo, in 1914, Mestrovic was in Venice. Not realizing he would be held suspect with other nationalists, he took a ship to Split. There an Austrian army officer urged him to sail at once for Italy, which he did.

His father, Mate, was arrested when war broke out and charged with conspiring against Austria-Hungary. Although condemned to death, he was reprieved before the sentence could be carried out.

While in exile in Italy, France, and England, Young Mestrovic formed a committee with Anton Trumbic and Frano Supilo to devise plans for the liberation of the Slavic people. After the Armistice, in 1918, the Allies used those plans in forming Yugoslavia. Things went awry, however; Mestrovic was pained by the conflict between Serbs and Croats as each fought to get the upper hand in the new government. He worked for compromise and so the extremists on both sides despised him.

Mestrovic also resented the dictatorial powers of Alexander I, first king of Yugoslavia. He resigned when elected to Parliament and refused when the king nominated him to the senate. The king offered him the post of prime minister and he again refused. His reasons were not entirely political. He did not want public life to drain the energies he felt compelled to give his art.

Right after the First World War, Mestrovic abandoned his dream of seeing the Temple of Kossovo become a reality. He gave the new state all of the massive works he had completed for the project. At this time his patriotic themes began to give way to religious themes. He now realized that the world's ills are rooted in a lack of spirituality.

Between the wars, Mestrovic designed chapels in Cavtat, Otavice, and Split and churches in Zagreb and Biskupiji. He acceded to a request of King Alexander, shortly before the king was assassinated in 1934 at Marseilles, to design a Tomb of the Unknown Soldier to sit on a hilltop ten miles from Belgrade. These projects are all enriched with his own sculpture. At Zagreb and Split he built homes for himself of such size that they resemble public buildings. All of this time, as rector of the Academy of Art in Zagreb, he was influencing young artists.

When the Second World War broke out, Yugoslavia came under the heels of Germany and Italy. Since Mestrovic had been outspoken in his disdain for Nazis and Facists, the Gestapo arrested him in Zagreb in 1941.

Fortunately, the prison guards smuggled him several writing tablets on which he wrote "Michelangelo's Dialogues with His Friends," later published by a magazine in Austria. The guards also smuggled in some brown wrapping paper from a local butcher shop; on it the artist made sketches, one of which was to become the monumental *Pieta*. When a critic observed the high quality of these sketches, years later, he said to Mestrovic, "Too bad they didn't keep you in jail longer."

An Austrian army general, one of Mestrovic's admirers, told Hitler, himself a frustrated artist, that the celebrated sculptor was being held in jail. Mestrovic told me that Hitler's response was, "I know it. But he is against us and has always been against us. A few years ago when I invited him to an exhibit he refused to come. I won't release him, but I won't take the responsibility of ordering his execution either."

Perhaps Hitler remembered the time, years earlier, when he had sent a Prussian general to Mestrovic's studio with a message. Der Fuehrer wished to speak with the artist about the unification of European culture and wanted him to come to Berlin to discuss it. In declining, Mestrovic told the general: "I am a little man in a little studio in a little province. But I do not have to shake hands with a murderer."

During the four and a half months in prison, the artist thought each day might be his last. Screams of the tortured pierced the walls; the footsteps of the condemned shuffled in the corridor, and rifle fire echoed in the courtyard. Finally, through the intervention of the Vatican, Mestrovic and his family were taken to Italy under guard. Pope Pius XII offered them hospitality in a Croatian convent, saying it would be a safe place because the Italian government considered the convent a part of the Vatican.

Mestrovic was not long in Rome when word came that Mussolini wanted to meet him. He sent back the message: "We are not friends."

In Rome he began work on the *Pieta* in 1942, but the project was not to be completed until after the war, in 1946.

In our conversations, Mestrovic did not make it clear why he was so anxious to get out of Rome. After nine months, some of his Swiss friends offered to forge passports for him. The flight from the country was planned for a night the British air force was expected to bomb the railroad terminal. The station was practically deserted and officials on duty were in no mood to check things closely. In an atmosphere of hurry, hurry, hurry, the artist and his family slipped across the border into Switzerland.

After the war Mestrovic refused to return to Yugoslavia because he did not approve of the new Communist dictatorship. Instead, he came to the United States to carry on his work at Syracuse University.

Among the many honors bestowed on him in this country were degrees from Columbia, Colgate, Marquette, and Notre Dame. He received the Gold Medal of the American Academy of Arts and Letters, the Christian Culture Award from Assumption College, and the Fine Arts Medal from the American Institute of Architects. When he became a naturalized citizen in 1954, President Eisenhower congratulated him at a reception in the White House.

He completed the *Madonna of the Immaculate Conception*, which stands above the entrance of the Cathedral of the Immaculate Conception in Washington, D.C., a *Pieta* in a park between a school and a hospital in Miami, and a statue of Father Martin de Mendoza Grayales, for the peninsula of Saint Augustine, Florida, where the priest had established the first parish in the United States. One of his most impressive works is a twenty-two-foot bronze called *Man and Freedom* standing above the diagnostic clinic at Mayo's.

Other works are scattered across the United States. The wonderfully dignified statue of his mother was for years in the Art Institute in Chicago but is now at Notre Dame. A larger than life pair of Indians on horseback stands at the Congress Parkway entrance to Chicago's Grant Park.

Museums in Buffalo, Brooklyn, and Detroit also have Mestrovics, and Syracuse University owns three pieces. There is a statue of Saint Jerome over the entrance of the Croatian church of Saint Jerome in Detroit, and there is Christ on the Cross, at a Lutheran church, in Rochester, Minnesota.

Tito sent a representative to Mestrovic offering to buy the *Pieta*, the one he had sketched on brown butcher-shop paper while a prisoner in Zagreb. The representative said: "I have been to the Metropolitan and asked them to set a value on the *Pieta*. They said $150,000. I'm authorized to pay you that and have it sent to Yugoslavia."

"Your government does not approve of religion," Mestrovic responded. "This is a religious subject."

"We will look on it as a work of art," said Tito's emissary.

"You aren't interested in art either. You are interested in having the people believe that I approve of the regime. I don't want to use the *Pieta* as propaganda, so I won't sell it."

One afternoon in November of 1955 from my office window in O'Shaughnessy I saw a startling sight. On the road that runs past the north end of the football stadium stood an out-size trailer truck; atop it was a seven-ton statue, twelve-foot tall, of Christ being lowered from the cross. Here was the *Pieta*, the one that Tito wanted so much.

How the Carrara marble glistened in the autumn sun! I took for granted it had been covered by canvas during its trip here, but learned otherwise from the November 13, 1955, issue of the *New York Times*: "Fully exposed to public view on its mammoth carrier, the 'Pieta' was the object en route of much neck-craning and comment. On occasion, motorists doubled in their tracks for a better look at the unusual cargo, the truck drivers reported."

The route had been carefully surveyed in advance. Bridges had been checked against the truck's heavy load and underpasses checked for clearance. The going was fine over the New Jersey and Pennsylvania turnpikes and over much of the Ohio turnpike, but the last 150 miles were the hardest. The Indiana toll road was still under construction and so the truck crawled over back roads into South Bend.

The insurance company required that the statue have armed protection en route. So no sooner did the truck stop near the Mestrovic studio than a black limousine pulled up behind it and three stocky figures emerged and took up strategic positions. With their black hats and black overcoats, and hands thrust deep into their pockets, they looked like characters in an old gangster movie.

The truck drivers were told to take the statue to the east side of Sacred Heart Church. There in one of the side chapels the floor had been reinforced with steel and concrete and a pedestal built, and the outer wall had been removed, for no door was big enough.

The *Pieta* had been on display at the Metropolitan from April of 1947 until the summer of 1950 in an exhibit sponsored by the American Academy of Arts and Letters and the National Institute of Arts and Letters. When the space that the show occupied came under construction, the *Pieta* was placed in museum storage. Just before starting its trip to Notre Dame the statue was taken to the Casavan Carrara Marble Company, at Ridgefield Park, New Jersey, for cleaning and polishing. That is why it glistened so in the autumn afternoon sun.

Each time I visit it in Sacred Heart Church I am impressed all over again by the artist's ability to take chisel and mallet and find inside a massive chunk of marble such sensitive figures. Mestrovic gave his own rugged face to Joseph of Aramathea and Olga's delicate features to Mary and to Mary Magdalene.

This work is an example of how Mestrovic simplified the monumental and still made clear all significant details. A young woman who had taught in a school of nursing and had taken my course in design said that in the *Pieta* the muscle structure and the bones are so wonderfully articulated that she could use it to teach a course in anatomy.

Notre Dame has the best collection of Mestrovic's work outside of Yugoslavia. Besides the *Pieta*, the *Return of the Prodigal Son* is in Sacred Heart Church. A bust of Moses is on the ground floor of the Memorial Library and one of Father Basil Moreau is in the seminary named after him. A crucifix and *Christ as a Young Boy Teaching* are in Stanford-Keenan, and *Virgin and Child* is in Lewis. *The Last Supper* is in the North Dining Hall.

A crucifix hangs in O'Shaughnessy. The Mestrovic park, in front of O'Shaughnessy, features *Christ and the Samaritan Woman at Jacob's Well*, flanked by two evangelists. In Mestrovic's former studio, now a part of the Snite Museum, are eight large drawings and some twenty pieces of sculpture, among them the wood *Ashbaugh Madonna* and the marble *Madonna and Child*.

Even after Mestrovic refused to sell the *Pieta* to Yugoslavia, Tito sent Ambassador Milovan Djilas to try to persuade the artist to come live in his homeland. The ambassador said, "Your homes are still there, come and use them, and anything else you need. We want to build a national museum; you pick the city, the site, and design the building. When it is finished we will put your works in it."

Mestrovic said, "I believe you when you make these attractive offers. But if I come back and work for the government I would be showing approval. What would my friends think! Many are persecuted, some are in jail. Archbishop Stepinac, for instance. No, I can't come back and seem to approve of what you are doing in Yugoslavia."

So I was surprised to hear in the summer of 1959 that the Mestrovics were off for a holiday in their homeland. After refusing three invitations, Ivan consented to visit in July and August on the condition that he be allowed to talk with his friend Aloysius Cardinal Stepinac, Archbishop of Zagreb.

The cardinal, under house arrest, was surprised to see Mestrovic at his door, for only a doctor had been permitted to visit him and then only twice a month. The cardinal seemed in fairly good health and assured his friend that he had not been tortured. He had been released from prison because of a circulatory problem and was now under twenty-four-hour guard in his native village of Krasic.

During the four-hour visit Mestrovic told the cardinal that Milovan Djilas, the former Yugoslav vice-president, had admitted to him, in 1955 in New York, that Stepinac was innocent of all charges. All Yugoslav officials knew that he was innocent, but his influence among the people was too great to be trusted. This part of the conversation Mestrovic did not repeat to anyone until the day of the cardinal's death a few months later, in February 1960.

Mestrovic spent August 15, his seventy-sixth birthday, in the Adriatic town of Split, where he had done some of his best work before the Second World War. Earlier in the week he had visited his native village of Otavice, where as a young shepherd he began carving heroes and saints.

Ivan and Olga spent a week on an island as Tito's guests. Considering how well they were received at this time, it only increases the mystery of the unfortunate events surrounding Mestrovic's funeral less than three years later.

When Mestrovic returned to the campus it was evident that the old antagonisms had cooled. He seemed more kindly inclined toward the Yugoslav government. If the cold war ever turned hot he believed that Yugoslavia would fight against Russia.

"I received a very cordial reception despite the attacks I have made on the Tito regime. And I found that the United States is a popular country because of the freedom it stands for and the economic help it has given to Yugoslavia. A shipment of grain during last year's crop failure made a deep impression.

"I have always thought Tito a capable man and I am now still more persuaded that he is. Things are not as perfect as he would like you to think, but on the other hand they are not as bad as the critics say. The truth is somewhere between."

As for the status of religion in Yugoslavia, he said: "The regime is trying to get to the youth, but they go to church all the same. Religion's popularity is due in part to the fact that the church is the one institution not pervaded with Communist thought."

I was interested in learning what Mestrovic thought of modern art but was not very successful at finding out. From research I knew that he stood aloof from contemporary artists and critics and yet they thought well of him. When, in 1947, he was the first living artist to have a one-man show at the Metropolitan Museum of Art in New York, *Art Digest* said: "It is singularly significant that he is almost unanimously revered by American sculptors of all schools as one of the greatest living sculptors."

When I could not get him to talk about modern sculpture I assumed that perhaps in his old age he had cut himself off from all other concerns to give full attention to his own work while the light still lasted. My assumption seemed confirmed when a friend said that Mestrovic had told him that a "German fellow" had visited his home on Pokagon. "What was his name?" asked the friend. Oh, some German fellow; I think his name was Wernher von Braun."

Another writer succeeded, though, where I had failed. Truman Moore asked Mestrovic, shortly before he died, for an opinion on modern art and got a direct reply: "I think nothing important is happening in art today. Art needs stability. There must be stability in the human mind and in the world. Art cannot be in equilibrium when all around is confusion. Art has always been connected with religion. Today religion is confused.

"So-called modern art is a little childish. I don't think it is very important. It is too concerned with novelty. It is not hard to do. You don't need to know much about anatomy to bend a wire."

A few weeks before his death, Olga said of her husband: "He has no other interest but his work. No hobbies. No vacations. Whether we were in Rome, Geneva, Paris, or London, the first thing was to find a studio and some clay or stone. He has not much need for money. He gave thirty life-size pieces to Yugoslavia. So much work! I hope they appreciate it. But he says he is not afraid of poverty because he can never be so poor as he was as a boy."

Mestrovic's response was: "The only way to be an artist is to work. Work, I'm used to it. My students want to work by the hour. Two or three hours a day. Nothing will be done that way.

"I have some good students, but they do not have enough time in the studio. They spend only a few hours a day, then they have to go to class. After only a few years they get a piece of paper saying that they have studied. That is not much."*

*Published in an interview by Truman Moore for *Think* magazine, March 1962.

The Master's last day of work was Tuesday, January 16, 1962. He arrived at the studio at nine o'clock as usual. His seventy-eight years weighed down on him. Of late he walked warily, as though the ground were mined. The past few months had been hard, but he was not one to wince. He had been in the hospital with a slight stroke; Olga, having suffered an accident, needed a pair of walking sticks to get around, and his son, Tvrtko, had died in Yugoslavia at age thirty-six, leaving two small children.

That morning the master picked up a mallet and a chisel but soon put them down. At noon he went to Saint Joseph's Hospital in South Bend. That night he suffered a severe cerebral hemorrhage and died.

How fortunate that he worked the day he died. Without work his life would have been a bitter existence. He was spared an old age that might have been as prolonged and bleak as an Arctic night.

Olga and his brother, Peter, survived him. So did his son Matthew Mark of New York, and a daughter, Marica Krstulovic, of Buenos Aires, and eight grandchildren.

After the funeral service at Sacred Heart Church at Notre Dame, on January 19, the body was flown to Yugoslavia for burial. From that point on all plans went awry.

The day after the burial in the family mausoleum, Matthew Mark Mestrovic told reporters in Rome: "My sister, Marica, and I are deeply disappointed that Yugoslav officials failed to live up to promises given my mother. They promised that my father would have full religious honors."

Yugoslav representatives in the United States had agreed that Ivan Mestrovic's body would lie in state for two days in St. Mark's Church in Zagreb, for another two days in the Church of the Holy Cross in Split, and that on January 28 it would be buried with solemn ceremonies at the family crypt in Otavice.

What really happened was that the body was hurried out of Zagreb fifteen minutes after arrival. Church officials had not been told of its arrival, and notices of the planned Pontifical Mass were mysteriously torn from the fronts of all churches in the city. So instead of being held in Zagreb until the family arrived, the body was shipped by special train to Drnis. When Matthew Mark complained about this, he was told that the hasty shipment had been necessary because of a threatening snowstorm.

The body reached Drnis late at night and the funeral Mass was held at dawn, before the family had time to arrive. The body was taken to the Mestrovic home and from there carried in procession to the mausoleum. About 3,000 people had assembled when Bishop Franic began his eulogy outside the family crypt. When he spoke of Ivan Mestrovic as "a Catholic and a Croat," some Communists in the crowd began calling him a bandit and a fascist. Several peasants who confronted the heckling Communists were arrested after the service.

Olga lived for another twenty-two years. After a Requiem Mass in Sacred Heart Church her ashes were flown to Yugoslavia for burial in the family mausoleum.

Will Ivan Mestrovic's work live?

"The past is present in his sculpture and there is an element of the future as well," said Norman Rice, when he was director of the Syracuse University School of Art. "The major works of Mestrovic have a quality of timelessness which does not depend on their style or current fashion for their artistic strength."

Through the centuries his work will probably have its ups and downs. It is my opinion that if one Notre Dame professor from the twentieth century is remembered a thousand years from now, it will be Ivan Mestrovic.

As I said at the beginning, whenever I enter the old studio, by way of the Snite Museum of Art, I picture the Master seated beneath the northwest window. That room recalls for me how strongly he held the old-fashioned belief in work and workmanship, an attitude that reflects a certain order of the soul.

Once you see such grace, the awareness always haunts you. And it serves as an uneasy measure of your own vocation.

– 17 –

A Man of Great Presence

In the summer of '52, Joe Boland and I commuted between South Bend and Chicago in the big orange coaches of the South Shore Line. He was host that summer of the NBC television show "Ask Me Another," and I was working, through arrangements made by Notre Dame, in three Chicago television stations, learning the mysteries of the new medium.

Since Joe was one of the more blithe spirits in our solar system, he was a delightful commuting companion. A large, looming man of great presence, his face was as Irish as you might expect of one whose father came from County Clare and mother from County Antrim. And his smile! It was a triumph over life's adversities.

During the two-hour trips on the South Shore, he constantly drew me out. Joe Boland was a great listener; he did not just half-listen, he *really* listened.

At first I thought he was just interested in hearing what I had learned about television techniques because the new medium would be demanding more and more of his time; eventually I realized he was interested in nearly everything. For instance, when spending an evening with Notre Dame professors he explored their specialties in history, literature, government, or whatever. Joe was always reaching for new information, new ideas.

During that summer, more than thirty years ago, I attended most of the weekly productions of "Ask Me Another," which went on the air "live," for video tape was still in the experimental stage. Joe was the host and the panelists were Johnny Lujack, a former Notre Dame and Chicago Bears quarterback; Kay Westfall, an actress; Tom Duggan, the bad boy of NBC who specialized in abrasiveness, and Warren Brown, sports editor of the *Chicago American*.

The show was a sports program of sorts. By asking questions the panelists were supposed to learn the identity of the athlete who was sitting behind a screen so that only his silhouette showed. Warren Brown usually knew at a glance the identity of each of the three guests, but through circuitous questioning stretched the show to its full half hour.

Guests that I remember were Dizzy Dean, Gene Sarazen, Lefty Grove, George Mikan, Satchel Paige, and two Notre Dame athletes, George Ireland and George Connor. After the show I often went with Joe and some of the guests to a pub on Michigan Avenue until it was time for the two of us to take the late train to South Bend.

Joe spoke of sports to the guests, but when he and I were alone he rarely mentioned athletics and certainly did not talk about himself. Only once do I recall that he dwelt on either subject. It was a winter night and I was home alone when Joe dropped by with a plate of fudge from his wife, Peg—a "thank you" for a clown I had painted to add to her collection of clown portraits.

Joe, evidently tired, seemed highly aware of the Law of Gravity. As he sank into a chair I put a log on the fire.

"The first time I was in this house," he said, "was when I was a student. Rockne used to have us come down here to Saint Vincent Street a few at a time. Guards one night, tackles the next, and so on. He talked football. Sometimes he would push the furniture aside and demonstrate something."

"That is why the floorboards creak," I said.

Joe recalled the time he had met Coach Rockne. It was in New York on a winter evening in 1923. His high school coach, Stan Cofall, a former Notre Dame quarterback, had written to Rockne saying that he had three players in Philadelphia who ought to be coming to Notre Dame. Rockne suggested that they have dinner with him in New York.

So Coach Cofall drove Joe Boland, Joe Maxwell, and Vince McNally from Philadelphia to New York in a canvas-topped Model-T touring car with isinglass side curtains. For his first night away from home Joe carried a nightshirt and a toothbrush in a brown paper bag.

At dinner the young men were puzzled that the celebrated coach said so little about football and spoke so much about education and personal discipline. Joe recalled: "Rock said that it wouldn't be easy. We would have to *work* for what we got. We could wait tables in the dining hall as long as we kept up our grades, kept out of trouble, and kept on the good side of the dining hall supervisor. Under those terms he would be glad to see us at Notre Dame." (Incidentally, the three Philadelphia football players helped Rockne win his first national championship.)

In the living room that evening Joe was in a reminiscent mood. Since he was tired, his defenses were down, and so I took advantage of this to keep him talking about himself. How much he spoke of his career that night and how much I eventually heard from other sources I don't know, but a few things stick in the memory:

As a sophomore Joe played fifty-seven minutes in the Rose Bowl game on New Year's Day of 1925. At right tackle he did his share to contain Ernie Nevers, the great Stanford fullback, while the Four Horsemen raced to a 27–10 victory.

As a senior Joe Boland seemed a sure-fire All-American, but against Minnesota, the second game of the season, he broke a leg and that was the end of his career as a player. It was the luckiest break of his life, he said; without it he would never have met Peg Limburg, a University of Minnesota journalism student who came to the hospital to interview him and to bring a plate of fudge.

Joe was equally outstanding in the classroom. He received the Hering Award for Excellence in Athletics and Scholarship for two consecutive years. He was graduated with honors in 1927 and later earned a masters in education.

Fresh out of college he was line coach at Santa Clara under Adam Walsh, a former All-American center at Notre Dame. It was then that Pop Warner, the Stanford coach, must have wished that Joe Boland would go away, for not only had Joe helped defeat Warner's team in the Rose Bowl, he now developed such an effective line that Santa Clara, a tiny school of 400, defeated the mighty Stanford University.

When offered the positions of athletic director and football coach at the College of Saint Thomas, in Saint Paul, Minnesota, Joe accepted. He was not long on the job when he and Peg Limburg became engaged. Rockne wrote to say that he hoped to attend their wedding in the log chapel at Notre Dame on April 6, 1931. A few days before that date Rockne died in a plane crash. Joe came to Notre Dame for the funeral on April 4, and stayed for two days until the wedding. As he and Peg turned from the altar, a married couple, they were pleased to see Knute's widow, Bonnie, kneeling near the aisle.

In the winter of 1934, Father John O'Hara, president of Notre Dame, put in a long-distance call to Joe Boland. The gist of it was that Elmer Layden had agreed to be the new head coach; would Joe be the line coach?

When Joe hung up Peg asked, "How much are they going to pay you?"

Years later she wrote: "He appeared to be in a sort of gladsome trance, and it was obvious that he had accepted the job. His tremendous grin adjusted to one of startling incredulity that anyone should ask such a minor detail."

Joe admitted, "I never thought to ask."

The salary was $3,000 a year.

Joe's job at Notre Dame ended in 1940 when Elmer Layden accepted the position of pro commissioner with the National Football League.

After spending a brief period at Purdue, Joe Boland returned to South Bend to become sports director at WSBT. Radio was not new to him. People had been saying for years, "You have such a marvelous voice you belong in radio." His rich baritone was heard on the air as early as 1933, broadcasting football games for the University of Minnesota; while at Saint Thomas he had accepted a part-time job with WCCO, Minneapolis.

In time Joe's baritone became recognized all over the world. That is because in 1951 he started the Irish Network to broadcast Notre Dame football games. By 1955 he had two hundred stations on the hookup. How delighted he was when Armed Forces Radio picked up his broadcasts and sent them around the world. During this time he also handled the home games of the Chicago Cardinals for CBS and broadcast a couple of Orange Bowl games, also for CBS.

His professionalism was so evident that Bud Wilkinson, coach of the University of Oklahoma, wrote: "No opposition sportscaster who ever followed us was fairer to us, or better informed about football, or described the game on such a high plane of sportsmanship."

Bing Crosby wrote to Peg Boland: "If you couldn't be at a Notre Dame game the next best thing was to listen to Joe's broadcast of it. Joe, with his wealth of football lore, and his intimate acquaintance with everybody on the field, called the game so realistically you felt you were sitting right next to him. You could almost feel the impact of that tackle. It was you who reached up and grabbed that spiraling football in the end zone. When Joe described a game, you lived that game."

Joe's professionalism and his great sensitivity to others are the two things people remember most about him. I was amused when he told me that one night when he was getting ready for bed he felt he was under observation. He tried to dispel the sensation; after all, the shades were drawn. Still he was aware of being watched. He looked carefully around the room and finally detected the beady eyes of a squirrel peering at him from the curtain rod above the window. How like Joe, I thought, so sensitive to every presence, even that of a stray squirrel.

Lawrence "Moon" Mullins, a football star at Notre Dame and later director of the National Athletic Institute, said that he probably would never have stuck it out at the university had it not been for Joe Boland's sensitivity to others: "I was the lonesomest freshman you ever saw on the campus. I knew nobody, and I had five dollars in my pocket. Joe was already a monogram winner. One day he stopped me to ask how things were going. Perhaps he sensed my loneliness. He took me downtown to a movie and bought me a soda. We talked a lot and he told me how everybody gets homesick and that I should hang on until I got used to the routine. He made me feel that I belonged."

With all this in mind, it is easy to understand how numb we felt on the morning of February 26, 1960, to hear that Joe Boland had died in his sleep. The policeman who came with the ambulance called Mayor Voorde before dawn to tell him the news. The mayor looked out the window, and seeing that the snow had fallen in the night, put a shovel in his car and went to 1101 Foster to clear the sidewalks. He knew that lots of friends would be coming there that day and that messages would be arriving from all over the world.

It would have been an inspiration to watch Joe Boland grow old. Shortly before his death his daughter, Meg, was looking at a photograph taken in his varsity days, with all of the thick curly hair still there and the 233 pounds well distributed. She turned to her father and said, "I like you better now."

Meg was right. Joe was always unfolding in the right direction. Were he alive today he would be an elderly gentleman full of grace and charm. That was the direction he was moving.

– 18 –

The Last Visit

Richard Sullivan was a new faculty member and I was still a student the first time I saw him. He was standing in the corridor waiting to enter a classroom, so I caught only a passing glimpse. Fifty years later the image is still clear in memory. He was short and compact, with wiry wavy hair, and showed the resilience of a gymnast. The vibrations of his vitality, more than anything else, impressed the picture on my mind.

We first met in the fall of 1947, when I joined the faculty. By some mix-up we were assigned the same classroom. Aware of his seniority I hurriedly found an empty room for my students, much to his chagrin, for he was always uneasy if he thought he had caused someone an inconvenience.

Right off we became friends. Perhaps because we both cared about writing and were also both collectors of anecdotes, exchanging them the way philatelists trade stamps.

The first anecdote Dick Sullivan told me was about Father Leonard Carrico, the dean of studies, whose directives to the faculty bore a wonderful definiteness. From those directives Dick collected sentences that he cherished. For instance, just before the start of the semester Father Carrico admonished the faculty to "teach in earnest from bell to bell." As final exams neared he admonished, "bluebooks are not to be used for miscellaneous purposes."

Dick treasured several anecdotes about Professor Dan O'Grady. Dan wrote a book of cosmology which he used as a text in class. At the close of a lecture one of those students who are always trying to score points approached the podium.

"Professor, what you said today does not agree with what you wrote on page 50."

"Let's see that," said Dan, taking the book from the student.

After giving the sentence a quick glance he said, "Oh, that! I have since changed my mind."

He ripped out the offending page and returned the book to the student.

141

Another of Dick's anecdotes about O'Grady had to do with the time
Dan and his new bride—Doctor Cooney's daughter, Catherine Anne—were
browsing in the stacks of the South Bend Public Library. Dan took a hefty
volume from the shelf—Maisie Ward's biography of Chesterton—and began
leafing through it. He handed the book to Catherine Anne, pointing to
a page on which Dan O'Grady was quoted.

"Oh, I didn't know about this!" said the new bride.

Dan, in a broad gesture that encompassed the long rows of books,
said with calm assurance, "Oh, you'll find such things in most of these."

One of Dick's favorite anecdotes had to do with Professor Don
Plunkett's car. When Don was living in the 900 block of Notre Dame Avenue
he happened to look out the window just in time to see a driver sideswipe
his car, parked in front of the house.

He recognized the culprit as a Notre Dame professor, a mathemati-
cian from Europe with an international reputation. Don waited until the
prof had time to reach his desk at the university and then phoned him.

"Did you run into a car just now?"

"What color was it?" the professor asked.

I contributed a few stories to Dick Sullivan's collection. One was about
a little nun, dressed in the bluest of blue, who lived in Sorin during a summer session more than thirty years ago.

On a sultry June afternoon, Sister lugged her suitcase across the main
quad to end a journey that had started in New Jersey. In a first-floor tower
of Sorin, on the southeast corner, she was thankful for the coolness, a gift
of high ceilings. Throwing herself onto the metal bed, she lifted aloft her
eyes, as a form of *Te Deum*. And lo, looking down on her from the ceiling
was a message. Block letters in blue ink. Nine words in all, she could tell
by the spacing, but could not read any of them.

The message was there the last thing each night and the first thing
each morning. She yearned, week after week, to climb up to read it, but
fought off temptation, ashamed that such unbridled curiosity should reveal
her fallen nature.

In six weeks her nerves were on edge. Body and soul were weakened
by August heat, unreasonable exams, and the stress of anticipating a new
obedience to be announced on the Feast of the Assumption. With her
defenses down, fallen nature began to break through for sizeable gains:
Perhaps the message on the ceiling is Providential. Perhaps it is something
that should be known. And acted upon! After all it is printed in blue.

With a sudden impulse the little nun pushed the bed to one side, shoved the desk into place, and put a chair atop it. Up she climbed, and, tottering in the encircling gloom, her lips formed: WHAT IN THE HELL ARE YOU DO-ING UP HERE!

Another story that I passed along to Dick was about Walter O'Keefe, a student here in the early 1920s who later appeared in Broadway musicals and was a personality in broadcasting.

While O'Keefe was living in Sorin Hall, the prefect of discipline laid down the law at the close of evening prayers in chapel: "I wish you fellows had more imagination! It gets tiresome hearing the same lame excuses over and over. If when you got into trouble you could give me a fresh alibi, one I have never heard, I might let you off the hook."

O'Keefe was already in trouble. Because of a transgression he was cam-pused, meaning he should not go south of Cedar Grove Cemetery until next semester. But a dance band was playing in South Bend, one that he just had to hear. Temptation triumphed, and Walter was caught coming out of the Oliver Hotel.

When appearing before the prefect of discipline the next morning, he said: "Father, you told us that if someone gave you an excuse you have never heard before you might let him off the hook. Well, I wanted to go to town and felt I had a good reason. I came here to ask your permission, but you were not in. I went to talk to the president, but he wasn't in either. So I decided to try the founder, and went out to Father Sorin's statue, and said, 'Father, may I go to town?' There was no answer and so I took silence for consent."

I heard O'Keefe tell that anecdote on the radio in 1946. Nearly two decades later, in Hollywood, I asked him if the prefect of discipline had reacted with good grace.

"Oh, yes! He admitted he had never heard that one before. As I was leaving the office he added, 'And I had better never hear it again!' "

An anecdote that Dick greatly enjoyed was one about the most disarm-ing alibi that a student ever gave me. Professor Stritch, with amusement, still reminds me of it thirty-eight years later. The memory of it pleased both because they felt I was as much a stickler for dependability as Paul Fenlon was for tradition.

I used to tell the class that in the mass media the cardinal virtue is dependability: "Observe that on the days that schools, banks, and businesses close because of blizzards, tornadoes, or floods, the newspaper still comes out. Broadcasters somehow get to the job and are on the air telling everybody that nobody is working. No matter what the conditions, you have to be able to be where you are supposed to be, doing what you're supposed to do. If you feel that this is not the real you, then search out another line of trade."

Tom Stritch knew I was especially allergic to the sentence: "My alarm didn't go off." So he followed the case with undue interest whenever I had a student of questionable dependability.

He and I were sharing an office in the Main Building, in 1949, when I was confronted with a classic case of what Stritch would call "a feckless youth who does not burn with a hard, gemlike flame." Of a less severe case he might say, "His work is quite competent but by no means devoted."

Just before leaving the office to go upstairs to the classroom I stood tall in the doorway and revealed my game plan: "He was absent again Monday! That's it! When he shows up today—if he shows—I am going to let him have it! Out! Out! Out!"

At the classroom door the prodigal lurked, and before I could regroup my scattered faculties he said: "Professor, I apologize for not being here Monday. I have a very rare type of blood. Saint Joseph's Hospital called and said they needed it. Somebody was dying."

At the end of the hour I returned to the office looking as though I should "seek professional help." At a glance Stritch saw that the adrenalin still surged.

"Well?" he asked in his resonate voice, the one that vibrates into the woodwork.

I threw up my arms and cried to high heaven, "What can you do when a guy gives his life's blood!"

My friendship with Dick Sullivan was strengthened because Professor Fenlon's sensitivity to tradition verged on the excessive. If you did something twice, Fenlon considered it an abiding custom and woe be unto you should you break it. Dick and I happened to go to Paul's tower room in Sorin—at that time on the third floor, northwest corner—on the day that Christmas vacation started in 1947. By chance, the following year we did the same, and that made it an enduring tradition as far as Fenlon was concerned.

Year after year he insisted that we three celebrate the ritual with a glass of Scotch—one ice cube per glass—just as December dusk settled over the Dome. The conversation was usually the same, for that was part of the tradition. With zestful elegance, Paul described the holiday he anticipated with his sister, Mercedes, in the house of his birth in Blairsville, Pennsylvania. Dick said he expected to visit his mother in Kenosha. I spoke of a trip that

Mary and I and the two boys would make to the farm in Kentucky to see my parents and sister.

Changes, of course, came with the years. The coming of old age caused Paul to move from the third floor to the tower on the northeast corner of the first floor. We all became more aware of our mortality when Dick's mother died, Paul's sister died, and my mother and father died. Still our ritual of Christmas continued.

Each year Fenlon added to our collection of anecdotes. For instance, he told of the time someone phoned him while he was on vacation in Pennsylvania to ask that he change a football player's grade. He refused. When Father Carrico, the dean of studies, next saw Fenlon in the fall, he said, "I hear someone tried to get you to change a grade. I'm glad you refused. Had you acquiesced, we may have had to dispense with your services."

Fenlon always told stories with footnotes. Each time he came across someone's name he slowed down the course of the narrative to give a footnote listing the subject's hometown, date of graduation, and similar things that had little to do with the story. It was not annoying; it was part of the charm.

Our Christmas visits always ended in a holiday mood. Amid a flurry of good wishes, Fenlon escorted us to Sorin porch. As we stepped into the crisp night air he would call after us, "Mr. Stritch"—for Fenlon's generation the word "mister" came readily to the tongue—"Mr. Stritch will come by in a few minutes to drive me to the station at LaPaz. I always take the Baltimore and Ohio." That, too, was a tradition.

As Dick and I walked down the main quad, Christmas lights blinked on and off in Walsh and Alumni halls. The clock in the tower struck six and the carillon, slowly, note by note, played "Silent Night."

In those days Richard Sullivan was at the height of his career. It had not been an easy road, though he had a way with words even in his college days. And, too, he had a way with a camel's hair brush. For a time it seemed the brush might win out over the typewriter. Dick splashed up quite a few canvases at the Art Institute of Chicago while on summer vacation from Notre Dame. In his senior year, he won the Mitchell playwriting award and that set the direction for his life.

After receiving his degree from Notre Dame in 1930 he enrolled in a division of the Art Institute known as the Goodman School of Drama. There he studied playwriting and stage designing for a year, with a bit of acting on the side.

He married a girl from Kenosha, Wisconsin, Mable Constance Priddis, in May 1932. After the ceremony in the log chapel at Notre Dame the couple honeymooned in Europe during the depth of the Depression. After Paris, Munich, and Rome, they returned to Kenosha with eight dollars to spare.

For the next few years Dick worked in his father's store in Kenosha. He used his spare time to write radio scripts, juvenile thrillers, Westerns, poems, and some high-grade fiction.

His first sale was to the *Midland*. The editor, John Towner Frederick, also reprinted that first story, "The Robin," in an anthology called *Thirty-four Present-Day Stories*.

The determined Sullivan found his optimism strained after completing "The Women," a story he always considered his best. He kept faith in it through thirty-three rejection slips. Finally it appeared in a little magazine, *Accent*. The story was reprinted in four anthologies.

When he joined the faculty at Notre Dame, in 1936, he began teaching courses in writing. He continued his own writing and soon his name began to appear above stories in the *Atlantic, Scribner's, American Mercury, New Yorker, Mademoiselle, New Republic, Columbia, Yale Review, Good Housekeeping*, and *Cosmopolitan*. His stories cropped up in such best-of-year anthologies as the O'Brien, Foley, and O. Henry collections.

He added book reviews to his chores and became a contributor to the *New York Times Book Review* and the *Chicago Tribune Magazine of Books*.

Soon he was turning out books for other reviewers to review. His first novel, *Summer after Summer*, was published in 1942. Next came *The Dark Continent* in 1943, followed by *The World of Idella May* in 1946. They were followed by several other novels, but I think he was always most satisfied with *The World of Idella May*, the story of a completely selfish girl who is a slave to her own romantic conception of herself.

Richard Sullivan was impressed by "the holiness of reality." He respected and was interested in any being God saw fit to create and hold in existence. That is why he could write as a "realist" and still reflect his optimism.

While both of us were trying to keep up our optimism we watched each other grow old, and finally one day I visited him for the last time in the hospital.

"It is strange the things you think about," he said. He paused, but did not add, "when dying," although his eyes were watching for death.

"About childhood?" I asked.

He nodded. "Mostly things you thought forgotten."

"Could you write them down?"

"I couldn't even spell a word." Another long pause. "Much less write a sentence."

He spoke in slurred phrases scarcely audible. And how frail. He looked older than his seventy-two years that fall of 1981. Perhaps it was frailty that started me remembering, sitting there in the semidarkness, of the abundant vitality he once enjoyed.

I remembered the days, thirty years earlier, when he would visit Tom Stritch and me in our office in the Main Building. He used to come bounding in between classes, and while standing there talking he vibrated with such vitality that I felt he was dribbling an invisible basketball very fast.

One day I drove him to the South Shore station; he was going to Barat, in Lake Forest, where his two daughters attended college. We reached the station as the train pulled out. Dick jumped from the car and ran after it. What high knee action! He wore new shoes; I could tell from the bright soles flashing in the autumn sun. Although past forty, he could still make the great leap of a Nijinsky to land on the rear step of a moving train.

As a pallbearer, I kept remembering Dick's vitality. While sitting next to his coffin in Sacred Heart Church, I wondered how many of those hundreds of mourners at the Requiem Mass knew that he had come to Notre Dame to play football.

He reported to Knute Rockne, in September of 1926, feeling optimistic. He had a right to feel that way because he had been all-state quarterback on the Kenosha high school state championship team. I learned this thirty years later when he and Joe Boland told me of their first meeting. Joe, a senior tackle, and Dick, a freshman quarterback, collided on Old Cartier Field ten days after the opening of football practice.

Rockne called for a drill that would test the souls of freshmen backs while perfecting the open-field tackling of varsity linemen. The coach stationed two varsity linemen on each ten-yard stripe, and told the freshmen backs to take turns running from goal to goal. Dick had been known in Wisconsin for his open-field running, and that skill got him past the first tacklers. On the twenty-yard line he met Joe Boland: 223 pounds crashed into 133. The laws of physics prevailed.

"Three days later," Dick said, "when I could hobble about, I turned in my suit and decided to plan a new life."

Through the years whenever Dick brought out a new novel, Joe Boland would say to him, "If I had anything to do with directing your destiny, I have no regrets."

Those two men admired each other's professionalism. Several times after Joe's death in 1960 I heard Dick say he thought Joe Boland was the best sportscaster he had ever heard.

While standing at Dick Sullivan's fresh grave I was pleased to see that just across the narrow road was Joe Boland's stone. The afternoon that Joe had bought that plot, he told Dick and me that he was pleased with the location: "It's near the Notre Dame golf course. Maybe when my friends pass by they will say a prayer for me."

I pass between the two graves often because many evenings of the year I walk the narrow roads of Cedar Grove. Those neighboring graves remind me that life takes more unpredictable bounces than a loose football.

When Joe ended Dick's football career in 1926, and when he told Dick about the new cemetery plot in 1956, how little either of them foresaw. It never dawned on them that they would be neighbors for all eternity.

– 19 –

Sabbaticals

Four times during thirty years of teaching I took leave of the classroom. The first time, three years after joining the faculty, I departed the campus at the request of the United States Army.

A hint of this came on Sunday afternoon, June 25, 1950, when a former student approached me in the Notre Dame dining hall, showing some agitation. Terrible things are happening in Korea, he said, and the United States may soon be at war.

I knew instantly I would be recalled, even though the statistics seemed against it: I was thirty-three, married, and the father of a two-year-old son with another child on the way. This uneasy feeling still hung over me when Thomas was born on August 2. When Tom Stritch returned from a holiday in Europe I told him of my uneasiness; his instant response was, "Nonsense!" At the start of classes in mid-September I went up into the attic and tried on my uniform.

Someone in Fifth Army Headquarters decided, in early autumn, that I ought to go to Korea as an escort officer for war correspondents; several had been killed or injured during the opening weeks of the conflict. Those orders were changed, though. Instead I was to work in the Office of Public Information at Fifth Army Headquarters, then located in the old Hyde Park Hotel, in Chicago. First, however, I had to spend six weeks studying journalism, broadcasting, and film and the Department of Defense Information School, in Carlisle, Pennsylvania.

When two dozen officers gathered there—from Army, Navy, Air Force, and Marines—we were given a speed-reading test to see how fast we could absorb a chapter from Bonnie Rockne's biography of Knute. Who decided that that particular piece of writing should be used for the test I never learned, but through the years many military men read of how Art Haley, business manager of the athletic department, used to drop by Rockne's house on Saint Vincent Street to discuss business affairs. There I sat in Carlisle, Pennsylvania, reading of things that had transpired in my living room a quarter-century earlier!

Those of us in the school who had served in India, Burma, and China felt encouraged when we heard that the North Koreans depended on the Chinese. Three months is all it will last, we said. It lasted three years.

We did not know how the Chinese military had improved. We remembered how things were when Chiang Kai-shek was trying to fight a cheap war, saving troops and equipment for battles to come. Chiang had reason to fear the future; Mao was not wasting anything on the Japanese. Mao defeated Chiang and took over China in 1949. Years later in Ireland, Father Hugh Sands, who had been a missionary in China before, during, and after the war, said to me: "I saw the difference between soldiers who work for money and those inspired by ideology. Mao's troops drew strength from the fanaticism that ideology inspires."

During my thirteen months in service I did nothing I felt was worth doing. It would have been an easy assignment had it not been that General Douglas MacArthur caused me some rough days and nights. One night in April 1951 I was awakened by a call from the *Chicago Tribune* saying that President Truman had fired MacArthur and what did I know about it. Of course I knew nothing—even MacArthur was surprised—but suddenly every newspaper, radio station, and television station in the Fifth Army area expected me to have something intelligent to say.

The real pressure came, though, when the generals in the Fifth Army decided that Chicago should give MacArthur a welcome that would rival those in San Francisco, Washington, and New York. When they heard that seven and half million New Yorkers had greeted MacArthur with eight hundred tons of confetti and ticker tape—a reception bigger than those given Lindbergh and Eisenhower—they were determined that Chicago should throw wide its arms.

The trouble was that the generals could not gracefully show they were on MacArthur's side and against their commander-in-chief. They sensed how much Truman despised them and were determined to have their way. When Merle Miller interviewed Truman for the book *Plain Speaking*, the president said: "I fired him because he wouldn't respect the authority of the President. That's the answer to that. I didn't fire him because he was a dumb son of a bitch, although he was, but that's not against the law for generals. If it was, half to three-quarters of them would be in jail."

It was not just the generals who were mad, the public was too. A Gallup Poll found only 29 percent of the people on Truman's side. Of the 78,000 letters and telegrams that poured into the White House, twenty to one were against the dismissal. Most newspapers condemned Truman's action. All over America, Truman and Dean Acheson were burned in effigy.

The generals wanted me to work closely with the journalists to do everything possible to ensure a good crowd in Chicago. I was to do it, though, without seeming to be involved. Thank God, General Douglas MacArthur got a rousing reception in Chicago!

My last afternoon in the Army was almost my last on earth. When told to go to Evanston on an assignment I was glad to escape to the great outdoors on such a lovely October afternoon. I signed out a driver and a staff car and we went tooling up the Outer Drive. At Foster Avenue some construction was going on, and a wooden barricade was built along the drive. For some unknown reason the driver fell asleep and ran through the barricade lengthwise. Wooden posts came feeding up through the car like ears of corn in a corn picker. I threw myself on the back seat and lumber came sticking in on top of me. With a severely damaged right hand I lay there listening to the corporal complain, "I only got my stripes yesterday, and now I'll lose them."

He looked at me trapped in the back seat and wondered if maybe he ought to get a doctor. Just then a military bus screeched to a halt and twenty-five men in blue jumped out and came running down the Outer Drive toward us. Twenty-five Air Force doctors. They were led by a figure in black. A Catholic priest.

My first leave from Notre Dame ended ingloriously when I returned to the classroom with a bandaged war wound. Each afternoon I went to the trainer's room under the stadium and there with Frank Leahy's lads thrust my battered hand into a whirlpool bath.

Twelve years passed before I took another leave from room 361 O'Shaughnessy. Arthur Mayer, who had found his delayed teaching career in that classroom, wrote: "When you come to New York at Christmas we must dine together." As we were being seated in the Russian Tea Room he asked, "How would you like to live in a castle?" He and John Fischer, editor of *Harper's*, had been asked by the Salzburg Seminar in American Studies to recommend someone to give lectures about films. Would I accept the appointment?

In early January of 1963 I went to the Brookings Institute, in Washington, D.C., for an orientation and to meet the three other members of the faculty: Ben Gilbert, city editor of the *Washington Post*, lecturer on newspapers; Rolland Tooke, executive vice-president of Westinghouse Broadcasting, lecturer on broadcasting; and Alvin Toffler, an editor of *Fortune* working on a book manuscript called *Future Shock*, lecturer on magazines.

We learned that we would be living in Schloss Leopoldskrone, a castle built by Mozart's patron, Archbishop Firmin. The archbishop's bones rest in Salzburg Cathedral, we were told, but his heart is buried in the castle's chapel. Among the castle's owners have been Ludwig I, King of Bavaria, and Max Reinhardt, the theatrical producer whose wife, Helene Thimig, an Austrian actress, had turned the place over to a couple of men from Harvard for a seminar in American Studies.

A few weeks later we were walking up the great stone stairway inside the Schloss, observing that in the old days they knew how to build these, for this stairway practically lifts you and carries you along. On the landings are suits of armor, collections of muskets, busts of two Roman emperors, and life-sized wooden statues of aristocrats long dead. The walls are covered with severe, dark portraits of the likes of Emperor Charles VI of Austria, the Emperor Joseph II, and the Empress Elizabeth.

The four of us from the United States settled down to a round of lectures, addressing forty-one Fellows, from fourteen European countries. All were professionals in mass communications, a bright and lively bunch averaging thirty-two years of age. They were selected because they were looking good in their home countries and might soon be leaders in their fields.

The three Yugoslavs took a special interest in me because I had known Mestrovic. What admiration they had for that man! Father Chester Soleta, C.S.C., was in Europe at the time, searching for an artist to take over the Master's studio. When he came by the Schloss for a visit, the Yugoslavs said they were thrilled to meet him and to shake the hand of a man who had shaken the hand of Ivan Mestrovic.

The seminars had started right after the war as a sort of intellectual Marshall Plan for Europe. They were effective indeed, at least in bringing together old enemies. Within a few days, students who had fought on opposing sides developed a strong *esprit de corps*. Several of us were talking about the war when a young German journalist said with feeling, "It doesn't seem possible, does it? It doesn't seem possible! How could people who respect and like each other so much set out to kill each other?"

My next leave of absence was the most off-beat of all. Years earlier, in 1949, when I saw Ann Blyth standing on the steps in front of the Notre Dame dining hall, I never thought that sixteen years later I would play opposite her in films.

The explanation for how this happened begins in the deserted Buddhist monastery in Burma. While I was writing the military history a film crew came by to ask for information. I said that if I were making their film this is how I would do it, and handed them a rough script. To my surprise that is how they filmed it, and I knew then I had a feeling for the medium.

Next came classes in film technique when I was recalled to military service and sent to the Department of Defense Information School. Two years later while working in Chicago to learn about television, I spent most of the time with film crews. When the Democrats and the Republicans held their national political conventions in Chicago, in 1952, I helped a production unit from New York make documentaries.

After starting a course in film production at Notre Dame, I joined the University Film Producers Association. Each summer its members met for a week and screened their productions for sixteen hours a day. After each screening came a detailed critique. In the audience were specialists in script writing, directing, film stock, lighting, makeup, sound, lab processing, and other things that go into filmmaking. When they criticized a film I learned to look and listen in light of each specialty.

After doing magazine pieces about films for years, I eventually wrote two books, *The Screen Arts* and *Film as Insight*. I had served as a juror at seven film competitions in this country when invited to be on the jury for the Venice International Film Festival. While in Venice, in September, 1962, I received a letter from the Vatican asking me to come to Rome to give some advice on the schema on Modern Means of Communication. It was being prepared for presentation at the Second Vatican Council, scheduled to begin on October 12. The project was directed by a special secretariat presided over by Archbishop Martin J. O'Connor, rector of the North American College in Rome and president of the Pontifical Commission on Motion Pictures, Radio, and Television.

A Polish monsignor, while asking questions, took me for an evening walk in the pope's garden. He pointed to a tower, saying that Pope John XXIII had gone there that afternoon to begin a private retreat before the start of the council.

I suggested to the monsignor that the power of modern communication is so great that it is impossible to insulate people against it. The only hope is to lead them through education to prefer things of quality. If the teaching lifts taste and judgment, it may even have the happy result of lifting moral standards. I would say the same today, only now I realize that the fight against vulgarity is more difficult than I dreamed it would be during that walk in a charming garden.

For several years my weekends were given to lecturing about film at schools and before various organizations. After one such lecture in Chicago, in early 1964, a film producer, Karl Holtsnider, asked me to consider coming to California to make a film.

After completing one I was asked to come back to make four more. All had something to do with film appreciation.

I was a cowboy in two, a professor in two, and a detective in one. Fortunately, I played opposite kindly people—Ann Blyth, Ruth Hussey, and Jayne Meadows. Those women and the stuntmen had all made names for themselves as professionals and yet they accepted me, a beginner, as an equal. They did not hold it against me for being an intruding university professor or, worse still, a film critic.

I never forgot for a minute that I was a beginner. When Miss Hussey and I went fourteen takes on one scene, she assured me she had gone more; I think she said it was twenty-one with Alan Ladd. And when Miss Blyth and I went nine takes she gave me confidence by telling of the time she and Charles Boyer went forty-one.

I enjoyed the experience but would not like to make a living in motion pictures. Too many people have to be involved. When someone asked me lately to work with him on a book, I said that in making films I came to realize what a loner I am. I need to face the blank sheets of paper by myself and not try to work with other people. During cavalry training I always enjoyed the assignment of the outrider. Anyone who grew up amid all of that aloneness of a farm in Kentucky is not apt to be a team player.

I was looking for aloneness when I took leave from Notre Dame to write *Everybody Steals from God*. Knowing the book would be demanding, I planned to skip the spring semester and settle in some remote place to ride horseback and to write. A warm place—Spain, or Arizona, or Australia.

At Christmas in 1968 Mary and I were on the way to Madrid and Rome when we stopped in Lisbon to visit Professor Ronald Weber and his family. He was teaching that year in Portugal. As we walked down the main street in Lisbon I spoke of my indecision for the coming semester, saying I must make up my mind within a few weeks. Ron stopped suddenly, I could still mark the place on the patterned mosaic sidewalk. He looked me in the eye and said, "Go to Ireland!"

Instantly, I knew he was right. Even though I had never wanted to visit Ireland, and knew that the coming months would be anything but warm there, still I was sure he was right.

Six weeks later when I came out of Dublin airport, walking on Irish soil for the first time, I stepped into a taxi piloted by a talky driver. Where might I be from? Notre Dame, I said.

"Might you be knowing a Father John O'Brien? He is not well thought of over here."

Father O'Brien's book, *The Vanishing Irish*, published in 1953, had made the Irish mad. It predicted the race would disappear: Young people leave the island for work abroad, many become nuns and priests, many marry late in life, and all too many remain spinsters and bachelors.

Were Father O'Brien alive today he would find the Emerald Isle so full of children that it might well sink into the sea. What happened? Perhaps membership in the Common Market stimulated the economy enough to bring about changes. Anyway, neither the taxi driver nor I could foresee these things when we reached the Shelbourne Hotel at noon on Tuesday, February 11, 1969.

Where to settle in Ireland? I had made a reservation for two nights at the Shelbourne, feeling that within forty-eight hours I would know the answer. In the lobby I knew I had made a good decision: There stood three American huntsmen, booted and spurred, with saddles on the floor beside them. They were intent on the bulletin board featuring announcements of the Wicklow Hounds, Kerry Foxhounds, Galway Blazers, and a dozen other fox-hunting clubs.

In the lobby of the Shelbourne, that first night in Ireland, I was delighted to meet Professor Paul Bartholomew, of the Department of Government and International Studies at Notre Dame. Paul and I had become friends in 1952, when he was an observer and I was making documentaries at the Democratic and Republican National Conventions in Chicago. Upon moving to offices in the new Notre Dame library, in the summer of 1963, he settled in room G27 and I in G26. Most mornings thereafter he knocked on my door at 9:30 and we went to the Huddle for coffee.

Paul suggested that we dine in the Shelbourne, in the Saddle Room, just off the lobby. Hardly were we seated when the chief justice of Ireland, Cearbhall O'Dalaigh, entered with his wife. Paul invited them to dine with us. While lecturing at University College Dublin that year Paul was writing a book about the Irish judicial system and so he knew the chief justice well.

"What are you doing in Ireland?" was the first question asked.

I said that I wanted to go to some remote place to ride and to write, but did not know where to settle.

The O'Dalaighs looked at each other and said in unison, "Bel-Air."

"Do you want to go to Bel-Air?" asked the chief justice.

Yes, I said. Later they told me how startled they were that I had said yes so suddenly, without asking what is Bel-Air, or where is it located, or how much will it cost.

Bel-Air is an old manor house in the Wicklow hills, about a mile out of Ashford and thirty miles south of Dublin, not far inland from the Irish Sea. Since it is hunt country, there were forty horses in the stables. Guests did not usually stay there in the winter, but the owners, Tim and Brigid Murphy, agreed to staff the place for my convenience because their friend, the chief justice of Ireland, asked them to.

The next evening the O'Dalaighs came by the Shelbourne to take me to Bel-Air. Paul Bartholomew, standing in the hotel doorway, said, "Look at this and remember how it looks. There is the chief justice of Ireland carrying your baggage to his car."

It was dark when we approached the manor up a long, winding driveway held close by trees and bushes. The house did not confront us until the last sudden turn, and then there it stood, a stone structure, silhouetted in the night. A part of the building, dating back to the eighteenth century, adds together in front around a square tower, but rambles freely toward the back. The long stone stables and several outbuildings make for something of a small village.

Only one window showed a light, a faint one at that. We entered the great hall, dark except for a flickering glow from the fireplace. The ceilings must have been twenty feet high. Large, dark paintings in ornate gilt frames and brass statuary lurked in the shadows. It was a setting that British mystery writers favor: dark woodwork, bookcases with thick calf-bound volumes, and heavy furniture from many periods. There were even ravens under the eaves.

My room, twenty feet square, was heated by a peat fire. It was evident that I would have to work within ten feet of the hearth. So I kept a writing pad on the mantel and stood there, wrapped in layers of sweaters, in a winter's chill that would give rheumatism to a wild duck. Take precautions against the dampness, an old Irishman advised, for "as we get older we don't get any younger."

Writing is such difficult business that something deep down inside keeps alert for attractive distractions. On the third day in Bel-Air I was distracted by the most penetrating sound in the world: the clank of horseshoe on anvil. Peter the Blacksmith had come down from Devil's Gap in the Wicklow Mountains to shoe the hunters in the stable.

I fought off temptation, for a few minutes, before abandoning the writing pad to hurry to the stable yard. I confessed to Peter the Blacksmith, "This morning I rode in the high hills. Most of the afternoon I walked in the low fields. Didn't get any work done. Not a bit."

"Ah, yes, but you were living," said Peter.

"I won't keep living, if I don't work."

"Now, now, don't be thinking that way. When a man dies he needs to leave only enough money to pay the man who digs his grave."

"What about the Irishman who refused to take out burial insurance? He said, 'When I die they won't dare leave me aboveground.'"

"Ah, no, that's not right. When a man dies he must leave enough money to pay the man who digs his grave."

After leaving Peter the Blacksmith, instead of returning to the writing pad on the mantel, I walked down the lane to the cottage of two spinsters, a laundress and a seamstress. Whenever I took laundry there I sat by the fireplace drinking tea and listening.

The spinsters told me a story about a neighbor, a ventriloquist, who in his declining years had retired from show business to settle in a cottage down the road. Each morning he rode his motorbike into the village of Ashford to buy a can of peas. He always bought the smallest can available, strapping it to the rear fender of the motorbike. Each day the villagers along the road checked to see if the can of peas was strapped in its usual place and often commented on how much that man liked peas. One day while riding his motorbike the ventriloquist was killed by a car. The neighbors went to his cottage to pack his belongings. In a cabinet they found unopened hundreds of tiny cans of peas. Stored with them was the little wooden dummy that had helped the ventriloquist make his living.

One evening I dined at the home of the chief justice, who lived in Newtownmountkennedy, a village with a name longer than its main street. Other guests were a Dublin surgeon, a lexicographer, and Paul Bartholomew.

Everyone wanted to know how I liked Ireland. I told them that Monsignor Philip Hughes, the historian, had told me several years earlier that my native Kentucky reminded him of Ireland. I know now what he meant, I said, because Ireland reminds me of Kentucky.

While the Wicklow Mountains have gentle contours that are similar to parts of Kentucky, it was not so much the land as the people that kept recalling things I had known as a boy. The Irish, for instance, have a "softness," that is not a weakness but a part of gentleness, a form of strength. If when walking along a path I met an Irishman coming from the other direction, he would step from the path several yards ahead to make sure that I did not have to give way.

The Irish also are like Kentuckians in the way they dramatize the weather. One February afternoon an Irish lady spoke in mournful tones about the terrors of that day's snow. I looked past her out the window to see snow with great patches of green showing through. In Kentucky it does not take much white stuff to cause people to stay home from work.

The kind of anecdote known as "the Kentucky story" is also popular in Irish conversation. It is not a man-made joke but an incident that really happened, yet is somewhat garnished in the telling. Guests at the dinner party began telling such stories. The surgeon recalled the time a helicopter was carrying the corpse of a woman from one part of Ireland to another when the coffin slipped its mooring and came crashing down. The relatives, though, could not find it in their hearts to be annoyed with the pilot. The deceased had landed on a village called Paradise.

The chief justice said that the people of County Kerry are averse to giving a direct answer. Kerrymen have a cagey cast of mind; when asked something they try to figure out why you might be wanting to know that, what is your hidden motive. An American tried to trick a Kerryman into giving a direct answer: When he saw a boy sitting on the steps of the village post office, he asked, "Where is the post office?" The lad gave a wary reply, "Is it a stamp you would be wanting?"

The lexicographer told of an Irish girl of easy virtue who finally returned to the church. When someone asked what penance the priest had given her she said: "He told me to offer the dregs of my virginity to the Lord."

Although in Ireland for less than a month, I had collected a few Irish stories of my own. I told the group around the table of the day I took a bus trip to an unfamiliar destination. Get off at the big tree, everybody told me. I asked the bus driver to let me know when he reached the big tree and he said he would. At one stop a country woman made the sign of the cross before boarding the bus. I began to feel uneasy; perhaps she knew something.

"Don't forget the big tree," I reminded the driver.

"Ah, yes, the big tree, Yes, yes."

Finally, he stopped and nodded to me. I paused in the door.

"Where is the big tree?"

"Oh, that's been gone these twenty years."

I also told about the night that Mary, wanting to speak about a trip to Ireland she had been planning, made a transatlantic phone call. Although she lacked my phone number at Bel-Air, she did have the address and gave that to the Dublin operator, a man. The address had been good enough for the postman to bring me her letters, but it was insufficient for the Dublin operator. He hemmed and hawed and sighed and finally asked, "I wonder now, could you tell me more about the place you say he is staying?"

"I don't know anything else about it," said Mary, "except that there are forty horses in the stable."

"Ah, yes," he said, "now I know."

Stories of uneasy happenings and of mysterious manifestations sooner or later creep into conversations in Ireland. And so it was that night in Newtonmountkennedy. We moved from the dining room table to the fireplace where the surrounding air was redolent with the faint, sweet smell of burning peat and everyone began telling of the kind of happenings that the Catholic Church calls *inexplicanda*.

The chief justice said that poltergeists were so playful in the rectory, just down the lane, that the priest tried sleeping in each room in the house but to no avail. His parishioners did not realize the seriousness of the situation until some young people on horseback visited the rectory. An ancient horse, never restive before, pricked up his ears and grew uneasy. Suddenly his eyes rolled white, nostrils flared red, and he lunged and reared, quivering all over.

While the parishioners had paid little attention to the complaints of their pastor, they took heed of what the horse was trying to tell them. Soon they made arrangements for the priest to move to another house and sold the rectory to a family from a distant village.

The first day there the maid, working upstairs, heard the bell downstairs. She went downstairs and the bell rang upstairs. Out the front door she hurried, never to reenter. The people living there now, said the chief justice, keep all lights burning all night.

Talk got around to Bel-Air. The dinner guests told of how two former residents of that old house had died from excessive pressure on their throats.

The Rev. O'Toole, parish priest at Wicklow Town, came to live at Bel-Air, then called Conroe, when Orangemen burned his house in 1799. As he was returning to town to make arrangements to have his rectory rebuilt, Orangemen waylaid him and strangled him.

The other Bel-Air resident who died of strangulation was Sir Roger Casement (the Murphys had bought the estate from Casement's relatives). At the fireplace where I was now doing my writing, Sir Roger used to sit and think long treasonable thoughts. Some of his unrest may have been caused by Charles Stewart Parnell, whose estate, Avondale, was ten miles to the south. Like Parnell, Sir Roger brooded over Home Rule.

When the First World War broke out, Casement believed that the time was right to cut the tie with England, and so he hurried to Germany to ask for arms and ammunition. The Germans agreed to give him a shipload, feeling that anything causing England inconvenience could be of help to them.

The Irish planned to use the weapons to capture Dublin on Easter Monday, 1916. Things went awry. The German ship reached Tralee Bay three days too soon, even though Sir Roger was racing along behind it in a German submarine trying to head it off. The Germans blew up their own ship when surrounded by the British.

Sir Roger Casement, captured by local police as he rowed a small boat to shore, was taken to London and tried for treason. His speech in his defense is considered a classic by patriotic Irishmen, but the English judges were not impressed. He was hanged.

Through the years I returned to Ireland about fifteen times. The chief justice continued to show me hospitality, arranging interviews with such interesting people as President Eamon DeValera and His Eminence Cardinal William Conway, prelate of all Ireland. Sometimes the O'Dalaighs took me to a play at the Abbey Theater and to dinner with the cast afterward. At midnight we would make the long drive to Bel-Air. Their hospitality was overwhelming.

The last time I saw Cearbhall O'Dalaigh he was president of Ireland. In August of 1975 he invited me to dinner, saying he wanted to celebrate my sixty-first birthday and hear about the writing assignment that had taken me to Korea that spring. Two *gardi* in a high-powered car picked me up at the place I was staying in Killiney and took me to the president's home. After some sherry we left for dinner at Hunter's Hotel in Rathew, County Wicklow.

I felt sure President O'Dailaigh was planning another assingment for me, and so he was. He introduced me to the owner of Hunter's Hotel, saying the place had been in her family for 200 years. Thackeray had come there to write and so had Sir Walter Scott. The present owner said she wanted a history of the hotel written, and the president of Ireland suggested that I live there while writing it.

It was the kind of opportunity that sounds good to the ear but does not reach the heart. Unless I feel an inner push to go ahead and do it, the work is not for me. Up until now, in this unfolding story, it may seem that I say yes to everything, but I really do say no quite often.

As we sat down to dinner the president told the owner of the hotel that he was expecting a phone call at any minute announcing the death of DeValera. That afternoon he had visited the former president of Ireland in a Dublin nursing home.

"How do you feel, Dev?" he had asked.

The answer was a slow, labored, "I am . . . not in . . . good form."

When Cearbhall O'Dalaigh died a few years later, the *New York Times* noted in his obituary: "He spent the last years of his life studying art and literature, watching birds, and riding horseback in Kerry." After reading that, a friend of mind said to me, "Now I know why the two of you got along well together."

All of these things came to pass because Professor Ronald Weber had stopped suddenly on the Avenida da Liberdade, in Lisbon, to give advice. There on a mosaic pavement, a pattern of arabesques, dark-green on white, he had said, "Go to Ireland!"

– 20 –
The Changes We've Seen

Tom Stritch began walking these blessed acres in 1930 and I started five years later. We did not know each other in those early days. It is fitting that our first meeting, in early May 1947, was on a campus path, one stretching from the old library to the church.

Often our walks have a theme. Trees, for example. Stritch might say, "Come let us behold the shadblow trees in bloom in the Hayes-Healy Garden." Or we may set out to admire the magnolias in front of the Main Building. Or thrill to dazzling colors of the sour gums by the Post Office.

He tells me the names of trees, but I remember only the usual ones. His interest is less than excessive in maples, oaks, and elms—they are too usual—but he enjoys locating the Kentucky coffee tree in front of the library, the copper beech beside Sacred Heart Church, and the gingko east of Walsh Hall. Four trees in front of the University Club he calls "Stritch's shame," for their names elude him. He has memorized Father Peter Hebert's guidebook of trees on the Notre Dame campus and regrets that it is out of date.

Although many of our walks are aimless, we prefer a definite plan. An ideal assignment came from Father James Connerton, who sent me a list of Eugene Kormendi's statues as he remembers them. Stritch and I took a walk to check the list.

Kormendi and his wife were on their way from their native Hungary to the United States, in September of 1939, when word reached the ship in mid-Atlantic that German armies were invading Poland. Shortly afterward he was invited to Notre Dame as artist in residence. The president of the university, Father Hugh O'Donnell, decided to keep the sculptor busy filling the niches in what were then known as the new buildings.

With Father Connerton's list in hand, Stritch and I left the library and walked southwest to the Law Building where two of Kormendi's best statues are featured: Saint Thomas More at the west entrance and Christ the King on the tower facing south. As a parenthetical observation Father

Connerton had added that since the latter was mighty heavy, it took some doing to get it up there.

Walking westward we reached Alumni Hall, where there is a statue — larger than life — of a graduate in cap and gown. It is facing south and located so high up on the tower that few people notice it. Several Kormendi statues are in the courtyard between Alumni and Dillon. On Alumni Hall are Francis of Assisi and Thomas Aquinas. In one of Dillon's niches stands Commodore Barry, the father of the U.S. Navy, probably put there because the Navy took over Notre Dame in wartime. Also in the courtyard are Saint Jerome and Saint Patrick, the patron of Father Patrick Dillon, after whom the hall was named. Father Connerton added as a footnote, "It has been recorded of Father Dillon that as prefect of discipline he was much beloved."

I led Stritch around to the west door of Dillon, facing the east side of the cafeteria, to show him my favorite statue. It is of Cardinal Newman in a pensive mood, not done by Kormendi but by John Bednar, who taught art at Notre Dame about forty years ago.

We cut northward across the quad to the court formed by Lyons, Morrissey and Howard. It is one of my favorite spots on campus. I mentioned this to Professor Stritch and he suggested we go to visit two of his favorites.

Walking westward we passed down the steps at the side of the Rockne Memorial. From a distance, I checked on the statue of Saint Christopher, above the memorial's main entrance. "It was not easy to find a muscular saint for this building," wrote Father Connerton, "although we might have thought of Father Lange," referring to the Holy Cross priest once rated as one of the world's strongest men.

Along the lake, just behind the ROTC building, is a stately stand of black walnuts. Passing between them down the cinder path brings something of the awesome experience of walking down the aisle in a Gothic cathedral. This, said Professor Stritch, might be his favorite view. This, or the graceful line of olive trees, so misty green, coming down the hill behind the community cemetery.

We stopped, as we often do, at the cemetery to read the names of good memories. There are the graves of men who had — as Mark Antony said of Julius Caesar — an "inbred goodness." They took things as they found them and gave them order and decency.

Father Howard Kenna (1901–1973), former dean of studies and provincial. How fitting that his discipline was mathematics. His life was as elegant as Euclid's geometry: everything counted, there were no dangling curlicues.

Father Leonard Carrico (1881–1944), dean of studies. He helped me understand what the Hindus mean in speaking in *darshan*, a kind of spiritual communion received when in the presence of an admirable human being.

Father John Farley (1876–1939), hall prefect. He tyrannized a whole Sorinite civilization. Pop sometimes kept us standing in a blizzard waiting for our mail as he played out his daily drama at noon on the porch of Sorin. He sniffed letters for hints of perfume, rolled his eyes heavenward, read aloud the return address, made comments, and sailed each envelope with true aim in the direction of the uneasy recipient.

A visit to the community cemetery makes us aware that life is as fugitive as a rainbow. Here we confront our mortality now that we have reached the age when a roaring in the head does not necessarily mean a touchdown—it could be high blood pressure.

We continued along rows of gray stone crosses, ranked in careful array, bearing names that are carved above the entrances of residence halls: Walsh, Dillon, Cavanaugh, Zahm, Lyons. Resting nearby are Brothers of Holy Cross whose tombstones read like a wonderful litany: Titus, Evaristus, Athanasius, Vital. Few universities have had the advantage of such a long-abiding influence.

As we came out of the cemetery onto the road that goes toward Saint Mary's we turned to a frequent theme in our walks, the subject of change. I said that my first walk across campus, in early September 1935, three Holy Cross Fathers came toward me along the path with birettas at rakish angle, short capes tossed back over shoulders, and a ropelike cincture girding the waist of ample cassocks. Although dressed in black they added a touch of color to the place, for they were of such good design that an artist might paint them into a landscape. That panache lingers only in Father Sorin's statue; priests today look as prosaic as the rest of us. The transmutation began in the 1960s when religious decided they ought "to be like everybody else." Priests were more in charge here that morning, a half century ago, when I walked toward Father O'Hara's office. Students arrived and departed, lay professors came and went, but the priests stayed, living on campus, many in student halls.

"How is religion faring?" elderly alumni are always asking us. They recall that when they were a part of the youth of the world, traversing these paths with greater alacrity, they were urged to attend Mass each morning, come to hall chapel for evening prayers, and begin each class with a prayer.

Father O'Hara published statistics as to the number of communion wafers used. I remember that each afternoon a tall, curly haired student, Edmund Joyce, who has now been executive vice-president here for thirty-four years, used to slide the *Religious Bulletin* under each door, and it was read.

I tell the elderly alumni that classes concerning the Almighty, formerly called religion, are now called theology. Since there are fashions in theology as in everything else, the religious mood is not the same today as it was fifty years ago. For example, God seemed somewhat crotchety in our time, but now is presented as more amiable. Perhaps the biggest change is that the Church at large is less militant and more humble.

But no matter what the mood of the hour, the University stands as a witness to the unseen; a sensitivity to "beyondness" saturates these acres. The spirit is still held in high regard here.

Because of an alertness to the transcendent, Notre Dame never lost its sense of mystery. It never tried to fool students into believing that knowledge solves mysteries to a real depth. In the community cemetery are men who realized that a real education increases an awareness of mystery and develops a sense of wonder.

Since a spirit of religion persists, it has always been easy to say yes to life at Notre Dame. While this place has known its cynics, it never developed a milieu in which cynicism was in and optimism was out. An affirmation of life is not considered corny on this campus. Perhaps that is why a blessing still lies on this place.

From the very beginning Holy Cross priests had a tradition that continues at Notre Dame today, the tradition of poise under pressure. Looked at in purely human terms, this place should have failed long ago. How close failure must have been when Father Sorin first stood by the lake in 1842, scarely twenty-eight years old, speaking little English, and having less than $600. Think of the odds against anything coming of that venture!

Time and time again Father Sorin continued showing poise under pressure. For instance, when he sent three Brothers west, in 1850, hoping they would find gold and relieve him of financial burdens, the scheme ended in disappointment. All Sorin got out of it was a dressing down from his superior, Father Moreau, for not getting permission to put so much money into the venture.

Father Sorin rose to the occasion on April 23, 1879, when he heard that the Main Building had burned. His school was wiped out. Students ate, slept, studied, and attended classes in that one building. He ordered a new one for September. In five months the present Main Building, with only man-power and horse-power, became a reality. Now to build such a structure the racket of power equipment disturbs the calm for two years.

An athlete might say that the school has been playing over its head since the day it started. Put in more spiritual terms, the Providential is more readily sensed here than in most places. Tom Stritch recalls that in 1932 Father Charles O'Donnell, in a year-opening sermon, called upon Our Lady for a miracle here. Professor Withey commented, "The miracle has been taking place for ninety years." You might describe Notre Dame's mystique as a long-descending blessing.

Tom Stritch and I agree that Father Hesburgh's appointment as president was part of the providential story of Notre Dame. The university was ready, in 1952, to make strides forward and Father Hesburgh certainly provided the direction for the next thirty-five years.

Not long ago he was giving a talk to the Ladies of Notre Dame in the penthouse atop the Memorial Library. When he asked if there were any questions, Mary spoke up. "When you became president there were forty-four buildings on campus and now there are eighty-eight. Of which are you most proud?"

He responded that he did not know there were so many. "The one that gives me the most satisfaction," he said, "is the one we are in right now—the library."

I cannot remember a time during Father Hesburgh's years in office that the sound of construction was not ringing across these acres. The university kept growing. He never neglected this growth, even when his own activities took on international dimensions. (The students used to say of the gigantic statue at the west side of the library that Moses, pointing skyward, is observing, "There goes Father Ted." Thank goodness he ignored any criticism that came his way and went ahead and made the university internationally renowned.)

In 1983 the president of one of my alma maters, Saint Joseph's, asked me to write the citation for an honorary degree that the college would be presenting to Father Hesburgh. I went through a stack of information provided by Richard Conklin, Director of Public Relations and Information, and was amazed at the vastness of the president's activities. It was frustrating trying to tell his story in a few sentences.

During the research I realized how much Father Hesburgh had brought the grace of reconciliation to his work. He served on fourteen presidential committees which dealt with civil rights, the peaceful use of atomic energy,

the treatment of Vietnam offenders, Third World development, and im-
migration reform, to name a few. Often he was the first Catholic priest
to serve in a given position; for example, as chairman of the Rockefeller
Foundation, as a director of Chase Manhattan Bank, and as United States
Ambassador to the Conference on Science and Technology for Development.

Father Hesburgh's vocation as priest-mediator has not gone unhonored.
In an annual survey of American leaders conducted by a national magazine,
he is usually ranked in first or second place in two fields: religion and education. Among his numerous awards is the Medal of Freedom, the nation's
highest civil honor, bestowed on him by President Lyndon Johnson. He
is in the *Guinness Book of World Records* for receiving more honorary degrees
than anyone in history. He may well hold that record for all time, having
gained it by surpassing Herbert Hoover with seventy-two. He now has well
over a hundred. What a wonderful time he will have in retirement writing
his memoirs!

Tom Stritch and I never tire of this campus so full of familiar things
and the recurring cycles of the academic year. In a world that has grown
more chaotic since Father Sorin's time, Notre Dame retains its freshness
because, for the most part, it has kept its tranquility. Visitors are impressed
with the serenity they sense here. It is a tranquility that comes in part from
the design of the campus; as I said earlier, in moving from one quad to
another, an ordered arrangement always meets the eye.

Notre Dame, like Professor Stritch, has always had a reverence for
trees. No tree is cut down unless it is so diseased that nothing else can be
done with it. Three oaks and a crabapple were in the way when the Snite
Museum of Art was begun, and so a professional was brought in to move
them with great care to the back of the arts and letters building. When
the library, fourteen stories tall, rose on old Cartier Field it looked severe,
sitting there in the wide open space of a football field with no transition
between it and the ground. By planting around it dozens of large trees, called
"instant forest," and a multitude of shrubs and ground cover, the severity
was replaced by a softening effect. And with those plantings, the serenity
spread eastward across the campus.

These acres reflect different moods, depending on the time of day and
the season of the year. On a cool, sweet morning in early June there is nothing in the world more lovely. On an October afternoon, with the lake reflecting bright colors and the dome shimmering in the Indian summer sun, the
whole world hums with contentment. When an August night is filled with
the whir of crickets and cicadas, it hints of autumn and of time running out.

Without care all loveliness turns shabby. Visitors here comment on how well kept everything is. Thanks to twenty-two grounds keepers and 253 housekeepers its well-keptness contributes to the aura of calm.

There is a special feeling, though, that goes beyond architecture and landscape gardening. I have found such benignity at few other places in the world. It is on the Aran Islands, off the west coast of Ireland, and in sections of Kyoto, in Japan, and in Kandy, Sri Lanka. Such places are greater than the sum of their parts.

To come closer to the secret of Notre Dame one needs to come closer to what Father Hesburgh speaks of as "the Notre Dame family." It is a family worth knowing, despite its faults. While working as a journalist, and serving in two wars, and traveling abroad on writing assignments, I have come to know some good people but have never found a greater concentration of goodness than on this campus. The "helpfulness quotient" at Notre Dame is high indeed.

I was reminded of this the day that two Japanese nuns visited here. They had come to say thanks at the tomb of John Cardinal O'Hara, the same John O'Hara who had given me a job when I came to his office as a green boy from Kentucky. They said that at the end of the Second World War the cardinal had helped lift their religious order out of the ruins of Nagasaki. As they knelt in the tiny chapel in Sacred Heart Church, they must have noticed twelve roses in a vase at the foot of the tomb. It would have pleased them to know that the roses are put there week after week as a token of gratitude from an unknown benefactor.

While on our walks Professor Stritch and I often recall with some nostalgia the years immediately following the Second World War. That was the best time to teach at Notre Dame, probably the best at any university.

I had predicted just the opposite. In New Delhi, on the day Japan surrendered, Major Donald Born of the Harvard history faculty and I talked about the GI Bill. We wondered if the men we had seen flying the Hump, building the Ledo Road, and fighting in the jungles of Burma could settle down to listen to some chalk-streaked professor talk theory. Surely they cannot, we said—but they did, as no generation before or since. Maybe that happened all over the world; George Macaulay Trevelyan wrote of the period, "Never had Cambridge been so full of strong and splendid life."

The strong and splendid life at Notre Dame came from mature students. Chronologically they were three years older than the usual undergrad, and psychologically about ten years older. They had suffered troubles not of their own making—a great encouragement to good sense.

When Vetville sprang up just north of the green fence of Cartier Field—where the two Pasquerillas and Grace and Flanner now stand—the men living there contributed to the general maturity of the place. Often a once-slovenly fellow settles down in marriage in a way that influences his grade point average. His motivation changes: He doesn't mind bringing home a sorry report to Mom and Dad, but bringing such to his wife is another matter. In a realistic way he finally sees the future as looming with requirements, competitions, and bills.

Jim Withey, Tom Stritch, and I hated to see the era of the vets end. When Frank Perretta was the last veteran in the department, we wished there was some way to encase him in amber, for his good sense favorably influenced the class.

The worst time to teach in a university came twenty years later. Those uneasy days, in the late 1960s, can be evoked by recalling William Kunstler, who urged radical students to break the law, even though he himself was a lawyer. In an interview he said that students should take over their colleges by occupying buildings, pending the administration's capitulation. If the administration refuses, students should burn down the buildings.

"You condone arson?" he was asked.

"Yes!" said Kunstler. "Arson is an appropriate response if a point has been reached when the mechanisms of society are not responding to serious grievances."

Arrogance ran rampant through the student body and cropped up in many ways. I recall a Saint Mary's student saying, "I have never made a film, but I will make one, and I will take up where Fellini left off."

I said, "That is as though I told you, 'I never played golf, but I will, and I will take up where Arnold Palmer left off.'"

It was pathetic the way poor little rich kids wanted to feel deprived. When a student told me that she was from New York City and I inquired as to what part of the city, she began to stammer and show uneasiness. I felt uncomfortable for having asked her to reveal some great embarrassment. She finally admitted, "Park Avenue." How she would have loved to have said, "Bedford-Stuyvesant." Some sewed patches on new jeans to give them the impoverished look. Many who could speak excellent English affected street lingo, saying that to speak with correctness is elitist. I kept recalling a Russian saying: "Having it too good drives them crazy."

With the lowering of morale, hoodlums from town became marauders on campus. At nine o'clock one Sunday night three students were watching television on the third floor of Alumni Hall when two young fellows, both armed, robbed them. At the time, Father Ferdinand Brown said, "If somebody had told me five years ago that I would feel uneasy walking from my office in the Main Building to Corby Hall after dark I would have considered that silly talk."

As I was leaving for Ireland, in February 1969, a festival of pornography was opening on campus. The last thing I saw that day was a group of grim art teachers returning from LaFortune, where they had been sent by the dean to determine whether the exhibit had any artistic merit. That evening when the porno film festival began, the girl in charge stuck a reel of film in her dress when the sheriff's deputy entered the room. He took the reel from her and she threatened to sue him for molestation. Her ambition, as I recall, was to make a documentary film about the making of porno films.

All of this began in 1965 when the job market for college students was better than ever before or since. In the spring of that year, in California, as we waited on the edge of the film set for the lights to be changed we spoke of strange things happening up at Berkeley. Riots started there when some students demanded the right to use obscene language in school publications. We thought that was just a passing matter and never dreamed the riots would spread from coast to coast and eventually reach Dublin, London, and Paris.

During those dark days I took comfort in my belief that all things run their course. I used to tell Tom Stritch, in walks around the lake at Notre Dame, and Paul Bartholomew, in walks around Saint Stephen's Green, in Dublin, that Marshall McLuhan was wrong when he announced with euphoria that this is the way young people would be for all time. When Stritch and Bartholomew asked if the change would come in our time I had to admit that I did not know.

The end came suddenly. The mood was darkest in the spring of 1970. That fall the lights came on again. We feared it was just a false dawn, but a new spirit was beginning to shine.

Some people say that Vietnam caused the trouble, yet the war went on for another five years after the change of mood. I think it is just one of the mysteries always abroad in the land, the mystery of the spiritual virus. How else explain the contagion that broke out in California and spread around the world?

Today's students are infected with likeableness, at least at this writing they are, but all of that could change by Thursday. They are even old-fashioned enough to be interested in traditions, perhaps realizing, as their older brothers and sisters did not, that traditions bring a sense of permanence and help a place become *someplace.*

When a student recently asked me about traditions, I told her that years ago there was a custom at Notre Dame that no undergrad would walk up or down the front steps of the Main Building until dressed in cap and gown on graduation day. The tradition disappeared with others in the bitter years. She thought a moment about the passing of such customs and said, "I feel cheated."

A student, when interviewing Tom Stritch about the changes at Notre Dame, asked, "What is the worse change on campus since your student days?" Tom answered, "The invasion of rock."

Our walks are sometimes spoiled when speakers are placed in windows, especially at Dillon Hall, to blare a beat at full volume across the quad. It is part of the general increase of noise in the world. Stritch and I know that there were also slobs in our days eager to lift the noise level of life, but they had to face up to such hall prefects as Tuffy Ryan and Pop Farley.

Even radios were scarce in those Depression years. When living in Corby, in the fall of 1935, I had to go to Howard to hear the broadcast of what turned out to be the celebrated Notre Dame–Ohio State game. In January of 1937 when the Ohio River was on the rampage, I went to the southwest tower on the third floor of Sorin to learn whether or not my home in Kentucky was threatened.

Lights went out at eleven o'clock for more than a hundred years. I enjoyed teaching eight o'clock classes until the lights-out rule was discarded about 1961. Since then, teachers find that dealing with students at eight in the morning is a frustrating business.

If Macbeth found life a "fitful fever," he should have been living in a Notre Dame residence hall during the past quarter-century. With lights all night, noise became so bad in the residences that library plans were drawn to include enough chairs so that half of the student population could escape to the reading rooms and be seated at once. That is how we happened to possess the biggest and most elegant study hall ever devised by the mind of man. For awhile it worked, but now a carnival spirit prevails at night even in the library. The old-fashioned librarian, the "shush lady," must have ridden off into the sunset. A few years ago I went to the Louisville Public Library, where I had spent so many happy hours in childhood, and was dismayed with the cacophony caused by the librarians themselves.

A few islands of calm remain. I am told that Cavanaugh Hall has kept a tradition of tranquility, and that in parts of LaFortune the off-campus students "shush" if somebody talks when they are trying to study.

Noise is such an ingredient of American culture that it is bound to have an effect on campus life. Two things have increased the decibel level until much of life registers eight on the Richter scale: the development of electronics and the growing popularity of the automobile.

In walking to the campus through the years I have watched the cars take over. Grass used to reach almost to the door of the Law School, but with time, blacktop oozed across the grass like lava from a volcano. When I heard Joni Mitchell sing, "We paved paradise and put up a parking lot," I thought of the campus. Now every day looks like a football weekend; thousands of student cars from all over the United States sit there rusting in the northern Indiana weather. Father Burtchaell once considered banning cars from the main campus; he would have found it easier to cut all salaries in half than to take down those coveted individual parking signs.

Of the good things to happen at Notre Dame in the past half-century one of the best was the arrival of female undergraduates. Stritch and I found that they lifted the tone inside the classroom and enhanced life outside it, too. Women, however, are not so new on the campus as most people think. As I said earlier, the nun who encouraged me to come to Notre Dame had received her master's degree in history here several years earlier. Through many long, hot summers Stritch, Withey, and I felt satisfaction in teaching nuns. We found them, for the most part, fine, sincere, intelligent, and dedicated women. There was mirth among them, and many even knew joy.

The summer program has been in decline since its peak in 1963. That is unfortunate. Notre Dame may have done more to enhance Catholic education in the summer than during the school year. The school year prepares young people for their personal careers, but the summer prepared teachers, mostly nuns, to lift the standards of their high schools from coast to coast. Those enthusiastic women returned to their schools and talked about Notre Dame, creating wider interests than those found on the sports page. They kept an eye out for likely prospects and encouraged their brightest to head for South Bend. As education was enhanced in their schools more able students arrived on campus.

The major change in our undergraduate student body came in the fall of 1965. I recall the morning in April when Jayne Meadows came into the studio and said, "Well, Notre Dame is going coed! I heard about it on television last night." That was the first I had heard that Saint Mary's students would begin crossing Dixie Highway in great numbers. It looked for a time as though there might even be a wedding, for the match seemed made in heaven. The sisters of Saint Mary's and the priests of Notre Dame are all of the Congregation of Holy Cross, honoring Father Basil Moreau as their founder. Students from their schools had developed a tradition of marrying each other and sending their sons and daughters to walk paths familiar to parents and grandparents.

Suddenly, however, the engagement broke off. Saint Mary's remained as it was, and Notre Dame recruited its own coeds. A shuttle bus now runs every fifteen minutes back and forth across Dixie Highway, some improvement over the distant past.

Stritch and I agree that one of the best things to happen to the faculty came about in August 1963. That is when the vast acreage in the fourteen stories of the library opened, and 250 professors were given office space in the basement. For years there had been few offices for teachers. Paul Bartholomew used to recall that as acting chairman of political science he lacked campus space and so ran the department out of his hat. Richard Sullivan used to meet with students on a bench in the lobby of the old science hall — now LaFortune Student Center — to discuss writing assignments.

Today each teacher, even each student, has a telephone. The day that Frank O'Malley had one installed the occasion was considered so unusual that Tom Stritch could scarcely wait to call him. When Frank put the receiver to his ear, a sepulchral voice asked, "What hath God wrought?"

On the same day in August 1963 that the faculty got offices and telephones, the Faculty Steno Pool opened. What a difference those women have made! I often wonder how we used to get along without having them prepare our letters and manuscripts.

In all our talks about changes, Stritch and I tend to agree on the favorable and unfavorable. Perhaps we agree on so many things because we grew up south of the Ohio River in an earlier world and appreciated its values. We care about the traditional and the well wrought. Maybe what makes us most akin is that we both fear the abstractions that disregard a mass of experience, theories that ignore the concreteness of life. Since so much of modern life is alien to us, we are much aware that we do not speak the sentiments of all men everywhere. And yet for some reason we do not feel adrift in an alien world. Maybe our roots on campus have spared us that.

We have explored these paths in tandem for nearly forty years. How fast it all went! Whatever happened to all of those yesterdays?

– 21 –

Years of Retirement

As we neared age sixty it was only natural for Mary and me to begin wondering where we should live during years of retirement. A few of our friends had returned to scenes of their childhood. Professor Thomas Madden, for instance, spoke often of "the old parish" and after his last class hurried to Ashtabula, Ohio, only to find that the old parish as he remembered it no longer existed. There was also the possibility of living abroad. Our former neighbor Natalie White and her mother were settled in Portugal. Most of our elderly friends, though, were staying in homes they had lived in during their working years.

As for scenes of my childhood, Mary and I continued taking our boys, Tom and John, there while my mother and father were yet alive. A walk around Bashford Manor became a sad ritual in the years when the white fences went down, section by section, and those left standing were askew and rotting. To make room for crops, a plough turned over much pastureland and a bulldozer knocked down most of the trees. Decaying bridges fell into the creek. In time, stables stood empty with only cooing pigeons and fluttering barn swallows disturbing the long narrow gloom. The world had changed since Azra, Manuel, and Sir Huon were restive in those stalls.

When mother and father died, Bertha moved to Louisville. We continued visiting her, but I did not get back to Buechel for almost twenty years. Not long ago I decided to see how things had fared there, even though friends warned, "Don't go back! Remember it as it was."

I found commercial hoopla cluttering Bardstown Road as it does the approaches to every large American city: Burger Chef, Arby's, Wally's Waffles. Somebody called Buechel Bill, "The Slim Profit Dealer," sold Fords amid a flurry of red, white, and blue pennants. Where I had crouched beside a country road, in October 1924, to look at a sports page that introduced me to Notre Dame, now stood the Speedway Self Service Gas Station with a warning sign out front: You Car Is Being Photographed. Please Pay Cashier.

One of the few things left from childhood was the two-story frame building, Seibert's grocery and saloon; now the Sahara Lounge and Liquor Store. The upstairs window on the southeast corner brought back memories of Christmas afternoon, 1922. In that room Mrs. Seibert had asked, "What did you get for Christmas?" I had answered, "Thirteen handerchiefs and a rubber ball." She told her son Bill to give me one of his toys, a man standing at a grindstone, something that gave off a spray of sparks when wound up.

I found one other landmark, the old Hikes place, where George Hikes used to raise gamecocks. Parking lots had replaced the long sweeping lawns after the sprawling white frame house became a restaurant, Bill Boland's Dining Room. For old time's sake Bertha and I went there for dinner. I reminded her of an afternoon, long ago, when I was coming out of the side door of this house and she came along and reported, "Dempsey just beat Carpentier." At the end of the meal I signed a traveler's check, only to have it refused. For years I had covered the world with traveler's checks, never having one unaccepted, but back in the old neighborhood it finally happened.

Where tense yearlings once cantered across lovely pastures I encountered a sale on Timex watches, Adidas T-shirts, and Hallmark cards. A shopping mall had replaced Bashford Manor, the white, three-story mansion where Colonel George Long used to tie thousand-dollar bills on the Christmas tree.

The Buechel Woman's Club had tried to save the mansion, but the final blow came when Ayr-Way and Thrif-T-Mart built out back, covering green pastures with asphalt parking lots. From then on vandals began breaking in. "We tried every way we could to save the house," said the former president of the woman's club. "We bought it in 1950 to use for meetings, bridge parties, and wedding receptions. We were stalling for time. We wrote to every historical preservation society around. Nobody was interested."

By 1970 it had to go. Ironically, Churchill Downs featured the seventy-fifth running of the Bashford Manor Stakes on the afternoon of the auction. Bargain-hunters, antique dealers, and curiosity-seekers crowded into the great dining room. Faded French wallpaper covered the walls, and from the ceiling hung the ornate crystal chandelier, the parts the vandals had spared. Buyers kept knocking on the highly polished furniture and doors to see if they were as substantial as they looked. A red velvet sofa sold for $500, a massive closet with a mirror on the door, for $95, and the mirrors from the two drawing rooms, for $100 each. A marble bust of Marie Antoinette brought $400. Even window shutters, banisters, and mantels were auctioned. A prelude to destruction.

As I walked from Bashford Manor Mall toward Old Shepherdsville Road I found five wire shopping carts overturned and rusting in Bear Grass Creek. The creek, where Falsetto and Proctor Knott had stood on broad flat stones, is now lined with concrete. Along Old Shepherdsville Road people looked at me with curiosity; nobody walks that way anymore. A sign says Radar Controlled. Where alfalfa once grew, 13,000 people work for General Electric; roads are jammed when 8,000 day shift workers start home. Wild flowers that made a glory of the roadside are long gone.

Where did the farm stand? The outlines are blurred. Blacktop and the sheds of a trucking company cover the space. Where the pond was, the Truck Alignment Service is. At the Preferred Body Shop a pickup waits with words painted on the door: Big Daddy, Little Mamma, and the Boss. We Haul Anything.

Where did the foundations of the house stand? Maybe where the oil stains are thickest. For some reason I recalled the hallway on a winter night, vast and hollow in the dark, and the long stairway that gave not a creak even after a hundred years. In the square bedroom the mound of a featherbed felt welcome, but the body heat of a boy took time to warm the space. All of a sudden I would awaken with a rooster crowing and woodpeckers drilling and mourning doves making sad sounds.

I remember the time, as a Notre Dame student, I had come across the sentence: "The corn grows now where Troy once stood." It had seemed so sad. Now I could say, "Where corn once grew parking lots stand." The farm in Buechel, the house where I was born in Louisville, the place in South Bend where I lived as a newspaperman, the location of the *News-Times* building, and the various places I lived in Chicago—all have given way to parking lots.

Will anyone ever learn to love the trucking office that stands where the beech tree grew? The beech that I walked around so often dreaming long dreams. On a crisp September morning I carved 9-11-28 into the soft gray bark that darkened in the rain. And then I left home for boarding school.

Where honeysuckles once bloomed the odor of exhaust and gasoline hang heavy in the air. Noises of motors and grinding gears replace the sounds of cackling hens, bullfrogs, and screech owls. The old simplicities are gone: cistern pump, quilting frame, kerosene lamp, axle grease, and harness.

In childhood only a few low barriers separated present from past, but now the separation is a high, thick wall. The Place has been obliterated "for further development." Progress has made Buechel so ugly that not even moonlight can save it.

Since the scenes of childhood had vanished, Mary and I could not consider retiring there. What about living abroad? In Europe might we find something to give a shape to our days, so that we would be more than just a pair of presences on this planet? In some foreign land might we develop our defenses against the ennui of the aged?

To answer such questions, I decided to do a book, *Why Americans Retire Abroad*. Mary went with me on some of the trips to Portugal, Spain, Ireland, England, Italy, and Greece. She gathered data in American embassies, questioned real estate agents, and checked the cost of things. My job was to seek out interviews of some of the 300,000 Americans retired in Europe.

By the time my book was published, Mary and I no longer considered retiring abroad. If roots go deep, we had learned, you had better not rip them up. Cherish them if they bring a consoling sense of things settled down deeply and tranquilly. Unless your past is exceedingly painful, do not go out of your way to disassociate yourself from it.

We believe that if you have accumulated layers of memories in a certain area, you might best live out your days there. Once you develop a feeling of "place," avoid tampering with it, for milieu is more important in age than it was in youth; you depend on it more as adaptability eludes you. You might not have much power in old age, yet you can have influence, which is better, but you can't have it amid the alien corn. So make your last-ditch stand on familiar ground.

About the time the manuscript for *Why Americans Retire Abroad* was completed, in the summer of 1973, I told Professor Weber, chairman of the department, that I planned to take an early retirement. There was this felt need to give full time to writing, the inward push that I am always talking about. And besides, my zest for teaching had waned during the days of incivility and did not give promise of returning. The department had three years to find a replacement.

Three years later Professor Elizabeth Christman agreed to join the faculty full time. For five years she had been teaching in the summer sessions. Her career, most unusual, might give inspiration to anyone seeking a change of direction in midlife. She had been with the Harold Ober Literary Agency, in New York, for two decades when at age fifty she decided she wanted to join a university faculty. With only a bachelor's degree, she began studying—not missing a day of work—until she had a doctorate from New York University. In 1969 she joined the Department of English at DePauw University, at Greencastle, Indiana. After age sixty she began writing novels and within six years three were published: *A Nice Italian Girl* (made into the motion picture *Black Market Baby*), *Flesh and Spirit*, and *A Broken Family*.

Professor Christman like Professors Cooney and Withey before her, insists on professionalism, demanding that deadlines be kept and that the spirit of the dabbler be filed away with adolescence. She has even told students not to get sick during the semester, explaining that they are blessed with the health of youth only so long as they get enough sleep, follow a proper diet, dress in a suitable manner, and, in general, lead a sensible life. Her students are lucky because she gives them something beyond the subject matter, something to aim at as a person.

She also gives the faculty something to aim for. Professor Sonia Gernes, nearly thirty years younger, said: "She's remained single and a professional all of her life, but she has never become strident or hardened, as some professional women do. I fear growing older myself, but when I look at her, I think that if I can be as loving and full of life when I'm in my sixties, I have nothing to fear."

With Professor Christman teaching in my place I now approach each semester without experiencing countdown fever. As the first class nears most teachers know the uneasiness felt before opening night at the theater—that is, if they are aware of how important a good start is. As I said earlier, the first class is the most important of the semester, the one that sets the tone. On opening day everyone is full of good resolve, except the problem children. That is the day to spot them. Chances are they won't show up for the first class. Or will have a mix-up in registration. Or will ask a silly question just for the sake of asking it. Problem children give themselves away early in the semester. All of them think they are clever, and so they never suspect how quickly a teacher who has been in the business a while catches on to them. Early in teaching I decided that about one student in ten causes trouble. Through the years I extended that rule of thumb to the world at large: ten percent of the people cause ninety percent of the sadness.

Character is what problem children lack; they have never learned self-discipline. No matter what subject is being taught, self-discipline should be a part of the course—even in graduate school. When I began to teach the sons of former students I realized that sons need to learn the same things their fathers needed. Sons arrive taller than their fathers, and maybe bring a few more bits of information—more mental clutter—but still they need to learn the same things. If a teacher merely adds to the clutter, the confusion is compounded. The teacher must help put together the pieces of the jigsaw puzzle, to bring some unity, some angle of vision. That can't happen without personal discipline on the part of teacher and student.

Every new generation needs to be encouraged to go to school. Not just register, but *go to school*: attend class, do assignments, frequent the library, and as Satchel Paige said, "be wary of the social ramble." I want to shake every freshman and say, "These are four precious years, kid. They won't come again. Don't wait until it is too late to find that out."

I have conversations with fewer students than I did before retirement. Some drop by the office, though, because a relative told them to. Now and again one will approach out of the blue. For instance, I was standing in front of the South Dining Hall when a girl came up and started a conversation announcing right off that she is a junior and an English major and that she is dropping out of the university. She said that she wants to be a writer and is going out to seek adventure. I told her to get ready for adventure by staying in college for three more semesters. No, she said, she wants to lead the life I lead, go to faraway places on book assignments. I tried to make her see that such assignments do not come at age twenty.

Not long afterward she approached me near the Huddle to announce that at the end of the semester, in two weeks, she would definitely not go home to Iowa. She had accepted a ride to Colorado where she hoped to work in a ski resort. Her mother wrote begging her to stay in school, saying how hurt the family would be. The girl answered that after traveling all over, if she fails to find whatever it is she is looking for she will return home. "After all I will still be your daughter."

I started to say, and perhaps should have, that maybe she won't still be her daughter. Legally, yes; a ledger in the courthouse will say so. But being her daughter is a matter of spirit more than a law or of blood. We go through life finding our family; those we are related to in spirit are closer than those related by blood alone.

The girl dropout admitted to me that she no longer wanted to impose discipline on herself. She wanted to go flitting around. Perhaps she is still flitting and may flit for the rest of her life. The irony is that she wants to write, work that demands more self-discipline than the courses she seeks to avoid.

When I retired to give full time to writing I knew it would be more difficult than full-time teaching. As a teacher I was never tempted to miss a class or enter a classroom unprepared: I did not want to look silly, and so that was a discipline imposed from without. Now each morning I must impose a discipline on myself: Nobody cared whether or not I faced a blank sheet of paper this morning. The temptation to avoid it is often great, as it is today. Freedom is hard to handle.

Few people realize how difficult writing is. While recovering from an illness, Flannery O'Connor asked her doctor if it would be all right if she starting working again. "Absolutely not!" he said. "Of course you can write if you want to."

I wish students could enroll in college already knowing what I did not learn until age thirty, while living in a deserted Buddhist monastery on the Irrawaddy River in upper Burma. There in seclusion my mind revealed a grasp that I never knew was there. It became like an undisturbed pool of water settling to such clarity that reflections had almost the same detail as the realities reflected. I could grasp great gobs of notes and organize them in a way new to my experience. When people came around it was like tossing pebbles into a pool: Things became less well defined. Most people go through life without knowing the full strength of their minds. What with commuting, and crowds, and the noise level of the new world, they never experience seclusion and serenity.

The experience in Burma influenced my life at Notre Dame. During thirty years of teaching I entered the classroom after the bell no more than twice. It was best to be there at least five or ten minutes early to allow the mind to settle. When students came bursting through the door long after the start of class, all churning up inside, I knew it would take a good part of the period for their minds to settle well enough to receive with clarity.

When walking to campus I sometimes hear cars roar by with such noise coming from the stereo that it sets the northeast neighborhood vibrating. How much clarity of thought is behind that steering wheel?

Because of my experience in Burma, in later life I sometimes organized a book by taking a suitcase full of notes and settling down in the Wicklow hills in Ireland. That is also why I still walk five or six miles a day in places not congested.

In taking an early retirement I expected to do this book first and follow it with the one I hope to write next. Then suddenly something happened to obstruct that plan. What seemed like a small matter changed drastically the next decade for Mary and me. The morning that made the difference was Saturday, April 6, 1974. I recalled that day several years later when in a convent in Tokyo I saw a poster: "The starting points of human destiny are little things." A little thing that redirected my destiny, and Mary's too, was a phone call from a stranger inviting me to breakfast at the Morris Inn on the Notre Dame campus. As I walked up Notre Dame Avenue I wondered why he felt so compelled to tell me "about an archbishop in Korea."

For half an hour my host recounted anecdotes about his friend Harold Henry, a Minnesotan, who as a young priest had gone to Korea and now forty years later, was an archbishop there.

"Would that make a good book?" he asked.

"A very good book," I replied.

"Will you write it?"

"Yes," I said without hesitation and immediately began to wonder, why should I, at age sixty, leave the pleasant life at Notre Dame to face the rigors of research, travel, and writing? I had never heard of Harold Henry and knew little about Korea. Although the project felt "right" to me, I tried to back away by asking why he felt I was the man to tell the archbishop's story.

My host explained that his daughter had given him *Why Americans Retire Abroad* as a Christmas gift but that he had delayed reading it until on a spring holiday in Florida. With each page he kept saying to himself that the man who wrote this book should tell the archbishop's story.

"What relation is there between elderly Americans living in Europe and an archbishop in Korea?" I asked.

He admitted he saw none and was also puzzled. The idea just kept haunting him, and so he stopped by the Morris Inn on his way back to Minneapolis to invite me to breakfast.

I made one last effort: "Maybe the archbishop and I won't get along together."

My host had an answer for that, too. "He will be coming to the States in a few weeks for an honorary degree. He can come to Notre Dame at that time and the two of you can decide whether or not you could get along."

In the South Bend airport the archbishop and I knew we could get along even before his baggage came down the chute. Late into the night he told stories about his off-beat life. The next morning, May 23, I put him on a plane for his return to Korea and that night I took Aer Lingus for Dublin to begin research for the archbishop's biography in the archives at the Columban Fathers' World Headquarters in Killiney, Ireland. That Thursday, as I will explain later, was important in Mary's life as well as mine.

Light in the Far East was the first of seven books I would write about members of the Saint Columban's Foreign Mission Society, a most colorful group. Research took me to Fiji, Japan, and the Philippines; it was unnecessary to go to Burma and China, for I had spent time there. The seventh book, *Journeys Not Regretted*, told of the experience of writing the series.

If my host at breakfast in the Morris Inn had asked, "Will you write seven books?" I might have lacked the courage to face such a task. As each manuscript neared completion something unusual happened to push me toward the next. Since this is described in *Journeys Not Regretted*, I will speak only briefly of what lured me into writing the Burma book.

That book became a part of my destiny because of an insignificant thing that had happened thirty years earlier in Bhamo. One noon, in early May of 1945,.I saw a tall, gaunt man "with the look of eagles" pause in the door of the officers' mess hall. He looked around as though he might be a stranger to the place. Since he wore suntans I took for granted that he must belong to the military. Although I saw him less than five seconds his face stayed sharp in memory.

Thirty years later, in the archives in Killiney, I came upon a photograph of the man with the look of eagles—Monsignor Patrick Usher, director of Columban Fathers in Burma. An hour later I found a photograph of a missionary riding across a stream on an animal that had the compact conformation of an Army mule. A few minutes later I turned up a picture of Father James Stuart, the only Columban I had known before meeting Archbishop Henry. The artist, Martha Sawyers, had used my monastery garden when she was painting the portrait of Father Stuart for *Collier's* magazine.

Excited by these findings I hurried downstairs in the Columban World Headquarters to talk with Father James Devine, who had spent much of his life in Burma. I was especially intrigued by the Army mule. Could it be one of mine? Father Devine said that it probably was. After the war he had learned that an Army sergent was trying to find a good home for some mules, and so he sent his catechist on a three-day trip through the jungle to investigate. The sergeant offered him forty mules, but the catechist accepted only ten. For years those animals did noble service for the Columbans in upper Burma.

What about Monsignor Usher? I asked. Father Devine said that he had died in Burma in 1958 and is buried there in Bhamo.

And Father Stuart? He too is dead.

Father Devine and I spoke of what a legend he had been. General Stilwell said, "The biggest mistake the Japanese ever made was not taking Father Stuart prisoner." And General Frank Merrill wrote to the superior general of the Columbans, "Father Stuart is the bravest man I have ever known."

I went to visit Jimmy Stuart's grave at the Columban seminary in Navan. He died August 11, 1955. The miracle is that he lived to age forty-five. I recalled the time a bullet struck the back of a chair in which he had just been sitting, and the time he flattened himself against a tree while machine-gun bullets chewed the bark off of each side of it. At the grave I thought of words he used to say when anyone died, "Ah, yes, he has gone to where the comfort is."

With all of these strange things happening, just as I was completing a manuscript, what else could I do but write another book about the Columbans. *Mission in Burma* is really a story of high adventure, a story of heartaches, satisfactions, and humor, experienced by fifty-one Columban Fathers living among Kachins and Shans from 1936 until 1979 in territory that American soldiers called Green Hell.

I spent the spring of 1983 in the Orient and finished the manuscript of *Japan Journey* early that fall. The day it went to the publisher, I did something I rarely do, I made a major decision out of my head. Usually, I trust only minor decisions to the head; the big ones come from deeper sources.

"I'm going to Peru to do a book," I said to Mary.

"Don't go to South America!" she exclaimed.

That surprised me. During our forty-five years of marriage I had gone on many trips to all parts of the world, some potentially dangerous, but Mary had never once said, "Don't do it!" or "Why must you go?" or "Do you think you should?"

So when she said "Don't go to South America!" I did not ask why. She would not be able to give a rational reason for something springing from a deep intuitive source. When Sister Mary Gabriel told me to go to Notre Dame, and Professor Weber said go to Ireland, and the man from Minneapolis asked me to go to Korea, I knew they were right, just as I knew Mary was right. I cannot give an answer as to why I accepted those suggestions, certainly not one that would sound sensible to somebody who works out of the head only.

I wrote a letter to a Columban saying that Mary does not want me to go to South America. He responded: "Your wife is right. This is not the time to go to South America."

What would have happened had I gone? We can never know. I do know that several weeks after I had decided against going, a Columban nun, one I would have surely interviewed, died a violent death in Peru. On December 14, 1983, Sister Joan Sawyer made a routine visit to Lurigancho Prison in Lima. That morning rebellious prisoners took as hostages Sister Joan, three Marist Sisters, and three social workers. The prisoners demanded that authorities supply an ambulance in which they might escape.

A Columban nun wrote home: "Negotiations went on all day, and by five o'clock that afternoon they had come to an agreement that the prisoners and the hostages would leave the prison together in the ambulance. The Sisters left in great fear, praying to God for protection.

"They were no sooner outside the gate when the shooting began. The ambulance was riddled with bullets from all sides. The hostages begged for mercy but the police responded by continuing to shoot indiscriminately. Our Joan must have died fairly quickly. She was struck by four bullets, one through the back of the neck, two through her leg and one through her finger. The other Sisters escaped miraculously as they lay under the prisoners who were mown down on top of them."

As suggested earlier, Thursday, May 23, 1974 was an important day for Mary and me, one that set a firm direction for the seventh decade of our lives. That is the morning I put Archbishop Harold Henry on the plane for Korea and that night went to Ireland to begin research on his biography. That same evening colleagues of Father Anthony Lauck, C.S.C., gave a dinner honoring him upon his retirement from the Art Department. Tom Stritch, the toastmaster, knowing I would have attended were I not over the Atlantic, asked Mary to go in my place. During the dinner, Father Louis Putz, C.S.C., himself recently retired, asked Mary, "What will you be doing tomorrow?"

"Playing golf," she answered.

He asked her to cancel the golf game because he wanted to talk with her about something he was planning: the Forever Learning Institute, a school for anyone fifty-five years old or older. He had access to the old Bendix estate, he said, and felt sure he could get retired Notre Dame professors to work as volunteer teachers. Would Mary volunteer to get publicity for this school, which he wanted to open in September?

Within a few days Mary was hand-delivering press releases at all newspaper offices and radio and television stations within the area. At one television station a producer invited her to go on the air to talk about the new school. After she had done so, he invited her to return for another appearance. Before long she was producer and hostess of "The Mary Fischer Show." In the following decade she taped more than five hundred programs and each was aired twice. Her guests were some of the celebrities that Notre Dame draws: Ann Landers, Don McNeill, Pat O'Brien, Mercedes McCambridge, Charley O. Finley, and Helen Hayes.

Meanwhile she continued the volunteer work she had been doing for years. For instance, as the need arises she gives guided tours through the Snite Museum of Art, the Notre Dame Memorial Library, and the Northern Indiana Historical Museum; on Fridays she helps out at Saint Joseph's Medical Center, and every day she works longer and harder for no pay than some people do for pay. She says, "The greatest luxury in life is doing something for somebody for nothing."

When Hugh Downs was host of the television program "Over Easy," the show's executive producer, hearing of Mary's attitude about doing for free things worth doing, sent a writer and a producer from California to prepare a script about her life. A week later a film crew came from the coast and began shooting.

The first sequence opens with a close-up of the golden dome. The camera tilts downward as Mary comes onto the porch of the Main Building. She descends the steps, puts her books into the bike basket and pedals down the main quad with the camera following. This was a fitting opening because of all the courses she has taken at Notre Dame: Shakespeare, tax law, gerontology, art history, Milton, modern drama, and others.

The documentary was shown nationally on "Over Easy" in February 1979 and has been repeated several times since. Each showing brings letters and phone calls from old friends long out of touch.

What now?

In her eighth decade Mary will continue, with the permission of God, to work at her many projects. She knows she must lead a life saturated with purpose, and Lord knows she has done that.

As for me, I will continue, also with the permission of God, to walk to the campus each morning and insert a blank sheet of paper into the typewriter. I hope to begin another book as soon as a period is put at the end of the last sentence in this manuscript. Several days a week I will walk the mile and a half to Saint Mary's dining room, have lunch with nuns I taught with thirty years ago, and after spending an hour in their wonderful new library, walk back to Notre Dame.

Writing this book has been satisfying. It was similar to working a jigsaw puzzle, fitting bits and pieces into a unified picture. The unifying forces in my life surfaced in part because I have a good memory, but mainly because I have put many words on paper in the past half-century. My news stories, magazine articles, diaries, letters, and books provided definite anecdotes, saving me and the reader from too many vague generalities.

In writing this memoir I came to agree with Carl Jung that there are no coincidences, and now I believe less and less in the improvisations of chance. The important events in my life arrived by what seemed small happy chances, what some people would call luck, or serendipity, but I favor those who speak of the Providential. Life adds up, it has meaning, and is not absurd. In the economy of God nothing is wasted. I read in a magazine in Fiji: "In some special way each person completes the universe." I have a hunch that all existence is one big ball of wax.

While filling these pages I have come to appreciate how much Doctor Cooney, Father Speckbaugh, and Mary meant in my life. They were all graced with a rich, understanding humanity, which the Scots call "innerliness." They diffused a gentle, compelling radiance. With something of the gulf stream about them, wherever they went they brought warmth, and people thawed out and unfolded, and some even bloomed.

Another thing I understand now is how much my adult life evolved from childhood. Human beings resemble plants, or vines, that grow in various directions while the roots hold where they were. Although more sophisticated in mind, I am still as old-fashioned in spirit as when growing up on a farm that was more pre–Civil War than twentieth century.

Chesterton said of his life that for the most part it was "indefensibly fortunate and happy." Mary and I feel that way; our lives have been more interesting than we had hoped. We understand how the Japanese poet felt:

> I have bought bread
> And I have been given red roses:
> How happy I am to hold
> Both in my hands!

– 22 –

The Ultimate Reunion

I began this memoir at the forty-fifth class reunion and now the fiftieth nears. I was reminded of its nearness a few days ago when I came upon an old man standing at the foot of the steps in front of the Main Building. He was so sure that I remembered his name that I could not gracefully admit that I did not, but I did remember that we had both lived on the third floor of Sorin Hall fifty years ago.

It was evident at first glance that in a universe where even the stars are collapsing we are both going along with the plan. A caring God, we are told, counts the hairs on our heads, but in our cases he has not had to work overtime in recent years. To put it kindly, more of history is etched in our faces.

It does not seem possible, we both agreed, that fifty years have passed since we sat on Sorin porch – endowed with all the juices of life and surrounded by lovely autumn afternoons. Time then was an abundance to be squandered. It never crossed our minds that we, unlike the gods of Olympus, are not forever young.

Those were the days we took tests under the Dome without once realizing how we die a little in the time it takes to put a period at the end of a sentence. We were still young enough to think that as we ran up Sorin stairway nothing changed. But in those few seconds everything in the universe was changing and has been ever since. In a literature course we read Elizabeth Barrett Browning's sentence, "The face of all the world is changed, I think," but did not really feel it.

We have since been told that many things we learned under the Dome have been outdated. For instance, Einstein cast a shadow over Newton and now some of the new theories are casting a shadow across Einstein, as he himself had predicted. We remember when Joyce and Eliot were rejecting things and by our middle years the Beat Generation and the Angry Young Men were rejecting them. And the *cognoscenti* assured us, some years ago, that the existentialism of Sartre had made old hat the Scholasticism of

Aquinas, but now Sartre is apt to be *passé*. The maps we studied only vaguely resemble those in today's atlas. To add to our sense of outdatedness we are hearing talk about quarks, quasars, and gene-splicing. Sooner or later every textbook needs revision.

In the past half-century, old Sorinites themselves have changed. We understand some things better now than when we first heard them under the Dome. For instance, we have more feeling for what Hamlet meant when he spoke of "the thousand natural shocks that flesh is heir to." We probably read and rushed on when we came to Aristotle's observation that the aged "live more by memory than by hope." We did not feel the poignancy when King Richard III sighed, "The silent hours steal on. . . ."

The day we heard about the myth of Terminus, the god who rules over boundaries, we did not understand it very well. Now we are so aware of endings that we realize why the Romans felt the need to create a deity to preside over all terminal things. While we are still unable, as Blake says, "to see the world in a grain of sand," we have learned with Lear that it is harder to be old than to be young, and are inclined to add that neither is easy.

Such changes had value, though; they helped us realize that current theories will, in time, be outdated, for the avant-garde changes with the seasons. Since learning the certainty of uncertainty we see that in a fallible mind even "truths" are cloudy, and our ability to comprehend anything has a border around it. Nobody gets the answer carried to the final decimal point; all answers are preliminary.

Even though some of the things we studied have become as obsolete as Ptolemaic astronomy, what we learned of the spirit has held up. This university never suffered the sterility of a culture lacking spiritual concerns. The agnostic and the pessimist were never in fashion here. Few members of the faculty got caught in the cycles of hysteria, and fads and cults did not thrive on these acres. Notre Dame has been a good place "to make your soul," an expression used long ago in Dublin.

Our teachers were not cynics; neither were they manufacturers of rose-colored glasses. The best ones were aware of the long adventure of the human race, and by passing along such awareness they helped us face the present with some serenity and the future with some hope. From them we learned that it is no easy matter to bring down the curtain on the world.

The Sorin Hall alumnus and I spoke with affection about professors long dead. Alumni always do that; it is akin to ancestor worship, for time hallows the dead the way it hallows events. All teachers, except the incompetent, are sooner or later fitted with a halo.

He pointed to Sorin Hall and recalled that in our time Professor Paul Fenlon had lived in the northwest tower on the third floor. I said that in later years, to avoid the stairs, Fenlon had moved to the northeast tower of the first floor. As student, teacher, and professor emeritus he had lived in Sorin for sixty-four years.

This turned the conversation to the bachelor professors who were housed in student residences before the Second World War—Tom Madden, Jim Withey, Paul Byrne and others. The alumnus spoke of how much he had admired one of them, Professor Joe Ryan. I told him that Joe could not leave the campus without missing it; he never changed the setting on his wristwatch, so that no matter where he was in the world he could look at it and say to himself, right now at Notre Dame such-and-such is happening. He felt uneasy away from Lyons Hall.

Uneasiness has filled much of our time on earth. We entered the world during the Great War and in high school and in college felt the Great Depression. We were just the right age for the Second World War and five years later were still right for the Korean Conflict. Some of our children were the right age for Vietnam. In the 1960s, when the pulse of the world beat with irregularity, we suffered a special pain because by then we were mature enough to cringe at such excesses.

We watched the coming of radio and television and saw the growth in use of the automobile, only to witness the abuse of these three gifts. Fine cities fell into ruin, and an excellent public school system declined. We watched the rush to communism and the rebirth of conservatism. So many ideologies flared out and faded like the fads of adolescents. From it all we learned something about the circularity of human affairs.

This sounds as though we were companions of calamity. A Spanish proverb says, "Whoever is not called upon to struggle is forgotten by God." If that is true, the Almighty knows some members of the older generation by their first names.

So many things, good and bad, have happened since five o'clock Sunday afternoon, June 6, 1937, when we emerged from the Fieldhouse, diploma in hand. There we were, each a unique, unprecedented, and unrepeatable person. We were ready to take the crosstown bus to Utopia, only to learn that there is no such place on the schedule.

Like every graduating class we stepped from campus life into a world of hard choices. Many of our ideas of reality were severely challenged, as we learned about the gap between intentions and results. And as we should have known, all of our plans were subject to God's veto.

All of this was long ago and in a different world.

Now our memories are fading like old letters in an attic trunk. For tunately, most memories soften—otherwise our psyches in old age would be one great bag of broken glass too painful to reach into. Only because of benign memories do alumni proclaim, like the poet Pindar, the glory of a golden past.

We are realizing more each year how completely alone everyone is, as isolated as a star in space. Many of those who helped us forget our aloneness have stepped outside of time and let the work of the world go on. They have been "promoted to Glory," as the Salvation Army puts it. As the ritual of the requiem grows more repetitive, we who are left are more "reduced." Seeing the many crossed-off names in our Christmas mailing list, and aware that we are living on the outer edge of Nature's permission, we find each day a dividend.

By now the sun was nearly down and a gust of wind blew across the quad. I said to my Sorin friend, "God willing, we will meet at the fiftieth reunion."

"Up until now we have beat the rap," he said.

The golden jubilee class will gather under the striped reunion tent, on the north quad, to touch up the past, painting pictures of it that are, like some watercolors, more charming than it deserves. In the winter of life, recalling the springtime, our memories tend to be warmly inaccurate, although some have the merit of truth. With age the faculties of discernment go out of focus until the real and the fanciful blur together.

Those of us who can make the reunion will share memories caught in the convolutions of our brains. The dendrites connecting the neurons create a chemical and an electrical activity, we are told, that keep reminiscences flowing. In the configuration of our neurons are preserved Pop Farley, Clashmore Mike, and the Saint Mary's tea dances. If speech is really controlled by the third convolution of the left frontal lobe of the cerebral cortex, that convolution will be working overtime under the tent when reunion time is here.

Another gust of wind blew across the quadrangle. My Sorin friend and I began moving apart. So much of life is meeting and saying goodbye. We wished each other a benign Indian summer. He started up the front steps of the Main Building with body weight making itself felt. I walked down the quad, also carrying all of those years, all of those memories. After such a meeting a thin solution of sadness stains the bottom of the cup.

Under the tunnel of greenery down Notre Dame Avenue, I thought for the thousandth time of how fortunate Mary and I are in being able to retire in this setting. The sense of perpetuity here is satisfying. It clings like ivy and brings an awareness of continuous unfolding. She and I agree with Cicero; in his essay *De Senectute* he observed: "What is more charming than an old age surrounded by the enthusiasm of youth!"